## THE El

**Deirdre Beddoe** was born in Barry and educated at Barry County Grammar School for Girls and at UCW Aberystwyth, where she obtained a PhD in History. She is Emeritus Professor of Women's History at the University of Glamorgan, Pontypridd.

She is committed to rescuing the lost history of women in Wales and to making their story available to a wide audience. She has researched and written extensively on both British and Welsh women's history and her books include *Welsh Convict Women* (Stewart Williams, 1979), the story of women who were transported from Wales to the Australian penal colonies; *Discovering Women's History: A Practical Guide* (first edition Pandora, 1983; second edition Pandora, 1993; third edition, Longman, 1998); *Back to Home and Duty: Women in Britain Between the Wars* (Pandora, 1989) and *Out of the Shadows: A History of Women in Twentieth-Century Wales* (University of Wales Press, 2000). She is co-editor of *Parachutes and Petticoats: Welsh Women Writing on the Second World War* (Honno, 1995). She also works in film, television and radio. She is a frequent broadcaster and gives talks and lectures widely on her work.

*Deirdre Beddoe.*

# CHANGING TIMES

Welsh women writing on the
1950s and 1960s

*Edited by*

Deirdre Beddoe

HONNO AUTOBIOGRAPHY

Published by Honno
'Ailsa Craig', Heol y Cawl, Dinas Powys,
CF6 4AH


First Impression 2003
© The Contributors


British Library Cataloguing in Publication Data
A catalogue record for this book is available from the British Library


ISBN 1-870206-53-3

Published with the financial support of the
Arts Council of Wales


Cover photograph reproduced with kind permission
of the National Library of Wales


Cover design by Chris Lee Design


Typset and printed in Gwasg Dinefwr Press, Llandybïe

*In loving memory of my dear aunt,*
*Kathleen Durbin, 1906-2001*

# CONTENTS

# INTRODUCTION

This is a very readable book. One by one, the contributors to *Changing Times* take us back to the 1950s and 1960s. We are transported to a world of Toni Home Perms, of sugar-starched petticoats and stiletto heels; of transistor radios, long-playing records and tiny black and white television screens set in walnut cabinets as big as sideboards; of Sunday school outings and sisterhood meetings; of prudery and old wives' tales; of sexual innocence and the social ostracism of unmarried mothers; of Saturday night hops and coffee bars; of the Coronation and 'You've never had it so good'; of council houses, hand-knitted cardigans, the scholarship and the key of the door at twenty-one. The accounts published here, written by women from all over Wales, enable us to revisit a world we have lost. This is a pleasure indeed, but there is a highly personal dimension to this book too. We are allowed to enter into the lives of individual women and permitted to share in the good, funny, happy, sad, bad and truly shocking times. That is a privilege. It is this combination of revisiting times past and gaining access into the lives of others through honest – sometimes astonishingly honest – accounts, written without artifice, that makes this collection such a compelling read. *Changing Times* is a real treat, which may be savoured slowly or devoured in great chunks: it is a book to return to time and time again.

Above all, what makes *Changing Times* so special is that it gives us a view of Wales in the fifties and sixties as seen through the eyes of girls and women. That in itself is a radical departure. Other books on this period have concentrated almost exclusively on men's activities. Here the women have written about what mattered to them. They write about simple childhood pleasures; about the looming shadow of the scholarship exam, with its power to make or break young lives; of adolescent turmoil, periods and first fumbling sexual encounters; of the power of the chapel over their lives, exerting strict control over their behaviour and at the same time being the hub of their social lives; of mind-numbing jobs and limited career options; of meeting their life's partners, of marriage and setting up home; of the appalling treatment of young women who broke the moral code and became pregnant outside marriage; of the 'swinging sixties', as seen through the eyes of insiders or, in the majority of cases, of outsiders looking in and who lament, 'The sixties passed me by'; and of political loyalties and passionately held beliefs. In submitting their contributions to Honno, the women whose writings appear in this book were given a free rein. As editor, I have organized their writings into sections, but the women themselves set the agenda in what they chose to write about. This book reflects their priorities. It is the very woman-centredness of this collection that differentiates it from other histories of this period. Interestingly, none of the usual cultural icons normally used to symbolize Wales in these years get a look in here: there is not a coalmine, male voice choir or rugby match in sight.

For older readers, delving into these pages is a bit like visiting a museum and wandering into a room with a reconstruction of a domestic interior, then suddenly saying out loud, 'That was our wallpaper,' or, 'Look at that enamel bread bin – we had one just like that.' But reading these personal reminiscences, we are reminded of more than just material things. Memories of our own past flood back – of childhood, schooldays, adolescence and young womanhood. There is a commonality of experience born of gender and place which binds women who grew up and reached adulthood in the Wales of the fifties and sixties with the contributors to *Changing Times*. We can submit to the warm embrace of nostalgia and share long-forgotten pleasures, and even anxieties, which loomed so large at the time, with the women who have written about their experiences here. But there is something else in this book which strikes a different chord. Sometimes expressed in overt protest and at other times merely hinted at in feint murmurings of unease, an undercurrent of discontent runs through some of the contributions. There is a distinct questioning of women's and girls' subordinate role and this is seen in resentment of sexism (though of course nobody called it that then) in schools in those days, in the questioning of attitudes which limited women's career choices and allotted differentiated gender roles to men and women, and, perhaps most clearly of all, in bewilderment at the cruel hypocrisy which permitted a dual standard of sexual conduct and exacted such a high price from single girls who became pregnant. But insight has come only with hindsight and as a result of developments since the 1970s. In the 1950s and 1960s we were only vaguely aware that something was not quite right. Something was out of place but we could not quite put our finger on it.

Younger readers will be stunned to read about what girls and women had to put up with and will marvel at our innocence, patience and compliance with the rules imposed upon us. But they are in for plenty of surprises too. Reading some of the accounts in this collection of rebellions against authority and of sexual encounters may perhaps cause them to view their elders in a new light.

*Changing Times: Welsh women writing on the 1950s and 1960s* is the third volume in the Honno Autobiographical Writing Series and follows on from the earlier works *Parachutes and Petticoats: Welsh women writing on the Second World War* (editors Leigh Verrill-Rhys and Deirdre Beddoe, 1992) and *Struggle or Starve: Women's lives in the South Wales valleys between the two World Wars* (editors Carol White and Sian Rhiannon Williams, 1998). These collections provide an important outlet for women writers in Wales, which is valued by established authors and is also particularly appreciated by women who have not previously ventured into the world of publishing. The series also serves another quite different function, of which I, as an historian, am keenly aware. In providing a platform for women in Wales to tell and share their personal histories, Honno is contributing to the process of rescuing Welsh women's history. However, readers should be aware that using autobiography as history is not unproblematic, especially when accounts are written so long after the event. Memories may fade or play tricks on us and we may, even unwittingly, censor and sanitize our lives. In the process of writing we impose order on our lives and, to a certain extent, reconstruct our past. It can be argued too that women who are able to write about their lives are *ipso facto* exceptional women. There is a great deal of truth in this, but, on the other hand, the contributors write about life experiences which are shared by many others and we are fortunate to be able to draw on the work of these 'exceptional ordinary' women. But having given this warning, and bearing in mind the paucity of written sources for Welsh women's history, it needs to be clearly stated that this is the best we have got. I would rather rescue women's life stories forty or fifty years on than not do it at all and allow their experiences to sink into oblivion. Whilst we must be aware of the limitations, collections such as this are a vital resource and there is a need for many more such books in both our languages.

Putting a book like this together is a slow process. Honno sent out the first call for contributions to this anthology of autobiographical writing early in 2000 by publishing letters in the Welsh press, making radio appeals and through its newsletter. By the summer of that year, we had received quite a good response of some sixty-odd pieces, of which about half appear here, but I was not totally convinced at this stage that we had sufficient material to produce a good book. We therefore made a second appeal early in 2001 and the net result is *Changing Times* which features forty-four autobiographical accounts written by forty-one writers, three of whom appear twice.

The contributors hail from many different parts of Wales, giving us a good geographical coverage of the country. There are accounts of life in our 'big cities', in towns and villages, and in valley and rural communities. We can read about growing up in Cardiff and Swansea, in the Rhondda, Rhymney and Garw valleys, in Aberaeron, Bangor, Barry, Carmarthen, Haverfordwest, Merthyr, Maesteg and Pontarddulais, on Lleyn and on Anglesey, and many other places. North, south, east and west are represented here, though central Wales is, like its population, a bit thin. Our writers come from both Welsh speaking and predominantly English speaking communities and represent the diversity of our cultural traditions. Since Honno is broad and inclusive in its interpretation of Welshness, a few of the contributors have written about communities in England. The notion of place is important to us in Wales and we have a particular enthusiasm for locating people geographically. On meeting someone new, practically the first thing we ask is, 'Where are you from?' or *'O ble dych chi'n dod?'* A sense of place comes over strongly in each of these accounts. In addition to this, each contribution is prefaced by a short biographical note, which enables readers to set the passages published here within the wider context of the writer's life.

In terms of the coverage of the women's lifespan, the accounts printed here range from early childhood up to marriage and motherhood. Obviously, since this collection looks back fifty years, there are no accounts of old age. In fact, there are no spring chickens writing here: the contributors range in age from their forties to their eighties.

The main criteria I used as editor for including pieces in the book was the inherent interest of the subject matter each writer had chosen to write about, together, of course, with the standard of literary expression. Every single piece here is of intrinsic interest and throws light on women's lives in the 1950s and 1960s and similarly every contribution is highly readable. There are some superbly written pieces from well-known Welsh authors, including Elaine Morgan, Molly Parkin, Mary Davies Parnell and Mari Ellis. There are many other very well written pieces and, taken as a whole, the book is of a high standard, but in many ways the quality of the writing is not important. What really counts is the story each woman has to tell. Where the pieces published in *Changing Times* were originally submitted in Welsh, this is clearly shown in the text. The fact that so much of the book is well written is really a delightful bonus.

One of the primary duties of the editor of such a wide ranging and diverse collection as *Changing Times* is to impose some order and organization on the many contributions by grouping them into certain clear sections, each dealing with a particular theme. This is intended to help the reader who has a particular interest in one theme or another and to place accounts dealing with common experiences conveniently together. The first issue I had to address was the fact that this collection covers both the 1950s and the 1960s. But, of course, the reality is that people do not neatly live their lives in decades. Many of the writers range freely over the whole period, so any suggestion of dividing the book into two halves would have been totally unworkable. In some respects, the two decades are quite distinct. The traditional view is of the restrained and hide-bound 1950s, set in its ways and essentially offering no radical departure from what had gone before. Some have labelled them 'the frustrating fifties'. Then this same traditional view waxes ecstatically about the innovative, convention-breaking and, above all, swinging, sixties.

But I do not believe that this view of a sharp divide between the two decades applies to women's lives in Wales. Of course, there were changes in the sixties in fashion, in popular music and culture, in Welsh politics and the economy, and even in sexual mores, but the overwhelming message which comes from reading the contributors' accounts is, 'The sixties passed me by.' Most women in Wales, though benefiting from educational change and a broadening of the labour market, were busy living their lives along almost exactly the same lines as their mothers had done. But because of the perception that the two decades were distinctly different and because of contributions from extraordinary Welsh women, who truly did swing, I have created a separate section devoted to the Swinging Sixties.

The other sections in *Changing Times* are a mixture of life phases and specific topics, which had a particular bearing on women's lives. The complete list is – childhood; education; teenagers; chapel; courtship, marriage and divorce; unmarried mothers; work; the swinging sixties; and finally politics. Unfortunately for the editor, people no more live their lives under discreet topic headings than they do in decades and many of the contributors cover a number of subjects in their pieces. I have therefore taken a flexible and elastic approach to placing the writings within sections. In reality, under each section we learn about a variety of aspects of contemporary life, all of which go towards building up a picture of women's lives then. In the following pages, I look at each section, one by one in the order in which they appear in the book, and at the same time point out how the personal testimony of the contributors helps us form an overview of women's lives in Wales in the 1950s and 1960s.

The contributors to the Childhood section, Jo Mazelis, Hazel Farr, Leona Jones, Mary Davies Parnell and Carolyn Lewis, evoke a lost age of innocence. They conjure up a world where children played safely out of doors and always did as they were told; where the sun shone brightly and skies were blue; where children grew up in communities calling their female neighbours 'Auntie' and where a treat was a toffee apple or a fish paste sandwich. The authors write about close families and childhood friendships; of special days long remembered, including birthday parties and family outings. They take us back to a time when mothers shopped daily in little shops – the butcher's, the grocer's and the newsagent's – when the Pop Man and the Bread Woman delivered to the door, and when sweets, still rationed until the mid 1950s, were bought in two-ounce bags from huge glass jars. Those privileged enough to enjoy holidays away from home spent them in caravans in West Wales or in post-war boarding houses in seaside resorts: there were hot pies for lunch and trays of tea on the beach, where mothers sat fully dressed – right down to their corsets and stockings. But alongside this old world were the harbingers of modernity. In addition to the joys of children's radio, came television, bought or rented by families to see the Coronation in 1953. For the first time too, cars became available to ordinary families, reflecting the growing affluence of the times. The authors in this section have conjured up an idyllic world of childhood and, indeed, in many ways the fifties and sixties were a marvellous time to grow up, in that they were free of the hardship of the war years and enjoyed a considerable prosperity when measured by what had gone before.

Of the five contributors to the Education section, three, Rachel Treadwell, Beth Clarke and Jane Salisbury, have written about their schooldays. They transport us back to a world of Victorian class-rooms, of rows of heavy desks with fixed seats, of inkwells and wooden pens with nibs, of the cane and regular visits from the nit nurse. Discipline was strict and pupils sought constantly to please teacher, responding instantly to commands such as, 'Hands on heads', 'Fingers on lips' and 'Sit up straight'. Several key themes emerge from these accounts. First, we see the low expectations which families had of girls and the continuing feeling that education was wasted on a girl. Rachel Treadwell deliberately made mistakes in her homework so as not to achieve higher marks than her twin brother. Secondly, looming over the lives of every girl and boy in Wales in these years, was the Eleven Plus Examination, what we all called the Scholarship Exam. No wonder it daunted us so much: passing or failing the scholarship could determine the whole of a person's future life. The 1944 Education Act introduced free sec-ondary schooling for all and set up a tri-partite system, in which, depending on examination results, a pupil was allotted a place in a grammar school, a technical school (where they existed) or a sec-ondary modern school. The aim was to establish a more meritocratic society, but this was far from totally achieved, as both social class and gender continued to influence an individual's chances of success. Jane Salisbury from Barry failed the scholarship in 1966. She came from what used to be called 'a broken home' and her failure is no reflection on her personal ability: nobody else in her class in Cadoxton School passed either. Now, having gained a Ph.D. and lecturing on educational policy at Cardiff University, she brings her analytical skills to bear on her own experience in an insightful account. The third important theme to surface in this section is the issue of Welsh language schools. Beth Clarke writes about community responses to opening a Welsh language primary school in Pontarddulais in the 1950s and of the 'English is the way to get on' attitude which influenced her father's choice of school for her. This piece links interestingly with that of Heulwen Williams, who as a teacher was involved in the campaign to open the first Welsh primary school in the Rhymney Valley (see Work Section). The 1944 Act paved the way for girls' increasing participation in higher education, but even so by 1967 only a third of the full time undergraduates in the University of Wales were women. The other two authors included here, Carys Richards and Ann Rodgers, both write of the more traditional form of higher education for Welsh girls – teacher training. Carys walked slap into anti-Welsh prejudice in a Cambridge college and Ann entered a world of strict rules, college uniforms and curfews at Barry Training College.

Teenagers were an invention of the 1950s and youth culture flowered in the 1960s. As in many other things, we were a bit behind the times in Wales, though that is not necessarily a bad thing. Welsh teenage girls brashly asserted their hold on modernity, but in the accounts published here it is evident that behind the trendy facades and the make-up, they were uncertain and perplexed. Growing up can be a difficult time, where having fun and insecurity often come into head-on collision. The contributors here, Marianne Jones, M. Muriel Hughes, Pam Clatworthy, Gillian Morgan and Joan Hilditch, illustrate the tensions of the teenage years. There is all the fun (and the anxiety) of going to the first proper dance and first 'adult' party – one with the lights off and experimenting with necking and French kissing. There is the joy of choosing Rimmel lipsticks from Woolworths, of buying Bill Haley, Elvis Presley and Beatles records, of drinking frothy coffee in coffee bars and of dressing up for nights out. There are the arguments with mothers about clothes. Girls wanted to wear petticoats starched in sugar solution and wide, felt skirts in the fifties or mini-skirts in the sixties. Mothers wanted them to buy their outfits in ladies' clothes shops and dress just like them. It was the same with hair. Girls favoured French combing, beehives and Mary Quant bobs; mothers liked perms. It was only really in the 1960s that Welsh girls stopped dressing like their mothers. The awkwardness that young girls felt about their maturing bodies is brought home here. First periods took them by surprise and some did not even have the advantage of modern sanitary towels and belts, but wore cloths, pinned on to vests or knickers, and later washed and hung on the line to dry for re-use. Old wives' tales abounded about not washing your hair when menstruating and it is clear that many girls relied for any sexual knowledge upon other girls. School sex education was practically non-existent, or so couched in birds and bees imagery as to be unintelligible. But not all of the youthful sexual experiences recounted in this section were fraught or fumbling, as Joan Hilditch's passionate piece, 'Sweet Sixteen', clearly demonstrates.

Church and chapel wielded an enormous influence on women's lives in this period, but even within the short span of the twenty years covered by this book that influence, along with membership of congregations, declined. As society became increasingly secular, so the hold of the chapels waned. Nowadays there is a tendency to emphasize the negative aspects of religion and to denigrate the power that chapels held over the lives of individuals. There is indeed something in this. Well into the 1960s, there are examples of young unmarried pregnant women being publicly drummed out of chapels in Wales. Lorna Pope picks up on the hypocrisy in her description of the service held to *re-admit* a young married couple whose child had been born too soon after the wedding. But it is wrong to concentrate only on the negative, because for many girls and women the church or chapel was the centre not only of their religious life but of their social life too. The other contributors to the Chapel section, Lynne Rees, Gaynor Cohen, Jude Brigley and Marian Tawe Davies clearly show this. There are memories of church services and familiar hymns; of Sunday school and Sisterhood outings; of smart new costumes for Easter; of Whitsun marches; of chapel teas, prayer meetings and the Band of Hope; and of falling passionately in love with young, handsome ministers. All of this emphasizes the positive role of chapels in providing not only the whole social life of large numbers of young women, but also in presenting them, through encouraging participation in church services and church groups, with confidence-building opportunities.

Courtship, Marriage and Divorce is by far the largest section, including as it does these three closely linked subjects. Marriage was for the great majority of women their highest ambition. Despite the so-called sexual revolution of the 1960s, marriage was more popular than ever in the 1950s and 1960s with the marriage rate peaking in the early 1970s. In the same period the average age at marriage fell: by the early 1970s it was twenty-two and a third of all brides in Britain were in their teens. Even by contemporary standards, however, Gillian Morgan, who married at sixteen in 1959, was extremely young.

The contributors to this section, Gillian Morgan, Judith Maro, Elaine Morgan, Eirwen Gwynn, Pamela Cockerill, Sally Gough, Mari Ellis, Marian Tawe Davies and Eva Goldsworthy, share their personal experiences with us and help us recreate the world of marriage in the fifties and sixties. This was an era when young women were likely to meet their future husbands at dances – as did Sally Gough and Pamela Cockerill – then in due course to become formally engaged and to marry in elaborate white weddings. Once married, young couples struggled to manage on very tight budgets. They saved up for each new item of furniture or household appliance and to buy their first home. Several of the contributors here draw on their own personal records and their excellent memories to provide financial details of living costs. There are fascinating accounts too of birth control, pregnancy and giving birth. These pieces are rich in domestic detail and one thing which clearly emerges is the stark difference between rural and urban life in those days. Three of the writers included here moved to live in rural Wales in homes without electricity, gas or hot water on tap. Judith Maro moved from Israel to Lleyn, where she and her husband set up home in a derelict castle. Eirwen Gwynn and her husband moved to the same area, where they became smallholders, keeping cows, pigs, poultry and sheep. Elaine Morgan and her children moved to a rent-free farmhouse in Radnorshire while her husband lived during the week in Abertillery to be near his work. With all the hot water having to be boiled in a bucket on the fire and the only lighting coming from paraffin lamps, she notes, 'Everything took longer than it does in town.' Interestingly, several of the contributors in this section are themselves professional writers. Elaine Morgan, the well-known dramatist and author of ground-breaking books on anthropology (including *The Descent of Woman* (1972), began writing scripts for television dramas in these years and Mari Ellis, in a selection from her diary for 1954, shows how she carried out her research work and her writing, while at the same time looking after two children, husband and elderly relatives. In a superb piece, originally submitted in Welsh, she presents a wonderful mélange of everyday domestic responsibilities interspersed with forays into exalted Welsh literary circles: one moment she is making marmalade and cakes, the next she is researching in academic libraries and having tea with Kate Roberts or Lady Megan Lloyd George.

The marriages discussed above were clearly happy and successful partnerships, but were all marriages so fortunate? Of course they were not. The whole question of domestic violence and unfaithful husbands was kept very much under wraps. There was no Welsh Women's Aid or refuges to turn to and marital breakdown left women in a parlous financial position. Marian Tawe Davies, whilst working in her mother's small shop in Godre'r-graig, became the confidante of worried female customers who told her their harrowing tales of violent and roving husbands. She tells of the treatment meted out to one abusive husband by two of her elderly great-aunts, who set about him with mops. It is reminiscent of the much older *ceffyl pren* (wooden horse) tradition in which wrongdoers were publicly shamed. The ultimate marital breakdown is divorce and the divorce rate, after falling in the 1950s, rose markedly in the 1960s. Before the 1969 Divorce Act obtaining a divorce was a complex and distressing business, which involved attributing moral blame to one or other of the parties: there were guilty and innocent parties and a woman who was judged to be 'a guilty party' was, in effect, publicly shamed. Such women were in a precarious position with regard to the custody of their children and also stood to lose out financially in the divorce settlement. Divorce could only be granted on certain grounds, primarily adultery, cruelty and desertion. Only when the more liberal 1969 Act came into force were divorces allowed on the grounds of marital breakdown. Eva Goldsworthy's divorce from her dominating and violent husband was heard in the High Court in London in 1969, but before the new legislation came into effect. In a remarkable, compelling and even entertaining piece, she recounts her courtroom experience of being cross-examined in detail and forced to speak in public about the sexual humiliation inflicted on her by her husband, before she was awarded her divorce on the grounds of cruelty.

I am aware that we are very fortunate to be able to include a section on Unmarried Mothers. That we are able to do so is entirely thanks to the courage of the contributors, who are willing to share with Honno readers their personal experiences, which even now, almost a half century later, are clearly still distressing to recall and recount. Quite frankly, becoming pregnant while unmarried and with no chance of marrying the father was regarded as the worst fate that could befall a girl. The fear of becoming pregnant over-shadowed the lives of young women and the very term 'unmarried mother' was a badge of disgrace. The dual moral standard was alive and well in the 1950s and for much of the 1960s too: women paid a very heavy price for sexual activity, while men got off scot-free. Yet it was very easy for a young woman to find herself in these circumstances. Birth control advice was for most of this period confined to married women or those about to marry. Women relied, often unwisely, on the man to take responsibility for contraception and although the pill gave women the chance to control their own fertility, it was not easy to obtain in Wales until the mid to late 1960s. Abortion was illegal until 1967, though women who could afford to pay the huge sum of three hundred pounds for a private termination could make use of loopholes in the law. Given these factors, together with the ignorance of their own bodies of many young women, it is no wonder that women continued to be caught out and found themselves in what was then the direst of situations.

The three contributors to this section, Dot Clancy, Eirlys Ogwen Ellis and Margaret Smith, show the trauma they were forced to endure – in dealing with the baby's father, having to tell their family about their condition and going into bleak mother and baby homes to give birth. Dot Clancy, a twenty-year-old student nurse, had to bear the consequences of 'getting carried away' at a party and submitting to the attentions of a dashing young doctor, who, of course, did not want to know. Margaret Smith, who was also rejected by the child's father, was regarded as bringing shame on her whole family, and Eirlys Ogwen Ellis, who came from a farming family in Gwynedd, became pregnant by a young student from the Sudan. There was huge pressure on these first two women to give up their babies for adoption, but neither would agree and both women kept them. Eirlys's baby, being of mixed race, was regarded as unsuitable for adoption by a family but, at her mother's suggestion, the baby was brought up by Eirlys's sister and her husband. It was not only the mothers who bore the burden of society's disapproval, but the children had to endure the stigma of being designated as illegitimate. These three women were forced to endure so much and their lives were made so difficult entirely because of the attitudes of the times. They vividly and movingly recount their experiences, which were to have a profound effect on the rest of their lives.

The numbers of women in paid work in Wales rose in the 1950s and 1960s. Whereas in 1931 just one in five women had gone out to work, by 1951 it was one in four. The trend continued to edge upward throughout the 1950s and 1960s and by 1971 over one in three women in Wales were in paid jobs. These figures were still low in comparison with England and the really significant increase was to come in the next three decades. Another clearly noticeable change in the character of the Welsh female workforce in the fifties and sixties was the rise in the number of married women workers: by 1961 about half the women in work were married. Increased participation by both single and married women was the result of greatly extended job opportunities in manufacturing, office work and the professions.

Three of the four contributions in the Work section come from women who entered the professions and provide us with a salutary reminder what the term 'professions' meant for Welsh women in these years. In effect, it meant teaching or nursing. Eiluned Davies took up her first teaching post in 1967 in a 'God-forgotten Comp' in a deprived area of south Wales, where she taught Welsh with only her academic gown and a broken chair leg to enforce her authority. Heulwen Williams not only taught in an English language primary school in the Rhymney valley, but also gave up her Saturday mornings to teach voluntarily in the Welsh medium school movement and from this grew the first Welsh language school in Monmouthshire. Her account conveys her enthusiasm and the great pleasure she felt in teaching and organizing a whole host of extracurricular activities in Ysgol Gymraeg Rhymni. Brenda Curtis acts as the representative of that other women's profession, nursing, and recalls her training in the prestigious St. Bartholomew's Hospital in London. Here she remembers the old-style uniform, the strict discipline, her ward duties and her leisure time too. But what about the Welsh women who worked in the many new factories which were set up in Wales after the war and which made everything from zip fasteners, lipsticks, gramophone records and washing machines to rayon, electricity meters and stockings? It is a weakness of collections of written autobiographical accounts that they do not attract contributions from working class women who did this kind of work. Fortunately, however, Jude Brigley, who was then a student, took a holiday job in the Revlon factory in Maesteg. She entered what was to her a totally alien world, but a familiar one to thousands of other Welsh women. In the factory, all workers had to wear caps with their hair tucked in; they clocked on and off and had to work at the speed dictated by the conveyor belt. She felt herself a total failure, as her lack of manual dexterity meant that she jammed up the line and had to be moved to less demanding work. Her experiences at Revlon of New York, Paris and Maesteg made her realize how fortunate she was not to have to do 'that grind' every day.

I have touched briefly on the topic of the swinging sixties earlier in this introduction and made it clear that I do not believe that the sixties did swing for women in Wales. Of course, Welsh teenage girls did get swept up in Beatlemania and screamed at Rolling Stones concerts and, although we lagged behind London fashions, mini skirts, fun furs and PVC raincoats all eventually caught on in Wales. But other sixties' concepts, like a psychedelic drug culture, free love and flower power, passed the great majority of us by. Single women found it very hard to get the pill and the idea of young unmarried couples living together was still unthinkable in most parts of Wales.

In short, Wales was not the place where it was all happening. For that we have to look to London, which was in those days the great magnet for young Welsh people.

In the Swinging Sixties section, we are fortunate to have a very lively, as well as an extremely thoughtful piece, from one of the great sixties icons, Molly Parkin. As fashion editor of the trendy *Nova* magazine, then of *Harpers & Queen* and eventually *The Sunday Times*, Molly was at the cutting edge of the sixties revolution. She was, as she says, 'the sparkling hostess of a party which lasted the entire decade,' but she paid a high price for all the fun and confesses that the sixties almost killed her. Her existence was a million miles from that of her childhood in Pontycymer and indeed from that of her married sister, Sally Gough, in Barry (*see* Courtship, Marriage and Divorce). Jen Wilson is also an exceptional woman and is a well-known jazz pianist. Jen has been playing gigs in Swansea pubs and clubs since the age of fourteen. Drawing on her old letters home from London in the sixties, where she worked by day helping problem families but kept up with the world of jazz, pop art and fashion in her free time, she concludes that swinging London simply did not exist for the poor families with whom she dealt daily. The other two contributions to this section are more typical of the broader experience of Welsh women. Jenny Sullivan brings us down to earth with the clear statement, 'The sixties totally passed me by.' Far from enjoying the much vaunted sexual freedom of the decade, she was told by her mother that she was no longer a virgin because she had used a Tampax. Similarly, Margaret Lloyd, a young wife and mother of four, living in her home town of Merthyr, muses on how she too missed out on the sixties phenomenon, but does recount a brush with hippies in Rhyl. It is ironic that many women in Wales today, who were young in the 1960s, still feel that they were alone in missing out on the sixties experience. They can take comfort in the fact that this was the common lot of Welsh women.

The coverage of major issues in the Politics section cannot claim to be extensive, though there are certainly sufficient entries to justify the creation of a section dealing with such an important topic. Nor can it be argued that the contributions here reflect women's involve-ment in mainstream politics: indeed, there are no pieces dealing with the dominant Labour and Liberal politics of urban and rural

Wales. Instead, what we have here are contributions by women who felt strongly, passionately even, about particular causes and issues. We are especially fortunate to be able to include Siân Edwards's superb memoir, 'Danger – Revolution in Progress'. Writing wittily and pointedly on her youthful involvement with Plaid Cymru in 1960s Carmarthen, she brings the campaign, which secured Gwynfor Evans's election as Plaid's first MP, vividly to life. She writes too of her passion for the Welsh language and how, via a stint in Holloway Prison, she eventually joined Cymdeithas yr Iaith. This is an important piece, giving a firsthand account of a period which was a key turning point in the history of Wales and of the language. We are pleased too to be able to publish the work of Hilda Price from Barry, who writes with equal passion on her long struggle to bring about a more egalitarian world. Hilda, who joined the Communist Party in 1941, evokes the optimism many felt at the programme of nationalization in the post war years. She writes about housing – a political issue with direct bearing on women's everyday lives – as well as her involvement with the Campaign for Nuclear Disarmament, with her trade union and in helping to run a blood bank in Cardiff for North Vietnam. The Vietnam War is also the main theme of poet Penny Windsor's early political memories: she gives us an eye witness account of the anti-Vietnam War demonstration outside the American Embassy in Grosvenor Square in 1968. Finally, Stella J. Schiller Levey examines her own political and national identity as a Jewish girl growing up in Wales. She describes her social and religious life in Cardiff in the 1950s and 1960s, and writes too about her membership of a Zionist youth group, her time on a kibbutz in Israel, and her work as a founder member of Ziona.

Taken together, the various sections of *Changing Times* help to build up a picture of women's lives in Wales in the 1950s and 1960s. Indeed, the idea of organizing the contributions into sections is to create the building blocks which can be put together to create a composite whole. But life is not as neat as that. In fact, readers will find hidden gems – tiny vignettes and insightful flashes – in unexpected places. The sheer wonder of electricity coming, as they said, 'on stream' is shown in Marianne Jones's piece in the Teenagers section; the most heart-wrenching picture of poverty and deprivation in the valleys of south Wales comes in Eiluned Davies's account of her first teaching post in the Work section; the Welsh Sunday is recalled in Judith Maro's piece in the Courtship, Marriage and Divorce section and the sheer joy of moving into a new council house is evoked by Hilda Price in the Politics section. On the other hand, I am aware that there are gaps in what women have chosen to write about and some fundamental points have not come over as strongly as I would have wished.

Amongst the gaps, I would pinpoint the fact that there is very little on women's social and cultural activities or on membership of women's organizations. These omissions may partly be attributed to the fact that the women are writing about their childhood, youth and early married lives, but it is still a pity not to have any accounts of belonging to choirs or sports' groups or taking part in activities run by women's organizations, such as the Women's Institute, the Townswomen's Guild or Merched y Wawr, though the last named group was not set up until 1967. With regard to certain points which have not come over as strongly as I could have wished, though some are implicit in much of the writing, I would single out just two.

The first is the fact that women were economically and financially dependent on their husbands. It needs to be clearly stated here that single women could not get mortgages and that women could not even enter into hire purchase agreements to buy a three-piece suite or a radiogram, without the signature of a male guarantor on the document.

The second concerns the fact that feminism was at a very low ebb, perhaps at its lowest point of the twentieth century, and there was as yet no such thing as equal opportunities. Siân Edwards and other young Plaid Cymru members, both female and male, in 1960s Carmarthen were on the vanguard of a new wave of feminism when they artfully challenged that male bastion, the men-only bar, but, for the most part, there existed amongst Welsh women only a vague unease that something was amiss. For a good illustration of this uneasiness, we can do no better than to read Jen Wilson's piece in the Swinging Sixties section and ask why did Jen's office boss refer to her as 'girl' but call the office boy 'Mr Phillips'?

Yet there is more to *Changing Times* than simply a resource from which we can recreate the past, valuable though that is. As readers of the many pieces printed here, we are privileged to view the lives of individual women from the inside. I am immensely grateful to all the women who have shared their stories with us. This is their book.

I also wish to express my thanks to many other people who have helped in its making. My thanks go to Chris Lee for her continuing support and help. I am particularly indebted to Catrin Stevens for reading the whole of the manuscript at an early stage and for her constructive advice on many aspects of the content. I also wish to thank Gwenllïan Dafydd and Janet Thomas of Honno for their unflagging support in seeing this project through from its conception to its final production. As always, it has been a pleasure to work with Honno, which has done so much for women's publishing in Wales.

I have enjoyed working on *Changing Times* and my sincere hope now is that Honno readers will find much to interest them in their journey back to the Wales of the fifties and sixties.

Deirdre Beddoe
Barry.

# CHAPTER 1

# CHILDHOOD

# Drawn from Memory

~

*Jo Mazelis*

**Jo Mazelis** was born in Swansea in 1956 and lived in the Sketty area until she was nineteen. After attending Swansea Art College for one year, she moved to first Aberystwyth and from there to London, before returning to Swansea in 1991. She has published a number of stories in anthologies published by Honno, Gomer, Parthian and Seren. She has won a prize in the Rhys Davies Short Story competition in 1995, 1999 and 2001. Parthian published her first book *Diving Girls* in 2002.

We are watching *Maverick* on the television. 'We' consists of mother, father, sister and myself. As a rule every evening is passed like this. It is the early sixties and I am four or five years old. My mother sits in her armchair with a chrome pedestal ashtray to her right-hand side, a cup of weak saccharin-sweetened tea, a pack of twenty Pall Mall cigarettes and a lighter close by. I am, I think, both madly in love with the 'Maverick' in the TV show, and also puzzled by him. It's his feminine side that both attracts and confuses me. His face is smoothly shaven, unlike the other cowboys, and it is boyish and attractive. I think I thought that he was pretty – I did not have the vocabulary to shape what I felt when I gazed at him. But I was inspired. The moment the show finished I went upstairs to my bedroom, and there, on the pale pink wall, I did a two foot high picture of my love with a waxy black crayon. The drawing surprised me – it looked like him. I had created him from nothing and he would be there on the wall for ever.

I suppose that a whole generation of children in the fifties and sixties grew up with television as the dominant cultural form. And that meant exposure to a lot of American programmes. America was scorched and burnt into my consciousness as surely and rapidly as the flames engulfed the map during the credits to *Bonanza*. The theme tune was all daring and galloping gusto: you couldn't help but have your appetite whetted by the stirring rhythms of its 'dum de de dum, de de dum, dee dee dum, dee dee dum dum'.

My very first boyfriend was a crew-cutted, well-fed and impressively strong little American boy called Hank. Hank had black hair. And four or five older brothers who also sported crew cuts, and one younger sister. They lived in a large house on the Gower Road near the police station, just up from Sketty Cross. They may have been Seventh Day Adventists. Their father may have been teaching at Swansea University. Or a doctor at Singleton Hospital. At that age one doesn't explore these facts. Instead obscure events lodge in the memory, like displaced dreams or invented truths.

My best friend's name was Christina and her family was of Italian descent. Christina also lived on the Gower Road a little further along from Hank's house, just before the junction with Sketty Lane where, on an invitingly large and blank wall, someone had painted the words 'Yankee go home'. I don't think they meant Hank and his family. That graffiti stayed there for years, it seemed. As did the 'Free Wales' graffiti with the 'W' crossed through on the pillars by the side of the Mumbles Road and the legend 'All mods are bent' which graced a wall near Oystermouth Bus Terminus.

Christina and I were the only two children from Sketty School who were invited to Hank's birthday party. This non-observation of the rules of party-giving marked Hank and his family as clearly different – and so I assumed that this was how all Americans conducted themselves on such festive occasions.

The other birthday parties which I attended, and which my parents gave for my sister and me, seemed to follow a fairly well tried and tested format, which went as follows. First, they were generally single sex affairs and thus all the female members of your class would be invited. The party would be held in your home. All of the girls would be wearing pretty party frocks and best shoes of patent leather, or plainer red or navy or white or brown sandals with white crêpe soles. The frocks had fitted bodices and big puffy skirts and were tied with a neat bow or, in my case, a stubborn straggly knot. Every guest would bring a present nicely wrapped by his or her mother and this would be handed over on arrival like an entry fee. The children would then play organized games, many of which ended in a prize being won. There was 'Pass the Parcel', 'Musical Chairs', 'Musical Statues' and 'Hunt the Thimble'.

Once, during a party at Christina's house, I performed the visionary stunt of entering the room where the thimble was hidden, pointing straight up to twisted crêpe paper streamers that hung from the ceiling and pronouncing the information that the thimble was there. I remember the look on her grandfather's face as kindly and amused, but yet also somehow dumbfounded. How did I know it was there? A lucky guess I suppose, but there again, it seemed, and still seems, such an obvious, though cunning, place to hide it.

After the games came the birthday tea. All of the children would be seated around a dining table, and extra chairs would have been drafted in, plain wooden kitchen chairs, or metal-legged ones, or folding outdoor chairs, or mismatched borrowed-from-a-neighbour chairs. I seem to remember that there followed a period in which our noise and excitement were stifled as we all gulped and munched sandwiches of white bread and fish paste, and slurped our lemonade or squash while our little legs dangled and swung about in their own happy gravity-free universes. After the tea there would be more games, the sort of rhyming, formation based circle games that seem finally, after hundreds of years, to be dying out – 'Oranges and Lemons', 'Poor Mary sits a-weeping', 'In and out the Dusty Blue-bells' and 'London Bridge is falling down'.

There is a cine film of one such party. It is a silent movie that my father, ever the photography and gadget enthusiast, had made. I have seen it only twice since reaching adulthood and its images magnetize me with loss and longing and wonder. It is a beautiful summer's day at the beginning of August and my sister and I, and all our friends, Janet and Sarah and Pauline from our street, as well as our friends from school are in the garden in our best frocks. We are playing 'The Farmer's in the Dell' and there is a slow, quiet intensity to our game. Holding hands, we walk around in a circle. My mother is doing the motherly thing by leading us in our game; she is wearing a sleeveless cotton shift of dark blue and white flowers. I am in the centre so I am the farmer, perhaps because it is my birthday. They circle me and chant the words of the rhyme but the sounds of our voices were unrecorded and so are lost in time.

The silence gives the ceremony a curious, almost funereal air, despite the pretty dresses, despite the sunshine and the flowers. Then, when it's time for the farmer to take a wife, I choose the person I love more than anyone in the world, my mother. She, however, protests. Silently on the film I mouth the words that shape my pleading, my love, but still she resists in that chiding, grown-up way of hers and thus she maintains the proper adult status which was perhaps typical of the age. I have found out that on the odd occasion when, in the spirit of history and nostalgia and recklessness, I have organized children, my own daughter included, in a game of 'The Farmer's in the Dell'. that, if I am picked, then I am inevitably the bone and end up rolling on the grass being pummelled with evident pleasure by hordes of devil children.

There were no such games at Hank's party and no birthday spread either. Instead there were tubes of Smarties and ice cream. But surely my memory is playing tricks on me; it cannot be that the only food given to us was sweets and ice cream? I doubt this memory because I distinctly remember sitting down at the table at Hank's. This sticks in my mind because someone stood behind my chair with their hands resting on its back for the whole time and I was desperate to wriggle and shunt and scrape my chair nearer to the table in order to be more comfortable. I liked to be wedged in firmly against a table, just as I liked the sheets and blankets to be tucked in as tightly as possible when I was in bed.

There were several things at Hank's party that remain vivid for me because of the strong emotions behind them. There was the discomfort and frustration of the unmovable chair. There was also the inevitable hunger for both Christina and I, as our mothers would have been careful to starve us a little before the party so that we could eat our dutiful fill. I also remember that lying around unused was a small wooden boat-like rocker of the sort that could seat two small children facing each other. I longed to have a go on this, as I had never in my memory tried such a toy, but something prevented me. For one, the toy belonged to Hank's younger sister, who was perhaps three or four, and I, of course, was a grown-up monster of five or six, and far too big and sophisticated to squeeze into such a rocker. Yet my eyes slid longingly towards this toy, my body aching for the joy of its rocking rhythms.

The final frustration was to do with the house itself and is, in a sense, an ongoing frustration, as the house still stands; now derelict and long empty, and due for demolition so that the road can be widened. The house was and is a very large late Victorian or Edwardian one. It stands at right angles to the road and the side wall and its windows are directly against it. There is a high walled garden in the front – now overgrown with nettles and brambles. And to the rear, like a little line of ducklings behind the mother duck, is a row of far smaller cottages leading back towards Sketty Cross. The frustration I felt and still perhaps feel is due to the fact that we were never allowed free reign of the house. We could not range freely in it, nor tiptoe into the older boys' rooms, nor inspect Hank's room and more importantly Hank's probably fabulous American toys. Even the boundary breaking request for the toilet only gained access to their downstairs one and did not allow the soft carpeted creep upstairs, while the voices of other children fell away and the cat-killing curiosity that burned in one was set free.

Sometime before or after this, I was at the swing park with Hank and Christina and we were on the spider's web roundabout – a metal barred thrill ride on which one could clamber or sit while someone pushed you round and round. If it was a parent, then you were unlikely to go very fast, certainly not dangerously fast and your parent would constantly be chiding you to hold on tight and not let go or climb about. Ironically, if Christina and I were playing on it unsupervised, pushing it around together or alone, then we could never get a good head of steam up and exhausted ourselves just to turn it at a slow walking pace. This was where Hank came in. Hank was a demon pusher. At age five or six, with his solid arms and legs, Hank had the strength and determination to push harder and faster than all the other spindly, flop-haired boys put together. Hank pushed Christina and me faster and faster. Faster than I have ever been pushed; thrillingly fast, scarily fast, dangerously fast. Christina and I whooped and screamed and folded ourselves downward as we fought the centrifugal force which wanted to pick us up and fling us far from the spider's web and impale us on the railings or entangle us in the swings or dash us against the slide. As I write this down, I picture the scene, remembering the exact position of the now removed-for-safety-reasons spider's web.

I remember the whirling, spinning houses of Cory Street and Park View Terrace, and the nearby tennis courts where the young Martin Amis may have been amongst the players who barely registered the gleeful screams of the little girls. Beyond the spinning ride and swings, just glimpsed, was the graveyard where Amy Dillwyn was buried and my grandfather, William Stanley Williams known as Stan, had had his ashes scattered, and where his daughter, my mother, would later be buried. What happiness I felt at that moment – to share the thrill of the ride with my best friend, to be entertained so loyally and royally by my boyfriend! And the sun must have been shining and the sky a giddy canopy of blue. And no one fell off that day, no one's hands were scraped and studded with gravel and stinging pain. No one cried until the snot poured out of his or her nostrils. No one got knocked out when they walked too close to the swings and got clunked on the head.

But after that shining memory, there is nothing. It is as if the TV set was switched off in the middle of the programme or the needle knocked from the record. I was removed from Sketty School and sent to Parklands, the new big infant and junior school that had just been built in the middle of the council estate. I was no longer the best friend of Christina – Christina who had loved me so much that when I was off school with mumps, she had refused to go to school. And I was no longer the girlfriend of the strong American boy called Hank.

One world was snatched away and another slipped into its place. I acquired a new boyfriend called Hugh, who wore an olive-green home-knitted jumper that had an unusual slash neck opening like a Breton fisherman's sweater. Hugh and I paraded around the brand new shiny black tarmac playground arm in arm. A gaggle of girls skipped behind gleefully singing, 'Here comes the bride', and I felt they were mocking us, mocking him and his jumper that his granny knitted. Then Hugh too, fades out, never to reappear in memory as if he, like Christina and Hank before him, were frail fragments of my young imagination, ghosts of belonging, mere walk-on parts in the drama of my being.

And all that is left is the sanitized and wood-chipped playground on Cory Street, and the two schools, Sketty and Parklands, and Hank's house on the hill; its garden overgrown, its roof sprouting a miraculous bush of buddleia, its rooms all empty, unexplored even by the ghost of me, forever denied access to its corners and secret cubbyholes of dream and desire. Who is Hank now? I wonder. Did he return to America to grow ever fatter, ever duller, ever older? And perhaps, more importantly, does he remember me? Do I exist, a tiny fragment of frail memory, a pale wisp of a girl as light as a feather, full of laughter? The past is covered over now, layer upon layer of wallpaper conceals it, but there beneath is the indelible stain, the black crayon outline of memory and longing, the place that cannot be returned to.

## In a Bubble of Innocence

~

*Hazel Farr*

**Hazel Ann Farr** was born in 1945 (on the day it was announced that Japan had surrendered) in Morriston, where she lived until she was twenty, when she married her first and only 'blind date'. She has two sons and four grandchildren. Her career has included working as a secretary, dinner lady, Avon lady, office cleaner, tea lady and school clerk. At the Swansea & District Writers' Circle, she won the Cup for three years in succession, and has had work published in *Nursing Times* and *My Weekly*, among others. She is currently writing a historical novel set in Swansea.

The first week of September 1950 introduced me to education and milk, which came in third-pint bottles left too long on the school steps. I drank one and was sick. I've never liked milk since. I remember little about that first day, except the milk and the railings that kept my mother outside.

She was forty-two when I arrived, my other four siblings being much older. So, I, an 'only child', played with imaginary friends under the table or behind the sofa, making dens, while the older ones played outside. Later, I was allowed to play in the *cwm* behind our house, in the 'sally-rhubarbs', with my friend Michael, who 'acquired' a packet of six Woodbines, lit one, coughed his heart up and turned green. I was so frightened I *never, ever* tried one. Michael and I enjoyed the innocent closeness of children, perhaps because his mother was 'ancient' like mine. 'The war's to blame, keeping my man from his bed,' moaned Auntie-next-door (I had an 'Auntie' in every house). My parents 'rested' (sex wasn't a word used then) on Sunday afternoons, while we were at Sunday school.

My maternal grandparents had a narrow terraced house in Plasmarl, with a small compact greenhouse that I hid in and got covered in green pollen off the tomato plants. But the exciting place was the bottom of the garden which overlooked the railway line. Across the sheer drop, I'd wave to the signal box and get my face covered in soot from passing trains. Oh, that smell!

Granddad was a lay-preacher, so I was a 'three times a Sunday' Methodist, changing my clothes after each visit. A costume and hat – not a 'suit' or 'outfit', well-dressed girls wore costumes. Mother went everywhere in a hat – it was etiquette. But off came my hat when 'chasing boys' after chapel, on 'Morriston's monkey parade'.

I must tell you about my wonderful Auntie May, my mother's sister, and also my godmother. I idolised every ounce of her body, and that, I might say, was a lot. Uncle Albert and she resembled 'Jack Spratt who ate no fat, his wife . . .' She was forever laughing your troubles away. On Sisterhood trips, she would dress up and have the coach passengers roaring at her antics. But on Saturday afternoons, she would set out, in extra large handwriting, the sermons of Mr Fenwick, our almost blind minister, who would still have to use a magnifying glass to read it. His sermons were, therefore, very slow and the congregation would fidget. But I would be thrilled to be standing alongside Auntie, who could also sing the hymns like an angel. I was so proud, I felt like shouting out, 'Hey, look everyone, I belong to her.' You could say that chapel was an extension of my home life, except my father never attended, his strict Baptist upbringing, I assumed, being sufficient for life. It was never discussed, and it wasn't until after his death that I discovered that his grandfather, during the late 1800s, had been a prominent revivalist

Baptist minister. Why hadn't he spoken of him? Skeletons in the cupboards!

The fifties' summers were idyllic. We never went away, but Sunday school trips were magic. I went with two chapels, Morriston and Plasmarl, on the train to Burry Port and Kidwelly – we thought, to the end of the world. And wonderful Aberdare Park! I can't remember it raining. There were family trips to the beach too. Swansea Sands and Caswell were my favourites. The bus trip to Caswell was an epic journey, nearly as long as train trips further afield. Nana and Granddad got on the bus at Plasmarl, but sat downstairs – Nana being 'asthmatical' couldn't join us on the single long seats above. When we got to the top of Townhill, the view was breathtaking. Swansea town and bay were at our feet. Sketty's posh houses came next, before getting back onto the Mumbles road. Here we'd get a fleeting glance of the pier before passing Oystermouth Castle; then came the top of Caswell Hill. Now that's another memory, coming back up that hill on a loaded bus, men being asked to disembark to make the vehicle lighter. And still we struggled up the steep incline, the male passengers walking behind.

Caswell was Nana's favourite, with her own special stone. It was a flat-topped boulder to the right side of the bay, which she sat on regally, surveying her subjects at play. At meal times, it was spread with a tablecloth and she'd expertly slice a loaf of bread, butter it and then spread on home-made jam. I can taste it now. Whenever we reminisce with our Essex connection, we always mention that 'stone'.

When I was eleven, we were hosts to our Essex relatives and, no doubt showing off, became more adventurous by going to Rhossili. For the benefit of readers who don't know the area, not many buses get to that point – if you miss the return bus, enough said. It's a most beautiful bay, and going down is no problem, but coming back takes longer.

The bus had gone! There were twelve of us, including a baby in a carry-cot. Taxis were out of the question in 1956, but along came a butcher's van, the type where you step in through a back door to the counter – a small space, to hold, shall I say, three customers. We all squeezed in, big Auntie included, me and the carry-cot on the counter. And, out of the kindness of his heart, the travelling meat purveyor took us to the next bus route. It's a wonder we didn't turn vegetarian, but there again, I'd never heard of that back then.

My introduction to personal transport was, for the fifties, fortuitous. We were first to have a car on our road. On Sundays, in between chapel (we were never allowed out to play on the Sabbath), I would sit in it, going far up the valley. Previously, my father (who I don't think ever took a driving test) would chauffeur our GP on fishing and shooting trips at weekends, he having a vehicle but no knowledge of driving. And I had an uncle who was official chauffeur to the owner of a large prestigious furniture store. He used to come and take us out on his days off. I felt like royalty in the back of the large black limousine, although I was too small to see out of the windows. But have you ever been in a 'brand new' car with leather seats reeking of beeswax, made acrid by the hot summer weather? Well, I have. I was sick! My eldest brother wasn't at all pleased with his kid sister's reaction to his treasured possession. A new car in the early 50s was rare. With his apprenticeship completed, and being unattached, his wages went on that car, so understandably, to 'swank', he took my mother and I out for a spin. It was the last time I was allowed in it.

Television was the next big event in my life. We'd had the wireless under our roof for a while, but it hadn't made any impression on me. Then in 1953 (as happened in many homes across the land) at the age of seven and ten-twelfths, it arrived in our 'best room' for the Coronation. I say best room, because we didn't have a parlour in the front of our house like our neighbours' terraced properties. Ours was 'doubled-fronted-posh': door in the middle with one living room either side – dining room and best room, separated by the stairs. A back kitchen with an 'inside' bathroom above it; two bedrooms atop of the living rooms, and most important, the toy cupboard under the stairs, which Welsh folk called a *cwtsh dan staer*. And to this day, we still refer warmly to the 'best room' and 'toy cupboard', the latter I will tell you about later. But getting back to the glass-fronted cube that brought strangers into our 'best room'. Relatives would gather on Sunday evenings to watch. I'd sit on the floor with my cousins, the adults having taken all the chairs. My father poured drinks for the men and my mother tea for the ladies.

On one huge occasion, my mother took me to the cinema. We had two in Morriston, the Regal and the Gem. I'd never been in one (my parents being of Victorian outlook), but this day was different. We were to see a religious film, *The Robe*. So that was my introduction to the 'big screen'. My husband went to their local 'flea pit' as he calls it, every Saturday morning to see westerns.

Photographs are not widely available from my early days, but I found one of me at the age of three, clutching a bunch of flowers in my Auntie May's garden (she had a magical garden where I'd spend hours making daisy chains). Apparently, I'd been persuaded to let the camera take a photo of the flowers, unaware that I would be in the frame as well. I'm glad the coaxing worked, so that I could see my early image – a mop of fair curls and a body with no waist. I remember complaining to my mother (as young as five) on a bath night about my lack of waistline, and I said that I'd never eat potatoes again, only chips.

Christmases were a blur, except for the time that I had a doll *and* a pushchair. I couldn't get over the excitement. I also remember sliding out from the blankets in the dark, to feel at the foot of the bed the 'bumps' that Santa had brought. Then I'd climb gratefully back and sleep contentedly until morning. But one Christmas was sad. I was seven and my mother and I had been to Swansea to 'buy' decorations – now that was quite posh, usually we made our own coloured chains. On the way back, we stopped off in Plasmarl to show Nana, who was in bed in the parlour. I jumped up and down excitedly on the bed, showing each item in turn. She smiled, gave a loud sigh, like a rush of air, and went into a deep sleep. As my mother tucked me in later that night, I heard her whisper to my sister, 'I'm worried about her, she hasn't cried.' I hadn't understood all the fuss about Nana going to 'sleep'. I was just annoyed at being ushered out of the room and my wonderful decorations ignored.

I was a very naive child. Children of today notice everything. I lived in a happy world of my own, until an earthquake shook it, waking me up. I haven't talked much about my siblings because they were never around. My sister (ten years my senior), took up nursing when I was seven and lived away from home. So when a nosy girl looking out of our classroom window at our chapel opposite, said to me, 'That's your sister going in there,' I replied sharply, 'No, she's nursing!' But when I got home there was a special tea laid out, and a telegram on the table from our 'Essex lot' saying, 'Congratulations on your marriage.' I wanted to cry. Nobody had told me. Or let me be a bridesmaid. Shortly afterwards, my nephew was born. When my school friends sniggered, 'Didn't you notice?' I began to wonder how thick I was.

Thick. Oh, yes, I was certainly that. Especially the day of the 'toy cupboard incident'. My mother (no doubt from the shock of my sister's 'shot-gun' wedding) had been taken ill with heart problems, my father and brothers were abed with the 'flu, and I was kept off school to help in the house. The Board Man (truant officer) came to visit. And, never having seen him, I answered the door and thought he was the electricity man. I didn't want to disturb my mother's rest, so I took the initiative and showed him the meter. This was deep under the stairs in our 'toy cupboard'. I opened the door and put my hand on his backside to usher him in. Luckily, my father appeared to save the day.

I hoped I entered the 1960s with a bit more common sense, but it was not to be. The very first day I was at the Secondary Modern School, having failed my Eleven Plus (I put it down to being the youngest in class – I should have been held back for the next year's age group) a girl came up to me and asked, 'Have you come?'

I stared at her, thinking how stupid she was, and answered curtly, 'Of course I have. I'm *here*, aren't I?'

It wasn't until a while later that I discovered what 'coming' was all about. Nobody had explained periods to me.

# Small World

~

*Leona Jones*

**Leona Jones** was born in Swansea in 1959 and grew up in Bryn-hyfryd. She moved to Cardiff in her early twenties, then to England, then back to Cardiff, where she now lives with a tall and patient man, two beautiful, bouncing girls and two golden fish. After a lifelong passion for reading, she started writing in 2000 and she is published here for the first time. She hopes to create more time for writing by perfecting her plans for a self-maintaining home.

Once upon a long time ago there lived a little girl. She lived with her mother and her father and her grandmother in a terraced palace on a hill known as Lovely in the east of the great land of Swansea. The little girl was very good – she never left the pavement to play in the middle of the street, and she always brushed her teeth so the tooth fairy wouldn't be cross.

The land the little girl lived in was far away and wondrous indeed. It was full of talk and chatter and movement – and people, people who performed strange and special deeds. There was the Bread Woman, who carried hot loaves to the doors in the middle of the nights, and the Milk Man, who brought clinking bottles at the dawn of the days. The little girl's favourite was the Pop Man, whose potion-carrying van was a fizzing, bubbling fantasy of dandelions and burdocks and lemons and limes.

Even Time knew where it was going. Every weekday the little girl's father came home from work at six o'clock. Every Sunday the little girl's grandmother took her Welsh-speaking fox with glass eyes to chapel. Every Friday the little girl and her mother walked to the butcher's, the baker's, paid for the papers, and bought good, fresh food from shopkeepers wearing aprons and telling tales.

The land thrived on talk. The people in the shops used it like brown paper, wrapping up goods. The people in the streets used it like umbrellas or sundresses. The people on the front steps used it like scrubbing brushes or doorstops.

Of course, these people were the big people. The little boys and girls who came out to play shouted and screamed and yelled and sang. The little people had not yet come to talk. They saw talk in quite a different way. Talk meant a chance to explore the details of the pavements, to pull moss from between stones in walls, to watch a cat watching them. It meant a time to pull on the big people's sleeves and make the big people say, 'Wait a minute, now!' It meant starting the meaningful hopping-from-one-foot-to-the-other dance which always interrupted the talk and began the quick walk back home.

At that time, the land was overflowing with sunny days, mixed with warm baking, mothballs, dinners roasting, and wild black clouds. Very often the little girl was sent on messages to the big people living in the neighbourhood. She would take a pot of home-made blackberry jam, carrying it carefully with both hands, or run with a small packet of sausages as the cold breath of the butcher's fridge frosted her fingers. Often the big people would give her something in return, a coin or a sweet perhaps. But the most special treats of all came from Auntie Maudie, a comfortable, soft fairy godmother who understood the magic of buttered Marie biscuits, and daisy chains picked from her warm, sweet-scented back garden. She was known throughout the land as the Queen of Talk. No-one else living knew as much as she did about the ancient Art.

Then, one day, a new person came to the little girl's palace. Her name was Daphne, and she was different because she could be heard but not seen. She lived in the special black and cream box kept on a small shelf high in the corner of the palace's main room. Daphne filled the world with songs and stories of magical animals, adventuring children and amusing elves, but only at the time that was specially hers. Daphne told children to listen with mother and asked if they were sitting comfortably, but the little girl's mother was always working in the kitchen at Daphne time. However, the little girl didn't mind listening on her own, and would stand as close as she could to Daphne's box, looking up at it, forgetting her true surroundings.

But Daphne time was also the Queen of Talk's time. Every day, Auntie Maudie would leave her lovely scented garden and visit one of the people of the land. As Daphne time approached, the little girl would watch from the window and hold her breath and wish and wish that Auntie Maudie would not call here today. But, of course, wishes are not always granted.

The big people always gathered in the main room to talk, and they did not understand the specialness of Daphne time. Big people talk meant little people should be quiet. But Daphne was asking if they were sitting comfortably and the little girl really *had* to tell her she was *standing* comfortably. Daphne was singing the special songs and the little girl couldn't help but join in. She was telling the wonderful stories – but the little girl wasn't able to hear what was happening. Big people talk meant Daphne's perfect voice disappeared. 'I can't hear!' she wailed. But still the big people kept on talking.

It was more than the little girl could bear. 'I want to hear the story!' she cried. The big people ignored her. In anguish she ran to the table and dragged a chair to her standing place. She climbed onto the chair. She stood on tiptoes on the chair. Daphne was closer but still distant. Desperately, the little girl turned to the big people with her finger on her lips. 'Sssh!' she implored, 'Please! Ssshh!' The big people turned their backs. She jumped off the chair and ran to fetch the small stool. She put this on the chair and clambered quickly on to it. If only Daphne could wait. If only the big people would stop talking. Daphne was still there, finishing the final song. The little girl grew as much as she could on her tiptoes and stretched to say goodbye. Suddenly, the little girl's mother turned and with a gasp swept her off the stool, off the chair, and away from Daphne's farewell.

Then the little girl was put in her tower room so she could learn the lesson of how to be quiet and listen.

## Summer Holidays in the Fifties

~

*Mary Davies Parnell*

**Mary Davies Parnell** lived in Trehafod, Rhondda until 1955 when she left to study French at university in Aberystwyth. She has published three volumes of semi-autobiographical anecdotal memoirs of growing up in the Rhondda, *Block Salt and Candles, Snobs and Sardines* and *Plateaux, Gateaux, Chateaux* (Seren) and since 1975 has lived in Cardiff (although she is still a keen supporter of Pontypridd RFC).

'Oh Lord! There she goes again!' These words, uttered by my long-suffering father, preceded by a thump, are what come to mind when I think about summer holidays in the fifties. The thump was the descent to the ground, fortunately never with any perceivable damage done to her person, of my largish maiden aunt, who accompanied my father, mother and me on the annual summer holiday to Weston-super-Mare or Minehead or Porthcawl or Ilfracombe or Llanstephan and once to pastures far indeed, to Pwllheli in north Wales.

Holiday mornings were usually spent walking around the town, leisurely surveying the scene, perhaps on the promenade, in the resort's 'Winter Gardens' as the park was generally called, along the harbour quay watching the fishing boats and sometimes, boringly, in the town centre where the shops were. While I walked in front with my father, setting the pace, so to speak, my mother and her sister would be dragging along behind, discussing hats, the relative merits of the shops in the place compared with Pontypridd, their corns and other things wrong with their feet, the various guests in the hotel or boarding house and the menial jobs waiting for them back home. At the sound of the thump my father would turn round with a sigh and hurry back to where my aunt would be sitting on the ground looking helpless and slightly embarrassed.

'Are you all right, Rach?' he'd ask with half concern, knowing she was uninjured, with only her self-esteem battered (once again). She had quite a large surface to land on after all. 'Come on then! Up you get!'

With that, he'd haul her to her feet while my mother brushed the dust off her skirt. 'It's these old shoes with high heels you wear, see, Rach. You ought to get a more substantial pair with flat soles that'll give you a better grip, or wear daps like I do on holiday.'

To be fair to my aunt, she normally only slipped onto her bottom on slopes, so after a first experience of Ilfracombe and a few unplanned sits on Capstan Hill, we avoided that resort as 'too hilly for Rach'. Minehead came into the same category, although it didn't seem all that steep to me. Perhaps it was just a slippery place. Combe Martin was another West Country town out of bounds when Aunty Rach was of the party.

Once the clocks went forward in the spring, the Davies family would start thinking about the summer holiday. At least the youngest Davies did and I would daily pester my parents with, 'Where are we going for holidays this year, Mam and Dad?' My father worked as a carpenter during the day and ran the corner shop we lived behind in Trehafod in the evening, so had little time for holiday planning. From the age of eight and joined-up writing, it was my job to peruse the small-ads in the *Western Mail* and write a letter to the landlady in response to finding something such as, 'Weston-super-Mare vacancies July/August. Full board £6 p.w. Children half price. 5 mins beach. Apply Mrs Bond, Minerva Hotel, Seaview Rd., Weston-super-Mare'. We never went for more than a week as the parents had the shop and loyalty to customers to think about.

By the end of May, our holiday was always booked, thanks to me. I longed to book a week at one of the new Butlin's Holiday Camps at Skegness or Filey, wherever they were, but my parents would have none of it. 'Oh no, they are too big, Mary, and you have to stay in small wooden huts and eat meals in a huge hangar with thousands of other people. Then they wake you up with a bugle at seven in the morning. And you're on the go all the time.' So Butlin's was out, though I wondered if perhaps I couldn't get us there by mistake, foul up the bookings by giving the wrong dates and there would only be Butlin's left. However, I was afraid they'd refuse to go and we'd have no seaside holiday at all – just spending the week visiting relations or having day trips, which meant either shopping in Cardiff with a placatory row on a boat in Roath Park, or Pontypridd with a visit to the baths in Ynysangharad Park afterwards. So it was always a small hotel or boarding house and always full board.

Packing for the holiday was a lengthy procedure starting a month before departure day. The suitcases were taken down from on top of the wardrobes and carefully dusted. My father's grey flannels, which hadn't seen the light of day since the previous summer, were cleaned and his tan tweed sports jacket brushed and aired. The white tennis shoes (daps) which he always wore on holiday were blanco-ed and his light coloured shirts, worn open-necked, were washed and carefully folded. I usually had some new white ankle socks to go with my Clarks brown leather sandals with the cut-out flower on the front, and a new frock. My mother always took a straw hat with false flowers or fruit on it and packed beige peep-toe sandals with lisle stockings and the obligatory corset to keep them up and her in, under her summer dresses. All this was laid out on the bed in the spare room and checked weekly against a list. At the last minute small things like a roll of plaster and a packet of lint were added in the event of blisters, and Rennies in case the food was indigestible. All I cared about was taking my bathing costume and swimming cap. This was also the only time of the year Mam wore her five diamond engagement ring and her gold Benson's watch. I think she was afraid to leave them at home for fear of burglars.

A necessary nuisance to pack, as they took up so much room in the cases, were a dressing gown each, another item only used during the summer holiday. They were necessary as a large part of the morning and evening, post getting-up and pre going to bed, was spent hanging about on landings, peeping around bedroom door-ways, often hopping in bladder-full anguish in the bedroom, waiting for the toilet to be vacated. As soon as the lavatory flush was heard, dressing-gowned people would suddenly appear to populate the corridor so it was like Queen Street Station in Cardiff and all heading for one door. Those were the days before 'en suites' and 'private facilities' had been heard of. You were fortunate indeed to have a bedroom next to the toilet, even if the cistern did keep you awake most of the night. It was an unpopular boarding house that had its bathroom and lavatory all in one, especially if your fellow guests took morning baths. I have known my father, on arising, utter a mild curse, dress hastily and before even washing and shaving, rush out to get the daily paper at the shop near the public urinals in the holiday town. Showers were quite unfamiliar. They were strange, alien things in foreign countries where people didn't clean them-selves properly anyway. There were also some recently installed in the local colliery, from where the miners emerged, not completely black as previously, but with coal dust ringing their eyes, so you always knew where they worked.

Sometimes we would remember to include two tennis rackets on the packing list. These would be not so much packed as strapped to the suitcase with leather belts, and were, in reality, a nuisance to take as they bumped and scraped against people's legs and often got dislodged. However, once in the resort, it was a welcome change to have a morning game of tennis rather than traipse around the shops. My mother and aunt would come to the park after their stroll about the town in their straw hats and sit, ostensibly watching my father and me running around, but really spending the time chatting and not paying a lot of attention to us at all. 'I don't know what your mother and Rach find to talk about all the time,' Dad would say.

My father's racket (like his bathing suit!) was a pre-war one with slack strings. Its frame had gone slightly out of shape in an elongated manner despite being clamped in a heavy wooden press with screws at each corner. Mine was far more modern, but despite this and his ancient racket, he could easily beat me. He would usually let me win, but that meant he didn't get much exercise and would stand more or less in the same place to hit the ball back while I ran around like mad getting red in the face. He had a friend who made tennis rackets, an Englishman called Fred Pearce, who had come to Wales during the war, liked it, and stayed. He had a sports, but mainly tennis, shop in Mill Street, Pontypridd. He'd made both the rackets and supplied us with a net of four balls which we carried hanging over the racket handle. My father didn't need to change his clothes for these games as he always wore white Dunlop All Purpose Soles (daps) on holiday and with a white short-sleeved shirt and his light grey flannel trousers he looked like the tennis players in the newspaper photos.

Best of all, I liked going to the north Devon or Somerset resorts. Not because they were any better than our Welsh seaside places of Porthcawl, Llanstephan, Saundersfoot or Tenby, but because we would go there by boat as opposed to the boringly familiar train or even more boring bus. The voyage was a mini holiday in itself. Paddle steamers called *The Cardiff Queen* and *The Bristol Queen* owned by the P&A Campbell company operated out of Cardiff docks and would transport you to these west country resorts so near by boat, so far and virtually inaccessible otherwise. Since I had unwittingly, through constant pestering, assumed the role of holiday organiser, I more or less had free rein in the albeit limited choice of destination. As a result, whether or not my family realised it, we generally spent the holiday at the end of a boat trip. My father was well acquainted with Cardiff and knew where to catch the tram to the docks once we'd arrived at Queen Street Station or at the bus-stop by the canal, around the corner from the New Theatre.

It was a thrill to see the white steamer waiting beyond the wooden landing stage (remnants of which are still there), with smoke issuing from its slightly rear-raked, elegant funnel and the huge paddles waiting to churn up the waters and carry us to Utopia.

Once the gangway had been negotiated, it was required to stow the luggage in special wooden racks (there was never any fear of it being stolen) and to locate seats for the sisters in the lounge at a window, to have a good view of the passing coastline. The steamer would stop at Penarth pier and sometimes the floating dock at Barry, where you could see the waiting people on the wooden quay, which would rise and fall gently with the sea swell.

If the weather was calm and the sea 'like a mill pond', my father and I would explore the boat. First on the agenda would be a visit down below to the engine room to watch the massive oil-gleaming wheels, arms and cogs move powerfully and rhythmically in their housing. An engineer would be close at hand regarding the awed gazers with an amused, laconic eye, superior in his knowledge of complicated machinery, but quite ready to share his erudition with the one-day sailors. Up on deck my father would point out the Isolation Hospital as we passed Flat Holm and tell me how the ground there was covered in small bones as sea-gulls and other birds would fly there carrying their prey to eat it in peace. Next was the inhospitable-looking Steep Holm, inaccessible according to my father, with its high charcoal-grey cliffs. If we were bound for Ilfracombe, Lundy Island appeared ghost-like in the distance.

If the sea was stormy and the boat pitching and rolling, my father would disappear, probably to the bar, to endure his sea-sick misery unseen and my less informative company would be my mother and aunt, who were amazingly good sailors, totally unaffected by the ship's gymnastics. With me in tow, fearful lest my aunt should come a cropper on the moving deck with no father in sight, aunt and mother would staggeringly make their way to the restaurant and eat a substantial meal on board, even though through the porthole you might, as though hypnotised, see a rapid succession of sky, distant cliff, shore, turbulent sea and back again through the itinerary to sky. I don't think the sisters would have cared had the boat somersaulted, and this insouciance surprised me as neither could swim. Not, I suppose, that this skill would be of much use should we capsize. As the steamer slowed to enter the harbour of the landing-place, my ashen-faced, but relieved looking father would reappear to marshal the family and luggage for a thankful disembarkation.

One summer, when we had the week booked in Minehead, we had to leave the boat at Lynmouth and proceed onward by coach. This involved getting into a launch out at sea, a manoeuvre which again had the family worried in the event of my aunt losing her footing. On hills my father could haul her up, in the sea it was an entirely different matter. Negotiating the transfer safely, if unsteadily, we reached the pretty resort at the mouth of the steep, wooded Lyn valley with its hotels and houses overlooking the little town, the stone bridge over the river, the harbour and beach. A week later we were back in Trehafod before a monumental storm broke over the Bristol Channel. The following day, the radio and newspapers reported how Lynmouth had been devastated by torrential rain turning the Lyn river into a raging monster. Buildings, the road, the bridge and quay had been swept away and several lives lost. It was impossible to recognise the happy little place we'd been in only a week previously from the photos of utter desolation in *The People* newspaper we bought on Sunday.

The afternoons were the time of day on holiday I enjoyed most, as, apart from Sunday, we went to the beach, probably as a concession to me. It didn't matter what the tide was doing, after lunch (three courses) it was down to the prom, hire four deckchairs and stay on the beach until it was time to return to the hotel for high tea (another three courses). After the daily puzzle of setting up the chairs and getting fingers trapped in the wooden bits, my father would have a snooze for an hour or so, as it was an unwritten rule that you couldn't bathe for at least an hour after a three course meal or you'd drown. In any case, sometimes on the north Devon or Somerset coast, you'd have to walk half way back to Wales to find the sea if you were unlucky with the tide during your particular week.

My mother would sit gazing round at the scene, resplendent in her straw hat, engagement ring and Benson's watch, and on very hot days would even remove her stockings, 'for a bit of sea air to get to my legs.' The corset, however, would remain intact. My aunt, on the other hand, would produce reams of silk scarves and towels out of a beach bag and if the sun looked as if it might threaten to appear,

41

proceed to cover every inch of exposed flesh about her person, ending up looking like a mummified queen of ancient Egypt under her wide-brimmed hat. Her face got redder and sweatier as the afternoon progressed. Movement was impossible, as the assorted haberdashery became dislodged and adjustments were difficult, creating more heat with the least motion. She must have hated the beach but never once complained and every day treated the rest of us to ice creams.

When my father deemed our digestive systems were ready to confront the sea (if we could find it), with the aid of a bath towel with the message 'Furness-Bermuda Line' written on it flapping around his lower half, and which he'd brought wrapped up like a Swiss roll under his arm, he'd laboriously change into his pre-war bathing suit. This was a navy woollen affair which had straps over the shoulders and inadequately covered his chest. At the front was a kind of mini-skirt, for modesty's sake I suppose. Although one saw a few similar, old-fashioned men's swimming costumes on the beach, the majority of men wore trunks, fairly substantial items of swim-wear in themselves, but my father would not countenance acquiring one. To my expressions of shame at his outmoded beach attire, he'd say, 'I like this one and it keeps my stomach warm. Anyway, there are no moth holes in it so why go to the expense of buying another one? I only wear it once a year, in any case!' So that was that.

In those days, children's costumes were either plain wool or of satiny material over-sewn in smallish squares with elastic cotton, squares which got larger and devolved into other geometrical shapes as the elastic gave out. Bathing caps were tight, usually white rubber bonnets with an adjustable strap under the chin. Photos of lady channel swimmers in the *Western Mail* always showed them emerging triumphant from the water at Dover or Cap Gris Nez with the strap undone and hanging down nonchalantly so I always contrived to come out of the sea like that even before I could swim.

At the end of the afternoon there would be more surreptitious glances around and frantic adjustments of towels when changing from bathers to clothes, desperately trying to avoid a knickerful, and, I suppose, a pantsful of sand.

If we were holidaying in Weston-super-Mare, all this changing palaver would be avoided as this town boasted a marvellous Lido at the far end of its prom. It was easy to persuade the family to spend the afternoon there because if the tide is out in Weston, the sea disappears altogether leaving deep sticky mud on the shore, unpleasant for middle-aged ladies.

This sticky mud came in useful once though. At the age of six or thereabouts, I had chicken-pox and the scabs were not completely healed when we went on holiday. My mother, being a farmer's daughter, had great trust in nature's remedies for ills. She told a story of how one of her brothers had rid himself of a wart on his neck by dabbing it with a little of the fluid that collects in the centre of a fresh cow-pat. Now she was convinced that if I rolled nearly naked in the Weston slime, let it dry, then washed it off in one of the sea-pools that then existed on the sands (built no doubt to keep children happy when there was no sea), any chicken-pox marks on my body would be cleared up. Well, her theory must have been right, because not only have I no scars from that illness, I remember having a wonderful time rolling in mud and thinking my mother must have taken leave of her senses to let me do this. Normally, cleanliness was close to her heart and mud quite distant.

The Weston Lido was the biggest swimming pool I'd ever seen and of an intriguing shape with arcs, unlike the staid, rectangular, practical, learn-to-swim one in Porth park. Above the deep end was an impressive array of diving boards and halfway to these were two fountains you could cling on to for a rest. There was a terrace overlooking the pool where onlookers sat at tables and drank tea and ate scones from a central café which sold ice cream as well. And of course there were cubicles where you could dress and undress with a minimum of anxiety about exposing your person to public gaze and ridicule. To me this place was paradise and I would feel a major depression coming on if we weren't able to go to the Lido every day we were in Weston, even in the rain.

After the beach, around four o'clock we'd find a seafront café for 'a nice cup of tea'. If we were at Porthcawl's Coney Beach, this would be at the Italian café in front of the fairground overlooking the sands. From here we could see the donkeys waiting patiently for small riders. Once hired, they would trot off in an alarmingly jerky mode, bouncing the worried-looking children on their backs, who would be clinging on for dear life, uncertain as whether to bawl or maintain a stoic, but decidedly dismayed demeanour.

If we had, on a rare occasion, caught a bus out to Rest Bay in Porthcawl, a bigger but more isolated and less developed area, the post-beach cuppa would be drunk sitting on the beach wall or the grass of Lock's Common, where it adjoins the sands, and bought from a 'Trays for the Beach' kiosk next to the Lifeguards' Hut. Then it was a trudge back over the Common to the boarding house in Nicholls Avenue (No. 22, I think), damp and sandy from the swim and pink-shouldered from the sun, for 'high tea'.

Everybody in those days appeared to take holidays with full board. I suppose you could have organised other arrangements but my family would not have contemplated anything else. Certainly around 12.30 and 6 pm, the streets of the holiday town would be deserted and just before those times, holidaymakers, apart from day-trippers having sandwiches on the beach, would be seen making their way hotel-wards.

'High tea' was a posh name for the evening meal, usually of three courses starting with soup, then meat and two veg, then apple pie and custard and, of course, the ubiquitous pot of tea. Lunch (or luncheon if you were at a hotel), would be two courses with a pot of tea, and breakfast the full English variety with more pots of tea. My father always encouraged the rest of us to eat everything up. He had a theory, and several brown paper bags. He was convinced that if you left any of the food that was served, the management would assess your eating capacity and not give you so much the next time. By the end of the week you could be on starvation rations. Consequently, after a few 'tuts', if any food was left uneaten, out would come the paper bag and potatoes, apple pie, half-eaten bread rolls, sausages, salad and especially rissoles would be stealthily secreted into it when the servers were out of the dining-room. The bag would then be passed along to my mother to hide in her handbag. She wasn't keen on these conspiracies, not being a big eater anyway, and would have preferred smaller portions, but would go along with my father's notions because he was more cosmopolitan. After all, he knew where nearly all the streets in Cardiff were located and had even worked in London and Wrexham!

Sometimes, to my glee, the food missed the bag and fell on to the carpet. My father would apologise profusely for the mess and could do this so charmingly, that the landlady or waitress would give the impression that it was a pleasure to clean it up and that he had done them a favour by dropping it. And of course, it was always on my father's side, as no-one else would gather up the left-over food. Our plates were returned to the kitchens, not so much empty as swept. The bagged food would later be fed to the seagulls or swans or put in a street bin if it was messy with fried egg, or peas and gravy. My mother tolerated these furtive operations but grumbled about the occasional stain inside her bag which she lined with cellophane paper, usually too late.

Besides parks or Winter Gardens, the beach, strolling on the prom and looking around shops, other holiday entertainment included a Sunday afternoon visit to a bandstand, where we sat in deck-chairs to listen to a local brass band play Strauss waltzes and popular songs such as 'You are my heart's delight' and 'The Londonderry Air'. On one evening my father would book tickets for the summer show in the theatre, usually comprising a comedian, a small orchestra, a male or female singer, acrobats and a dancing troupe of women in bathing costumes with feathers. We once saw Tommy Trinder perform in the theatre on Weston pier. The audience roared with laughter at what he said and clapped enthusiastically but I only found it mildly amusing. I couldn't understand half the jokes and stories.

If the evening suddenly turned wet, there would quite likely be a trip to the cinema. I always hoped for a film with Laurel and Hardy or George Formby. I could understand their jokes and found them really funny. My aunt preferred Bob Hope and Bing Crosby. The best seats in the circle cost 1s 9d.

On the Friday evening of the week, my parents considered it a great favour to allow us to go to the fair or amusement park. Beforehand my mother would say, 'If you're a good girl and not in your wants for this and that, you shall have an evening out in the fair.' Why they thought this was such a great bonus for me, I was mystified, as I wasn't keen on fairs, apart from the Penny Falls and the 'Allwin' (Rarewin would have been a more appropriate name) machines which had metal balls like marbles we called 'bompers' which had to drop in certain cups to win.

I had been promised a ride on the Water Chute in Porthcawl fair one year, had worried about it all day, had climbed apprehensively into one of the painted carriages with my parents and aunt, had left my stomach several feet up in the air, had got soaked and was promptly sick on getting off. The others were all right though. I watched with horror the Figure of Eight and other vile machines with cabs on the end of metal arms flailing about in the air. Even the roundabout of prancing horses made me feel queasy. I didn't mind the Ghost Train, as you simply had figures in white sheets popping out of the darkness at you making spectral noises, and quite liked the Round the World cruise. Nothing in these latter two turned you upside down or swung you about so there was no worry of letting yourself down by vomiting or yelling with fear.

One of the most amusing things in a fair was watching the stall-holder make a new fangled thing called candy floss. The stuff appeared from nowhere in a fast revolving drum, vivid pink, on to a stick held by the man. It tasted like sweet cardboard cotton-wool. Far nicer were the gleaming, dripping toffee apples, ice cream wafers you had to lick on each rectangular side to stop it trickling over you, or pucks of Walls ice cream wrapped in thick paper. Ice cream carts were to be seen around the seaside resorts, bins on bikes, where the man would cycle along, raise a parasol above his cart, organise cones in glasses and wafers in boxes and put his metal ice-cream tools in a jug of water, before starting to serve the customers.

There were jolly sailor hats with mottoes for sale in the promenade shops and stalls, tin or rubber buckets and spades, sunglasses with lurid frames, simple kites and beach windmills and pink rock with the place's name embedded through it, suitable to take as presents for friends and relatives at home. Racks of postcards, views mainly in sepia but some in washed-out colours were displayed, together with funny, often rude, postcards of seaside holiday life. These cost a penny (a red stamp) to send, and little more to buy, or tuppence ha'penny (a blue stamp) to send in an envelope.

The seaside holiday was undoubtedly the high-spot of the year for most families. Personally, despite having spent holidays since in many parts of the globe, I can't say that these were any more enjoyable or memorable than those in the fifties with my family in Wales and England. I certainly look back on those times with a great deal more nostalgia.

# As Good As New

~

*Carolyn Lewis*

**Carolyn Lewis** was born in Cardiff in 1947 and spent her childhood in Fairwater, attending Fairwater Junior School and Canton High School for Girls. Following her first marriage she lived in Caerphilly, and later returned to Cardiff. Following the breakdown of the marriage, she lived with her three daughters in Dinas Powys. She now lives in Bristol, is remarried and is taking an MPhil in Writing at the University of Glamorgan. Her work has been published in *New Welsh Review*, *Myslexia*, *QWF*, the *Moonshine Anthology* and *Suspended Sentences* (Redcliffe Press).

Two small children, my sister and I, perched on the back seat of our father's Morris 8. Andrea was eight years old and I was ten. My feet almost touched the floor of the car; hers didn't, they dangled. We sat on an old car rug, harsh wool on the backs of our bare legs; the rug covered bed-linen, sheets, pillowcases and, underneath all that, towels, blankets and tea towels. There was no other place for these items. The car was fully loaded. We were going to Tenby.

We went every year, my mother, father, sister and me. We travelled in the early hours of the morning to avoid the traffic jams. It was holiday time and that meant factories, large warehouses, the mines and Welsh Brick Industries, where my father worked, had closed down for the summer holidays. Holidays always meant an early start, driving in the dark, my father's hands steady on the steering wheel of his beloved Morris 8, my mother in the passenger seat, knees slightly apart to accommodate a Thermos flask, sandwiches, apples and the map. The map wasn't needed – she had accompanied my father on that trip for nearly ten years – but trips in the car and especially holidays, meant maps, the following of holiday roads by torchlight in the dark interior of the car.

For two excited children, these trips took a long time. Hour after hour, the car moved from our home in Cardiff towards the front at

Tenby. We always started our journeys between the hours of two and three in the morning. My father insisted on this early start to 'avoid the traffic'. It became a litany throughout all those early years. It did seem, however, that every other person in Cardiff had the same idea. Looking out of the back window, I could see twin headlights of other cars forming an almost continuous line, like blurred yellow bones in a long spinal column moving steadily through the quiet streets of Cardiff, then along the A48 towards Tenby. I asked my father once why everyone went on holiday at the same time. 'Is there anyone left in Cardiff? Is it empty? Has *everyone* gone? The buses will be empty, and the shops, and the hospitals.'

My sister chimed in with, '*And* all the dentists, all the schools, even Woolworths will be empty.'

We steadily became sillier and sillier, as bored children do, the excitement that began with the packing evaporating rapidly. Told firmly to, 'Cut that out and stop being so daft,' by our Dad, 'driving is a serious business,' we sat back into a heavy silence, relieved only by the wriggling that we both did in an attempt to ease the scratching on our legs caused by the harsh blanket we were sitting on.

There were many stops on those long journeys. Not just the necessary stops for the toilet, but my father needed breaks to check the old car, to nurse her on her journey. The ritualistic checking of the oil, peering in the dark at the dipstick, checking the water levels and, of course, checking the suitcases that were lashed tightly on to the roof rack and covered in black plastic sheeting. We could hear that plastic as the wind whipped through it, tearing great chunks out of it and reducing the plastic to ribbons which flew like banners as we drove.

Preparations for our holiday took months and, although we *always* went to the Clifftop Caravan Park, and we *always* took the same route, *always* going at the same time every year, the planning was military in its precision. Weeks before departure, the clothes that we'd all wear on holiday were washed and ironed, piled high on a spare bed and were not to be touched again until our arrival at the caravan. We had to wear old clothes for the week before departure. Everything else was kept for the holidays. Lists were pinned up on the kitchen wall, one list headed by: 'Elastoplast', 'Germolene' and

'Aspirin', printed in big, bold letters, less important items written underneath. Each one of us had a list of our own written by my mother and she would cross each item off as she placed yet more things on the spare bed. My list included two swimming costumes, shorts and T-shirts, and enough knickers for the holiday. There were never any additions to the lists. We were all allocated what the car and the caravan could hold. There was no room for anything else. Even when my sister and I were teenagers and we brought boy-friends along, those four lists would be pinned up on the kitchen wall.

The long, dark drive through the night always culminated in a disappointing arrival. The need to *beat the traffic* and *make good time* meant that we arrived at Tenby sea front before the sun emerged. The grey, unlit sky gave only token illumination to the seaside town. For tired children, like Andrea and me, there was nothing to soften the early morning appearance of a Welsh holiday resort in the 1950s. Shutters were up on the ice cream parlours and the fish and chip shops; the tiny kiosk where windbreaks could be hired was closed. There were no amusement arcades, no bright neon signs, not even a flag fluttered on the beach. We were always so early that we arrived before the previous holidaymakers had vacated the caravan. Every year we sat in the old, dusty car, waiting for the sun to come up, waiting to move into our caravan home and waiting for our holiday to start. My sister and I never questioned the parental logic of early starts and subsequent hours of waiting, we just sat, tired, bored and restless.

We'd sit for hours cocooned in the car, watching as the sun eventually broke through the morning sky and the shops opened their doors and shutters. We watched as the owner of the fish and chip shop wrote out 'Catch of the Day' in chalk on a big blackboard, placing it near the door, and the man in the kiosk carried out boxes of striped windbreaks and put them outside on the pavement. People appeared on the streets, children carrying buckets and spades, parents holding a picnic basket between them, all making their way towards the beach. I felt segregated from the emerging holidaymakers; we could see them crossing the street, buying newspapers and fresh bread. We were crumpled and travel-stained and, to an impatient ten-year-old, it felt as if our holiday would never start. It could only start when we moved into the caravan and, even more importantly, when we changed out of our old clothes and into our holiday clothes and then, and only then, would we be like everyone else.

Finally, my mother said it was time to move and we drove slowly from the beach to the Clifftop Caravan Park and into our caravan. The caravans were neatly lined up in a field overlooking the beach. They all had wide, bay windows facing the sea. Each caravan was painted blue, a bright garish colour at odds with the deep blue-green of the sea. The thundering noise of the waves could clearly be heard between the regimented rows of caravans.

Unpacking the car was laborious but, at last, my sister and I stood outside the caravan. We'd washed and changed our clothes. We were holidaymakers. The holiday had started, the new shorts and clean T-shirts proved it. Andrea and I knew it too because the atmosphere was different. Our parents were more relaxed, my mother in par-ticular had visibly altered. All her planning, the strict adherence to the lists, the early start, the slow drive through the night, it had all worked. We had arrived safely without mishap or argument; the caravan was the one she had booked and paid for, she could relax. She was vindicated, the control she exerted over the holiday plans could be eased.

Sometimes during that holiday, she'd pause as she stepped from our caravan and glance around at all the others on the site. Our caravan looked the same as the others and, I think, that was what she wanted to see, that we were just another family amongst so many. She liked the uniformity of the terraced rows of caravans where the occupants had lined sandy shoes up outside the doors, where bathing suits and beach towels flapped on makeshift washing lines and empty suitcases were pushed underneath the caravans.

Our days at Tenby followed a pattern which rarely changed and it was this predictability that initially delighted my sister and me. Once breakfast was over and the caravan locked up, we walked in single file, my mother at the front, my father at the back, Andrea and I safely protected in the middle. We walked past the rows of blue caravans, negotiating our way down a steep path to the beach. Andrea and I carried buckets and spades, my father held the old car rug and my mother carried her shopping bag, now magically transformed into a beach bag. We had a special place on the beach, it was our place, with enough room to spread the rug and a large rock to act as windbreak.

Then, as now, the beach was wide, flanked by sand dunes and rocks. The rocks were home to many generations of crabs and Andrea and I spent hours searching for them to take back to the caravan as trophies. The sea held no terror for me although I was a non-swimmer. I'd wade in, delighting in the feel of an enormous wave exploding around me. Lunch was almost always a hot pie. Andrea and I took it in turns to place the order as soon as we arrived on the beach each morning, handing over the money to the man wearing a chef's hat, patrolling the beach and ringing a noisy bell.

'Four hot pies, please.' Our order never changed.

We both ran back at one o'clock, joining the queue of people lined up outside the chef's van, the smell of warm baking hovering over our heads. 'Don't let them get cold,' we were told every day, so we always ran back to our parents, juggling the hot pies in our hands, trying not to get our fingers burned.

On the days that it rained, we drove to Saundersfoot and once we drove in to Swansea. We'd wander through the streets wearing plastic macs and eating ice cream. On those days we took a packed lunch and ate it in the car. My mother said that restaurants were 'not to be trusted'. I didn't know what she meant by that, perhaps they weren't clean enough? It was only years later that I understood. Meals out were not included within the framework of our holidays simply because the cost was unknown. The precise planning included sticking to a very tight budget and there was not enough money for anything as spontaneous as a meal out on a wet day.

By contrast, after days of fresh air and frantic exercise in the sea, our evenings were spent in the small clubhouse built from corrugated metal sheets into a corner of the campsite. 'This Club is for the Exclusive Use of Residents Only', said the sign, written in uneven black lettering on a white board, nailed across the front. The brochures advertising Clifftop Caravan Park, described the interior of the clubhouse as 'comfortable and clean'. It had started its life as a cowshed and now, just for tourists, the corrugated walls were freshly painted in glossy white paint and green vinyl chairs placed on the uneven floor. Large, round tables held misshapen ashtrays, rejects from a local pottery. The clubhouse was illuminated at night by fluorescent tubes and the light from these was harsh, shining on the spartan interior, bouncing off the corrugated walls. Every night at eleven o'clock, these lights were switched off, plunging the clubhouse and the rest of the caravan site into darkness.

My parents spent their evenings inside this smoky haven, drinking Welsh beer and talking to the other caravanners. They were a tightly knit band of holidaymakers who returned, not only to the same caravan every year, but here, in the clubhouse, they sat at the same tables every year. Their evenings were spent reliving previous holiday memories and catching up on their lives outside the caravan park. The children of the site, Andrea and I included, played outside, making use of the natural hills and valleys to be found in the sand dunes. We made occasional forays into the clubhouse to ask for more crisps or, better still, a bottle of Tizer complete with straw in the neck of the bottle.

Andrea and I counted the days of our holiday, making a chart which we hid under the pillows of our bunk bed. Not counting until we could go home, but counting how many days we had left. It was a tantalising torture, coming to the end of the fortnight, crossing off another day, getting closer to the final Saturday when we had to go home. But, even before that, came the *Checking of the Car*. That was important, spoken about in reverential tones. There were five members of our family, mother, father, two daughters, and the car.

'She did well; the old girl never lets us down.' My father spoke lovingly and regularly of his Morris 8. Other cars on the camp site were sleek, shiny vehicles; they had chrome bumpers, white-walled tyres, radios and aerials. The bodywork on our car was bright, geranium red, hand-painted by my mother from a tin chosen from Woolies. A battered old tray had to be put underneath the car every night to collect the drips of oil and the front seats were hidden by fake leopard-skin covers to disguise the cracked and sagging leather. Part of me desperately wanted a sleek, shiny monster of a car like all the others, the ones that had flags in bright, rainbow colours and the names of holiday resorts flying cheerfully on the aerials. And yet, when my Dad lifted the bonnet of the old Morris, wiping his hands on an oily cloth, the other drivers crowded around to hear the story of how he had replaced the engine and gearbox. I felt differently then. Anyone can drive a new car. My Dad had rebuilt ours.

Every year, just before the end of the holiday, came the *Checking of the Car*. Each time we went away, the suitcases were lashed tightly on to the roof, because the boot was always full. Engine oil, petrol cans, tools and overalls took up all the boot space. To Andrea and me, it felt as if the Morris was a demanding old aunt, needing her medication to get her through each stage of a journey. My father would never trust a garage to take care of his car. He alone knew every one of the Morris's frailties. 'Can't trust garages, they're no good. They'll handle her all wrong. I know what she needs.' He'd disappear under the car, tools laid out close by, my mother hovering anxiously, offering cups of tea to help the operation along. Certainly the questions she asked would not have been out of place in an intensive care unit.

'How is she? . . . Do you think she'll make it?'

My father took the whole matter very seriously and he'd give us, the waiting relatives, the good news. 'At one point it was touch and go, but she'll make it now. She's as good as new.'

We all breathed a sigh of relief, Andrea and I especially. That news meant we could have our last day on the beach with an easy conscience. Along with our buckets and spades, we carried an air of desperation with us on those last days, trying to hold on to the closing moments of the holiday; stretching them out, making them last as long as possible. We needed to fill every minute with an almost tangible essence of the holiday mood. To jump amongst the waves, to paddle in the rock pools, eating a last meat pie and licking a last ice cream.

It wasn't just the holiday or the being away from home and school. At our ages, eight and ten, we still revelled in the predictability of our holiday. The list making, the long early morning drive, the same caravan in the same fortnight, the lunchtime pies, the hours spent outside the clubhouse; these were all part of the rock solid ritual of our lives in Tenby. The format itself was part of our holiday as much as the hot meat pies. The format remained the same for many years. The *beat the traffic* litany was accompanied by the *leaving nothing to chance* refrain. My parents had a deep distrust of anything that they felt was outside their control. If we did the same things every year, nothing could go wrong and the holiday would be a success. Perhaps it was the equivalent of the childhood game of jumping over cracks in pavements: avoid the cracks and all is well, step on a crack and disaster is imminent.

Although our holidays to Tenby continued in the same format, the Morris 8 was eventually laid to rest and, in its place, an Austin 10 Roadster became our transport. Hand-painted again by my mother, only this time in a sedate black. My father thought fewer tools would be needed for this graceful old lady, so our suitcases were stashed in her enormous boot. The stiff canvas hood was put down, enabling us to enjoy the sunshine, but only on occasions when there was no threat of any cloud in the sky. 'Can't take any risks,' my parents said.

By the time Andrea and I were fifteen and seventeen years old, holidays with our parents had lost their attraction. Even more than this, along with the acquisition of boyfriends, we could see the ritual of the planning, the packing, the sheer predictability of it all as others saw it. Andrea and I teased them, 'Come on, take a chance . . . be devils! Why don't you go in June, or early September? Try the Norfolk Broads or what about Scotland?'

My Mum and Dad smiled at each other, tolerant smiles conveying their understanding of this youthful teasing. 'We've always done it this way because we know it works. There are no problems. We don't get let down because we leave nothing to chance.'

Sometimes with boyfriends, sometimes with friends, Andrea and I embarked upon a series of holidays without our parents. We camped in a field in Carmarthen whilst listening to a rock band, we battled with the workings of locks on narrow boat holidays and we also took caravan holidays in Devon and Cornwall. All these trips were fraught with problems: lost deposits, booking at the last minute, ruined friendships, travelling at the peak of holiday traffic and any packing that we did was defiantly haphazard. Whenever my parents learned of yet another holiday disaster, they shook their heads, telling me that what I was doing was, 'Not worth the risk, why take these sorts of chances?'

I'd always told them of my holiday catastrophes with a bravura performance, dramatising the event, laughing at the consequences. With the arrogance of youth, I tried to demonstrate to my parents that taking chances was what life was all about. 'You'll learn,' my mother said, 'holidays are serious things.'

As I grew older, I travelled extensively, camping all over Europe, flying out to Canada and America, taking a safari holiday in Africa. None of these trips made any impact on my parents. 'Very nice,' they'd say to me whenever I brought a souvenir home from my latest trip abroad. They'd put whatever I'd bought them on a high shelf, where it couldn't be seen. They continued holidaying in Tenby; their only concession to getting older was staying at a small B & B near the front.

Years later, after the collapse of my marriage, I took my three daughters to Tenby. I drove there, setting off this time down the M4, after our breakfast. I took it steadily in my old Austin Metro and my children jostled with each other on the backseat. We kept up games of I Spy and we sang chorus after chorus of 'Ten Green Bottles'. We stayed in a small cottage; from there we could walk to the beach every day.

I was able to watch the girls searching for crabs in the same pools that Andrea and I peered into. My daughters and I sat together on an old car rug, eating hot pies, protected from the wind by a bright red windbreak, hired from the kiosk on the seafront.

# CHAPTER 2

# EDUCATION

# Girls Didn't Need to be Clever

~

*Rachel Treadwell*

**Rachel Treadwell** was born, with her twin brother, on 24 July 1960 at home on a housing estate in Harlow in Essex. Her parents came from London, moved a lot and eventually settled in Stafford, where she started school. She married at eighteen and moved to Wales, where she has lived ever since. After living in a remote cottage for sixteen years, she is now in the seaside resort of Fairbourne. Since beginning writing four years ago, she has had many articles and nearly forty poems published, including an article in *Country Quest* and a series of anecdotal articles in *Dial 174*. She recently self-published a collection of poems, *Poems from Blaencerniog.*

During the nineteen sixties I was too young to be aware of the significance of any changes happening in the world. I spent most of my time at a Catholic primary school. My parents were not strict Catholics. We knew people whose families were much sterner in their approach to their beliefs. However, they did hold very old-fashioned views about the roles of boys and girls and their place in the world. These views had a great effect on my life and my image of myself.

My foremost memories of that time at school were of struggling to compete academically with my twin brother. It was decided from an early age that he was the cleverer twin. At about seven years old, I decided to give up the struggle and to settle into my given role as the girl, who was not supposed to stand out academically.

This came about when reading became competitive. Our reading books were colour coded: each time the end of the book was reached you moved on to the next colour. Because my brother would become upset and cry if I was 'better than him', I felt that I could not move on to the next book unless he did so first.

Although this may sound as if I was not looking out for my own interests, you have to understand what it was like to be a twin. I realise that my behaviour says something about my personal psychology and my relationship to my brother, but I also believe that I was conditioned from an early age to think less of myself for being born a girl. We were not, of course, identical or of the same sex, but we did share a strong bond. He was my best friend and closest companion, especially as our mother did not allow us to go out to play with neighbouring children. When you are seven years old, you do not wish to upset or cause your best friend to cry.

He believed that he was a complete failure as a boy if I, as a girl, were to achieve better results at school. If he became upset, he would be comforted and told that he would do better next time, whereas I was given extra books to work on at home and told that 'girls don't need to be clever'.

In the year before our eleven plus exam, we had to complete a homework book every week. I found them quite easy and for the first few weeks gained marks of eighty to ninety per cent, but then of course my brother was distraught because he was scoring marks in the seventies. I can remember my mother telling him that it didn't matter as, again, 'girls didn't need to be clever'. Once more I decided that I needed my best friend, so I put down some wrong answers to enable him to get a better mark than I did.

By this time, I had begun to believe my parents' views about girls and when the exam came around I was convinced that I was destined to fail and that it wouldn't matter if I did. I believed that girls were only made for having babies. I was pleasantly surprised to find the questions very easy and I passed the exam. My brother also passed, as was expected, but he pointed out the questions that he found difficult and I was amazed that I hadn't struggled with them. I kept the knowledge to myself as I had learned not to complain if I failed or show pleasure at succeeding.

This success gave me more confidence in my own academic abilities and, although the attitudes of the time continued to affect me in my schoolwork, I can still remember that secret pleasure at passing my eleven plus exam. Looking back, I know that I didn't achieve my potential at school because of the attitudes of Catholic parents towards their daughters during that decade. It has taken me many years finally to throw off that mistaken image of myself, but I think that struggling to do this has made me a stronger person.

# The Spectre of the Scholarship

~

*Beth Clarke*
translated from Welsh by the author

**Beth Clarke** was born in Pontarddulais in 1944 and lived in the area until 1990 when she moved to Radnorshire. After Pontar-ddulais Primary School and Gowerton Girls' Grammar School, she went to the Glamorgan College of Education, Barry, to train as a mathematics teacher before returning to teach in the Gorseinon area. In 1979 she was appointed Head Teacher of Felindre Primary School and in 1986 of Ystalyfera Primary School. After taking early retirement in 2001, she has turned her attention to writing, painting and foreign travel.

When I was about ten years old, my thoughts turned to sitting the scholarship for a place at the local grammar school. Winning a place at the grammar school was my goal. I'd heard so many stories about the initiation ceremonies for new pupils at the local secondary school, commonly known as 'Top School', that I was scared witless of becoming one of its pupils. I was prepared to do all that I could to gain a place at the grammar school.

Ten years after the 1944 Education Act promised to give all children an education to suit their age, aptitude and ability, pupils living in the old county of Glamorgan had two opportunities to sit the scholarship examination. I remember the day of the exam clearly. Pontarddulais Primary School had a group of three class-rooms divided by glass and wood screens, which could be folded back to make a large hall. On the day of the exam, these screens were folded back and individual desks were set out in rows for the candidates. Teachers from neighbouring schools acted as invigilators and ensured fair play. It was a long day with examinations in mathematics – mental, mechanical and problems; Welsh or English comprehension, grammar, essay, and a verbal reasoning paper. My parents had paid for extra 'coaching' for me in English to ensure I was capable of reaching the required standard. When I started school it had a two-stream entry policy, an English stream and a Welsh stream. I started in the Welsh stream and learned to read, write and count in Welsh before I could speak English properly.

The 1950s saw the growth of interest in Welsh medium education and it was decided to open a Welsh medium primary school in Pontarddulais. The opening of the Welsh school caused a great deal of discussion and controversy in the village. Many were opposed to the concept, thinking that it would divide the community. Others thought that teaching only through the medium of Welsh was a retrograde step. Most of the pupils from the Welsh stream transferred to the Welsh School.

My father was born in 1907 and had been a pupil at the National School, run by the Church. This had been an English medium school and had long since closed. He worked at the Teilo tin plate works in the village and valued the importance of a good education and the ability to communicate well in English. If you sought to enhance your career or gain promotion, English was essential. Welsh was the language of the 'worker', English the language of the 'boss'. The importance of education as a means of lifting people out of poverty and providing a route for social progression was a strong incentive for parents who wanted better for their children. At the end of the day, my parents decided that my brother and I should stay in the English school. The removal of the Welsh stream from Pontarddulais Primary School resulted in the school turning, almost overnight, into an English medium school and losing its Welshness. Until the introduction of the National Curriculum in 1986, very little Welsh was taught in the English medium primary schools. Today all children in Wales are taught Welsh and are given an insight into the culture, history and language of their country.

Going back to my scholarship days, I was by now in Miss Bushell's class. Having started school in the Welsh stream, I was now in a class where English was the premier language. The class teacher lived near my home and had taught my mother. She was a teacher with little empathy for her pupils and very little time for Welsh-speaking families. Her classroom was not a friendly place! It was a very dark room, called the dungeon by the children, because it was about fifteen feet below ground level with high windows at pavement level. The children sat in rows of double desks with sloping lids. I shared my desk with a boy called Dilwyn who lived in my street.

One day the class was given a spelling test and Miss Bushell warned everyone that anyone who had two or more spelling mistakes would be caned. After the test, Miss Bushell called out the names of the offenders and I was one of them! I had left the 'u' out of 'queen' and I have long forgotten what the other word was. The teacher moved along the row of frightened children, boys and girls. I stood next to Dilwyn and saw him hold out his hand. Next it was my turn. I held out my hand for the first and last time and felt the crack of the cane sting my hand. I did my best to fight back the tears and hold my head up high, but the tears rolled down my face. The pain and the shame of the punishment were too much to bear. I knew that everyone in the school would know about the caning by home time and someone was sure to tell my mother. When Miss Bushell realised how upset I was, she angrily sent me out to the lobby to wash my face. As I went through the door, I saw Dilwyn laugh. Once again, I relived the caning and instead of going to the lobby I ran home to my mother.

My mother was a strong-willed woman, always prepared to protect and defend her children. After hearing the tale, she put on her hat and coat and marched me back to school, straight to the Head Teacher. After wiping the floor with him, she insisted on seeing Miss Bushell. My mother's argument was that if I had been badly behaved or rude, I would have deserved the punishment, but since I was in school to be educated, the punishment was grossly unfair. The outcome was that I was moved out of Miss Bushell's class into Mr Lewis's class, a far more caring teacher. It was after this incident that my parents decided I needed 'coaching' in English. I was given additional lessons by a retired teacher who lived about a mile out of the village. Her home was in a very dark and lonely location. I had to wait for a bus on my own – my parents never accompanied me – and strangely enough I don't remember feeling frightened.

After the scholarship exam, the next significant day was the day of the results. The Head Teacher would be sent a list of successful candidates and he would come into the classroom and call out the names of the children who had passed. These children would then be allowed to run home to tell their parents the good news. I will always remember the first time I tried the scholarship and failed. I had visions of my mother peeping from a bedroom window, watching for the children running home, and was very conscious of her bitter disappointment on realising I had failed.

Primary school pupils all over Glamorgan sat the same scholarship paper. It was a huge county, stretching from Pontarddulais in the west to Caerphilly in the east and Merthyr in the north. Over the years the authority had realised that pupils in some areas could gain a grammar school place with fewer marks than in other areas: this meant that in some areas, able children were being denied grammar school places. Llwchwr and Gower districts, which sent children to the Gowerton Grammar Schools, were two such areas. The authority, therefore, decided to allocate a percentage of places at Pontardawe Grammar School to pupils from Llwchwr and Gower. In 1955, Dilwyn and I were the two pupils at the bottom of the list of successful candidates with the same mark, but there was only one place on offer. Since it was Dilwyn's second try and my first, it was decided to allocate the place to Dilwyn. I had to stay in the primary school and try again the next year. The English 'coaching' must have done some good because my parents now decided I needed help with mathematics and I was sent to Pontlliw, again on the bus, to improve my maths. Eventually I passed my scholarship and gained a place at Gowerton Girls' Grammar School in 1956. Having a sister in the sixth form at the time did not help to allay my fears on that first day. The journey from Pontarddulais to Gowerton took about forty minutes and I was not a good traveller. For the first three months, I travelled on the platform of a double decker bus, feeling sick and sorry for myself.

The Head Teacher was Miss Huldah Bassett, a lady for whom I developed a great respect. I must admit that I enjoyed my days at Gowerton with its high standards and strict rules and regulations. Young people today would neither accept nor abide by them. All the girls, even in the sixth form, wore full school uniform and ankle socks, no jewellery other than a watch and no one dared speak to the boys from the Boys' Grammar School, when they wolf-whistled at us from neighbouring woods while we played tennis in our shorts! It was rumoured that when Miss Bassett telephoned the Head of the boys' school to complain, his reply was, 'Boys will be boys'! We all had indoor and outdoor shoes, which had to be changed before we entered the school, and I remember girls being excluded for a week for colouring their hair or being caught talking to boys in the woods. I also remember special arrangements being made for a girl who was pregnant to sit her O level exams in private in the secretary's office, so that her education was not wasted. These were days when unmarried girls who were pregnant hid away at home hoping that no one would find out. How times have changed.

After seven years at the grammar school, my friends and I thought we were very worldly-wise and better educated than most. Now, after thirty years in the teaching profession, I realise how much more there is still to learn.

# Sixties Schooling

~

*Jane Salisbury*

**Jane Salisbury** was born in Barry 1955. She is co-ordinator of postgraduate studies at the School of Social Sciences, University of Wales, Cardiff, where she lectures in education policy, qualitative research methods and post-16 education and training. She has published papers on classroom ethnography, vocational education and training, and the sociology of work. Some of her recent work has been published in *Educational Reform and Gender Equality in Welsh Schools* (Cardiff, EOC, 1996).

The floor of the infants' school hall was painted with rows of penny-sized dots. 'Find a spot and sit on it!' instructed the Headmistress to the children trickling in from the classrooms which bordered the hall. This is one of my earliest memories of being at school. 'Quiet, fingers on lips,' 'Hands on heads,' 'Which table is sitting up the straightest?' 'Who's got the neatest line today, the boys or the girls?' 'When you've stopped talking, *Susan Burford*, I'll know that the class is ready to go out to play!' 'What are you doing with Julie's hair, Terry? Boys do *not* play with girls' ribbons.' These statements were typical of instructions and cues used by teachers during my education at the infants' school. The questions required no answers, but demanded a prompt physical response, and established control. They were amongst the means by which generations of pupils were taught the hidden curriculum.

In the early days of infants' school, I learned the norms of classroom life: along with others I chorused dutifully to my teacher's elicitations and questions. 'Who can tell me what happens when . . .?' 'What day comes after Sunday?' and 'Hands up if you know the answer!' This was an era of teacher pleasing, of signalling rapt attention and compliance. To secure a gold star for a perfectly traced alphabet or sheet of correctly counted shapes was my goal. With my peers I quickly learned to make sense of the teacher's red-inked ticks, crosses and question marks. Equally important in the classroom arena was being able to interpret her negative and positive body language: her tuts, frowns and perplexed black looks, with which she managed our class, were crucial clues.

I can recall quite clearly prancing around the infants' hall, directed by a distant voice from the BBC's School Service. In navy knickers and vests we collectively metamorphosed from leaping frogs into roaring lions as we tried to impress our teacher, who sat knitting next to the huge square radio speaker. I loved these sessions and the posh lady's voice, which challenged our little bodies to stretch and grow from, 'teeny weeny acorns into large, proud, tall oak trees.' Mornings were used to teach the basic 'three Rs' and to progress us through our 'Janet and John' readers. I only learned much later in my thirties, how limited Janet's activities had been in comparison to her brother John's and how some scholars linked these textual role models to teenage girls' 'poverty of aspiration'.

On each afternoon of the week during my last infants' year, the class was divided into groups for different creative activities. Casting on and off, we learned to knit on plastic needles with soft coloured string and to weave through large-holed canvas called Binca work. These crafts were no doubt deemed to develop our fine psycho-motor skills and eye-hand co-ordination. Six children always got to paint on the three 'A form' easels near the sink, whilst another group worked on bits for the classroom frieze controlled by the teacher. I loved fringing yellow wool to make blonde people but hated handling the Gloy pots; like lumpy wallpaper paste it frequently spoiled my attempts to create smooth surfaces and our resulting stickiness clearly irritated our teacher.

At least twice a year, like lambs to the slaughter, we queued outside a screened-off cloakroom to experience the indiscriminate tugging and combing of the Nit Nurse. Oil of sassafras was used in the perennial battle against headlice. Of course there were the usual 'accidents' and our mothers had to return the school's loaned knickers within the week. Puddles of urine and splashes of sick were promptly covered with sand for one child's regurgitations often triggered an automatic reaction in others. The stained blocked floors seemed to smell permanently of disinfectant.

Inevitable nostalgia tints the viewing of old class photographs, yet I am always struck by how poor the children staring out of them appear. In one particular infants' class photo, the majority of us look so 'homespun' – many wearing hand-me-downs from older siblings. Cardigans and sweaters were, without exception, all hand-knitted and made in generous proportions in order to last. I recall how carefully such photographs were choreographed. The girls were seated, those with white sandals and hair ribbons being placed on the front bench. My brown serviceable T-bars did not qualify for prime position. The boys were all standing (trusted to balance on tiered benches) and framed the girls like guards. 'Knees together, ladies, and boys stand tall!' were typical instructions which 'gendered' our postures. Our gap-toothed smiles as we 'cheesed' for the school photographer convey a beaming optimism about our unimagined futures. This childhood innocence is quite poignant, viewed some forty years on.

My personal recollections of being prepared for the eleven plus are very vague. Indeed, there was nothing of the practice and 'build up' that pupils facing SATs (Standard Attainment Tests) experience in junior schools today, where parents and pupils are fully *au fait* with test dates and expectations. A blankish memory on my part is perhaps not surprising given the unhappy circumstances of my parents' marital breakdown and acrimonious divorce. My mother and I were back living (once again) with my Nanna and her son, my uncle Reg. We had left my father, and two homes, and returned to him on several occasions, for futile attempts at normal family life, only to return to my Nanna's home six or eighteen months later. Sadly, his instability and violent temper eventually resulted in my mother seeking a divorce. As a little girl I witnessed some fairly horrific incidents of domestic violence (a rather sanitized term, I believe), which at the age of six I didn't understand at all. Images remain vivid even today and I am often unable to watch scenes of marital violence on TV or film.

My family problems not only caused me emotional distress, but they had a direct impact on my education. I frequently had to transfer from one school to another. Between 1960 and 1965, I attended four different primary schools from five different addresses. It was something of a relief, and the beginning of a much happier period of childhood, to return to the sanctuary of my Nanna's home and finally settle into regular attendance at Cadoxton Junior Mixed.

From the Old Village, I trudged up the steep hill of Church Road, calling for a friend on the way. The school appeared enormously tall and was perched somewhat proudly on Cadoxton's highest point. At the sound of the hand-rung brass bell, all children lined up promptly in the seriously sloping yard. Boys and girls formed separate lines and, of course, each gender filed in through different entrances. It never struck me as odd, even though some five minutes later, each class group was lining up regardless of their sex outside their own classroom door.

We sat in tiered rows of oak desks, bolted to the floor by iron frames. The teacher stood at the front and addressed the whole class at once. There were few distractions: the windows were high and the walls relatively unadorned. In classrooms of this kind I seemed to spend what felt like an inordinate amount of time perfecting handwriting skills. It was a constant battle maintaining cleanliness and neatness – an almost impossible task given the vagaries of bent nibs, cheap paper and runny ink. Undoubtedly, this description is a typical stereotype of schooling from this era. The boredom factor was fairly pronounced, which is why I particularly remember the severe winter of 1963, which broke the monotony of classroom life for many children.

The snow seemed to linger for months and like many other

'urchins' I wore my uncle's old laddered socks over wellington boots to avoid slipping. Our school positively steamed and cloakrooms reeked of stale wet woollens. Our mid-morning milk bottles were frozen solid, despite teacher's attempts at thawing them next to ancient radiators. At midday, and buttoned against the weather, we formed long crocodiles in pairs and were marshalled by teachers across roads to walk the 100 yards over to the dinner hall in a nearby Methodist Hall. The school meals service dished up 'fairly' hot stews, which had been cooked elsewhere and transported in greasy vats and urns. I remember many of us being far less fussy during this icy period, the cold having stimulated our appetites. Playtimes were bitterly cold on the top of Cadoxton Hill but all pupils were forced to leave the premises. My visual memory is reminiscent of a Breughel painting; we donned balaclavas, pixie hoods, shawls, mittens and scarves. We were totally unconcerned with fashion. Icy patches around burst pipes became sites for skidding games. We snapped icicles from dripping railings and pretended they were lollies. Boiler problems meant that many schools were closed, forcing pupils to stay home. The luxury of these 'unscheduled gift holidays' – which allowed me to lie on my bed reading – will remain with me forever.

Much of my junior school education was unstimulating. Creativity was again linked to Binca canvas; threading blunt bodkins of Anchor thread over and under or in and out of existing mesh was tedious yet we dutifully progressed from bookmarkers, placemats and a tray cloth in the dreaded stuff, which was grey with over-handling by the time we came to show our mothers! Fourth year girls went to Miss March's class one afternoon a week for sewing. We made gingham waist aprons, gingham peg bags and an embroidered gingham tray cloth. She was very strict and we worked almost silently. The skills she equipped a generation of girls with remain today – I still work sixteen running stitches to the inch and feel disabled without a thimble.

In sharp relief to the strict regime of the learning, chanting multiplication tables and silent reading, were the years I spent with Mr Bowen. He read aloud to us often twice a day and his animated performances transported us into times past and mythic. We learned about Ancient Greece via *The Odyssey* and also studied the Norse Gods, Oden and Thor. Much time was spent re-enacting these stories and in small groups we improvised episodes to the rest of the class. Our classroom was messy and colourful but its 'drama corners' with a box of old curtains and the nature table, stacked with various phenomena, engaged us all. This was probably sixties progressivism. On sunny days, Mr Bowen took us on rambles to study habitats and collect waterboatmen for our pond. These were very happy times and it was a joy to go to school.

The preparation and selection processes for the eleven plus tests remain fragmented in my mind. I remember vividly, however, being lined up outside my regular classroom and 'shushed' rather formally by Mr Bowen, who issued each pupil with a new, freshly sharpened pencil. We were instructed to file into class and fill up the desks row by row. The shock of seeing our classroom transformed from its cosy group table formation to regimented rows of equidistant desks conveyed to the entire class that something very serious was afoot. The 'face front' geography of the classroom, the neatly printed instruction on the blackboard along with Mr Bowen's agitated commands of 'Silence please! Fingers on lips!' signalled much more than his occasional spelling test! This was our first taste of formal assessment and we were urged from time to time to 'Do your best' and 'Move onto the next question if you're stuck' by our teacher, who paced the aisles.

I failed the eleven plus grammar school entrance exams. Indeed none of 4B, Mr Bowen's class, secured a place and only about twelve of Mr Latham's 4A class went onto local grammar schools. Friends who went on to Barry Girls' Grammar with whom I am still in contact have relayed how Mr Latham drilled them and tested their arithmetical and comprehension skills weekly. They also confess to how they had envied 4B's nature trips to the Cadoxton Dock Ponds and sketching visits to Cassey Common!

The exact details of how my family learned about the eleven plus outcomes are unclear. This lack of collective memory is perhaps significant. My retrospective understanding is that my mother was given the names of the secondary schools I could attend, none of which included the Grammar School. Like many other working class families of this time, we probably failed to recognize the importance of this potentially life-changing event.

The options for my secondary education, which would begin in

September 1966, were two girls' secondary schools – Holton Road and Jenner Park – and St. Cadoc's Roman Catholic Secondary School, which had recently been built and to which I went. This new Roman Catholic School was undersubscribed in spring 1966 and although Catholic children were bussed in from the Vale, Penarth, Sully, Dinas Powys and Barry, there was ample capacity, so its doors were opened to local non-Catholic pupils. My mother's decision, she informs me, was based upon the fact that my friends were going, it was near my Nanna's home (where we were currently living), but beyond these practical matters, she had felt that being 'mixed sex' was more modern and natural and of course St. Cadoc's was, in her words, 'spanking new'. Its greenfield location off Argae Lane in rural Cadoxton was attractive and its slick white concrete and glass architecture was a stark contrast to the austere Victorian red brick buildings she herself had attended. Furthermore, 'newness' was a quality much valued as Britain emerged from its post war greyness and gloom.

In 1966, the curriculum at St. Cadoc's Roman Catholic Secondary Modern School was broad-based enough and I found it totally thrilling at the start. In retrospect, however, it was more limited than the curriculum of my age mates who had secured a place at Barry Girls' Grammar School. Whilst we 'sec mods' studied general science, the 'grammar girls' studied Physics, Chemistry and Biology along with Latin and two foreign languages. Of course, ignorance is bliss and I was far from discontented at the time. I can recall feeling really grown-up and self-important on entering the science laboratory on my second day. It seemed technical: the whiff of the gas taps, weird things in glass jars, oak benches each with its own sink and, of course, the mysterious 'Table of Elements' chart. Huge laminated wall charts displayed the 'viscera of the abdomen' and a section through the human eye. It later became sheer joy to put on the teacher's second white coat and to assist him on the front bench – only later did we undertake our own group experiments because the boys were caught flame-throwing with the Bunsen burners.

I can still visualise many of the specialist classrooms clearly. Geography was taught in an airy room lit by two walls of large windows. A huge globe was suspended from the ceiling and the teachers occasionally lowered it on a pulley system to make points about meridians and the equator. We learned about life in the Borneo stilted houses of Sarawak and, when older, the rather drier details of the industry of the Rühr in Germany. It was through my geography lessons that I realized how small and insignificant my village of Cadoxton was in the great scheme of things. Such glimpses into other worlds fired imaginations.

We were challenged on a weekly basis to 'use your imaginations' by our Art teacher Mr McGirr whose vast collection of wine bottles formed the still life groupings which he made us draw and paint in various media. There were well over seventy of these in different colours, shapes and sizes. 'From all over the world,' he said. We did use our imaginations and silly rumours were rife: he was an alcoholic with a penchant for Chianti and his wife ran an off-licence somewhere in Cardiff! Our Art lessons were informal chatty affairs and, once grouped around a still life, he let us get on with it, circulating occasionally to cross-hatch a shadow, enhancing the solidity of our bottles before our eyes.

Cookery lessons were always 'double', allowing time to cook and clean up. They took place in what was a modern open plan fitted kitchen. It twinkled with new white electric cookers and gleaming double drainer sink units. I had seen nothing like this in any of the homes of family or friends. A little flat led off the kitchen and in it was a teak dining suite where we were taught how to create a 'dining ambience' (full cutlery, candles and napkins). In the bed-room, the single divan bed with its Welsh tapestry coverlet enabled us to practise mitring bed corners. In general, most girls loved cookery and progressed from rock cakes to soused herrings. We accepted the learned skills as a valuable contribution to our futures as wives and mothers. Boys did woodwork and never crossed the threshold of the kitchen. Similarly, we girls never ever got to hold a hammer, chisel or master the craft of the secret dovetail joint.

PE and games I largely enjoyed despite the compulsory end of lesson shower. The girls' changing room was nevertheless a site of struggle, with the pleasures of netball and hockey frequently offset by the PE teacher's monitoring of our monthly periods. We never actually saw what she jotted on her closely held clipboard but all learned to vary our excuses for missing a shower! It was all so public. Surveillance from peers was also uncomfortable: there was much ogling of and verification of bra sizes. The polarisation of girls with bras and those without was marked; each group occupied a different territory in the changing room. As a 'late developer', I felt my 'bralessness' acutely. At fourteen, and wearing a fibre-filled 32AA 'Berlei Teen-Form Bra', I finally crossed sides.

Along with a number of other moody fourteen year olds, I was switched on to poetry in our English lessons with Miss Cole. Listening to the lyrics of 'Elinor Rigby' – the Beatles' 1996 number one hit – made us feel sophisticated and modern. In the library at lunchtime we listened to her Joan Baez and Bob Dylan records (for their lyrics and poetry, of course). A newly qualified teacher, Miss Cole had the knack of exemplifying lesson points using contemporary pop culture. Her explanations of poetic form, imagery and devices of style like onomatopoeia and alliteration were both fascinating and accessible. She also drew our attention to the human element in literature: Lady Macbeth's ambition for her husband, Piggy's vulnerability in Golding's *Lord of the Flies*. The comments and annotations on our own creative writing conveyed Miss Coles's infectious enthusiasm for her subject. Our English portfolios submitted for the Certificate of Secondary Education (CSE), which had been launched in 1965, were testimony to this young teacher's splendid efforts.

I have said little about the majority of teachers who shaped my education. Some were colourful, others less so. My detailed recollections of the curriculum are fragmented, yet still with me some thirty-five years later are a whole collection of facts, alongside sets of useful life skills. So vivid was a science lesson on the life cycle of the tapeworm that I was unable to eat pork until well into my marriage.

Like many schools then and now, St. Cadoc's had an annual eisteddfod and sports day but the Catholic dimension meant that Christmas and Easter were prominent celebrations. Under the creative direction of our Head, Mr Brook, parents and pupils witnessed the most sophisticated illuminations of religious events. His detailed designs for costumes and sets with proscenium arches and apron stages were exquisitely realized and he swapped his black academic gown for overalls and worked alongside pupils and staff in the Art, Woodwork and Sewing classrooms.

For an Easter production of the morality play *Everyman* (in which I played Death), medieval tiles were screen printed and stencilled onto stage flats. After school one day, we sat in awe and wonder to watch the erection of columns and arches to the haunting music of Vaughan Williams's 'Variations on a Theme of Thomas Tallis'. I also remember one Christmas marvelling at the angel's wings our Head made with layers of feathers sculpted from paper and tinted in pinks and silvers. He created the most aesthetic Gabriel I have ever seen; she was a walking reproduction of a Fra Angelica fresco. Looking back, Mr Brook introduced us to many cultural dimensions which were not easily accessible to children from a working class background.

Over the years people have enquired of my actual experiences as a non-Catholic pupil in a Roman Catholic secondary school. These were broadly positive and amusing to look back on. My awareness of our differences occurred in the very first whole school assembly during the recital of the Lord's Prayer. The entire school population of Catholics stopped after 'forgive us from evil', leaving the non-Catholic children droning on with increasing lack of conviction and embarrassed awkwardness to complete the final three lines. My friend Carole whispered, 'They don't believe in God's kingdom or power – it's all Mary stuff with them!' Such rumours were rife and contributed to the sense of 'otherness' that each group of pupils felt. On an unfamiliar ear, the 'Hail Mary' sounded strange and Protestant pupils gawped open eyed at their Catholic classmates in prayer. It was not surprising, therefore, to find that separate assembly venues were soon established.

We Protestants were crammed into the long science laboratory for a somewhat cursory affair consisting mainly of school announcements and presided over by the two most forceful disciplinarians with the loudest voices – the male and female PE staff. The Headmaster led the more spiritual gathering in his academic gown from the stage; the Catholics sang along with the grand piano in the spacious school hall. Separate worship was discontinued one year later, however, when the further influx of local Protestant children rendered the laboratory too small. It took no time for 'the strange to become familiar' and soon all pupils said 'Hail Marys' and edited versions of the Lord's Prayer together.

The initial pride with which I wore school uniform faded: its novelty wore off as I approached the end of my first school year and began to emulate the nuances of senior pupils. Like hundreds of 60s teenagers elsewhere, we subverted school rules, particularly in relation to skirt length. Hemlines shifted several times a day; for lining up, filing inside and assemblies we wore them long – not a girl's kneecap in sight! At break and lunchtimes, the girls' toilet witnessed the ritualistic and precise rolling over of skirt waist-bands – a mass exercise. A pair of fourth form seniors 'went too far' one day however, and were shoved up on to the stage where each of them was seen to display at least four inches of red nylon bloomers. I remember this incident vividly: 'What is this? What do you think you are doing? Do you realize what you look like?' barked the Headmaster as he circled them like an agitated bat.

'They're bloomers, sir,' offered the cheekiest one. 'It's really cold, sir.'

The rapt attention of the whole school gazed on. Although implied, the Head managed to restrain himself from using the word 'tart', but he, and we, all knew that she was one of those 'available' girls who found alternative uses for the long jump pit! However, the consequence of this incident was the sudden popularity of bloomers as a fashion accessory for girls throughout the school, but worn with more prudence than the original instigator of the trend.

As I walked across the yard one day (shirt worn out to conceal the 'tyre' of rolled up skirt and sporting new white tights), I received my first wolf whistle: 'Hey you! Wednesday legs!'

I smiled over at the boy in a 'Do you mean me?' sort of way.

He yelled, 'Wen's day gonna snap and stick up your ass?'

He and his mates collapsed into raucous laughter whilst I scurried off in linked arms with my best friend Carole. Such bullying and humiliation was rife, often centring around sexual maturation or lack of it. For example, I was referred to as 'titless Donovan' whereas my well-endowed friends were baited with, 'Tarzan tits, how are they swinging?'

The secondary school education I received, like that of the infants' and junior school, was heavily gender-stereotyped. At St. Cadoc's, I learned how to be conventionally feminine, how to cook and sew and, as a prefect, how to look after new intake pupils. Nevertheless, the sound subject teaching of the official curricula had a personal impact. I became increasingly motivated and enjoyed coming top of the class. Support from home was one hundred per cent. Though I shared a bedroom with my mother, it had sufficient space for a collapsible wallpapering table which served as a useful desk. My uncle Reg followed my studies closely and was enthusiastic to test me on Norfolk's crop rotation system and the Industrial Revolution.

Retrospectively, I can now see how these home circumstances and being a single child were fruitful conditions for learning. The endeavours of some of my teachers and increasing academic success enhanced my enthusiasm for further study.

I left St. Cadoc's in June 1971, returning only in August for my examination results. I was allowed to telephone my mother at work with the good news that I had passed ten CSEs at grade one. This was sufficient to allow me entrance to the much-revered Sixth Form of Barry Girls' Grammar School two weeks later.

# That Welsh Accent

~

*Carys Richards*

**Carys Richards (1930-2001)** was born in Porthmadog, spent two years at the University of Wales, Aberystwyth, and then trained as a teacher at Homerton College, Cambridge. Shortly afterwards, she was selected as an announcer by BBC Wales in Cardiff, where she worked for four years, then joining her husband, Christopher Bell, in working for the BBC World Service in London. After the birth of their daughters, Rhiannon and Branwen, Carys worked as a freelance for radio and TV and, increasingly, as a writer. She published six Welsh novels, plus a Welsh translation of K.M. Peyton's *Pattern of Roses.* She was a regular writer on Arts topics for *Y Faner* and *Y Cymro* and contributed to the 1989 Honno anthology *Ar Fy Myw.* For many years, Carys and her family spent much of the summer in Porthmadog and when she suddenly died, in 2001, she was working on a novel set largely in the surrounding district she loved so much.

'Would Miss Richards go to Miss Whitby's room after dinner?'

This was one of the notices read out in the dining hall of the teachers' training college where I had arrived in 1950, after being unable to complete a degree in Philosophy at UCW Aberystwyth. The summer had been spent at my parents' house in Porthmadog, trying to get well again and finding it impossible to shake off the guilt of sitting in that examination hall, unable to write a word.

However, here I was in Cambridge – such a different place from Aberystwyth. The first thing that struck me was the absolutely appalling standard of singing: a short service was held daily in my women's college and not only were the English hymns new to me, but also the singing, or rather the shouting, attempted in boring unison, with no soprano or alto harmony. Now, I am not a natural nightingale, but the hard sounds and glottal stops sprinkled where none ought to be grated very badly on my ears.

What could Miss Whitby want? I muttered a groan to my friend Pat Donohue from Tonypandy and walked slowly up the gleaming stairs to the Vice Principal's office and knocked on the door. 'Come in.' I entered the elegant room, all white panelled walls, a vase of flowers on a low table, on one wall a print of some pale green apples on a plate by Cézanne. Here was the portly Vice Principal. After some practised queries on how I was settling in, 'The course should not be too difficult for one who had studied philosophy – ha, ha,' she paused. I kept my eyes on Cézanne's apples, wondering when she would get to the point.

'And now, Miss Richards, we've all been discussing this on the staff, so I've asked you to come and see me.'

She paused and I perspired.

'We do think it would be wise if you got rid of that boring Welsh accent.'

I whipped my eyes off Cézanne's poor apples, that I would never enjoy seeing again. For the first time since my examination blackout, I felt a human being, not a miserable failure. I felt gloriously angry.

'No, Miss Whitby, I won't do that. I am Welsh and proud of my language and if it affects the way I speak English, I shan't try to change myself.'

The V.P.'s smug face altered very slightly as she chose the English way of becoming as impassive as possible, showing the superiority of her self-control. In a little while, she continued to advise me that my chances of finding a post in a prestigious English school would be damned at the interview once I opened my mouth and spoke with that Welsh accent, which might be passed on to my pupils.

'But I won't be applying to schools in England,' I said brightly. 'I shall go back to Wales.'

How that interview continued I can't recall, but I do remember that I won, and the life-giving anger stayed with me for days as I told the tale to the other Welsh students at the college – Anne Bowen Thomas, Anne Issacs, my dear friend Pat, and half a dozen others.

'I shall go back to Wales,' I had told the V.P., but it wasn't going to be easy. I applied to join the waiting lists of all twelve education authorities in Wales, but they were all full, so when my course was ended I had to look elsewhere. London County Council took me as a supply teacher; I found a shared flat in Golders Green with my Irish friend Sheila and started what was one of the most exhausting periods of my life. Having asked for schools near Golders Green, I was allocated across the city in Islington. In the six months of my teaching career, I worked in twelve different primary and secondary schools, each with its own system of taking the register, the dinner money, the milk money. I rarely had a chance to use my training as an art teacher.

# College Days

~

*Ann Rodgers*

**Ann Rodgers** was born in 1932 in the small village of Sarn near Bridgend and educated at Bridgend County School for Girls and

Barry Training College. On qualifying, she was unable to obtain a teaching post in Wales, so taught in London. She married in 1954 and returned to Barry. She left teaching when her sons were born, looked after her parents and mother-in-law, and then returned to teaching, spending twenty happy years at Barry Island Primary School. She wrote the lyrics for two musical adaptations, *David the Shepherd King* and *The Legend of the Spiders*, and some of the songs have been published in a book of Christmas songs for children. She has published a collection of poems and is currently working on a novel for children. She enjoys needlework and embroidery and gives talks to many local groups.

Nineteen fifty marked a turning point in my life. It was the year I went to Glamorgan Training College, a single sex teacher training college, which was ruled over by Principal Ellen Evans, a true martinet of the old school. Our lives as students were hedged about by rules and regulations and the strictness of the regime earned the place the nickname of 'the nunnery'. But as far as our parents were concerned, such rules were designed for our security and Barry was the only college which my mother deemed safe enough for her young, innocent, naive, wilful and wayward elder daughter.

I was fortunate to be going to college at all. My brother, who was two years older than I, had done his two years' National Service. He had passed his exams before doing his conscription. Now at twenty, he was ready to go to college too. Times were hard and wages were low. There were no student grants: in fact most students going to training colleges paid fees. These were not high by today's standards, but in order to maintain two children at college (and with another child still in school) my mother went back to her pre-married work as a nurse. She worked nights in order to earn enough for me to have the same chance as my brother. I would like to say how very grateful I was. Alas I cannot. I do not think it even crossed my mind.

My home was in a little village called Sarn about three miles outside Bridgend and I had attended Bridgend County School for Girls. During the war, of course, no one had been able to travel very far, so going to college in Barry was a great adventure. The new trunk had to be bought, together with clothes and books to go in it. There was the exciting trip to Cardiff to buy my new college uniform at Roberts'. The college colours of brown and cream were not very inspiring. However, most girls wore their new blazer proudly the first day they arrived. I seem to remember we had to wear it that first day.

I was the only girl from my school going to college in Barry that year. It was with trepidation that my packed trunk was despatched to the station at Tondu, not to be seen again until it was delivered to my cubicle in dormitory four. When I say despatched, that is not quite accurate. My trunk was, in fact, fetched from home by a railway porter, who tied it on to a little porter's trolley and wheeled it, yes, wheeled it back the two miles or so to Tondu Station. This happened in reverse at the end of each term and again when my brother went away or came home.

The first time I left home for college, I allowed my father to accompany me to Cardiff bus station. When I saw the crowd of college girls waiting for the Barry bus he was hastily sent on his way. I did not want to look like a baby to the other students. After he had gone, my heart sank; everyone seemed to know someone except me. We crowded on to the bus and were on our way. My spirits sank lower and lower the nearer we came to Barry. The bus stopped at Williams's Stores and emptied of everyone for college. I was carried along in the crowd. As we entered the gates, I saw that the upstairs windows were open and girls were hanging out, calling out names at random. These were the second year girls who had been given charge of a first year girl, our 'College Mothers'. To my great relief, I heard through the babble my name, Ann Owen, shouted out. I waved frantically to show I was there. 'Wait,' shouted a voice and I stood and waited. This was my first introduction to my college mother, Ceri Jones from west Wales. Ceri was older than the average student as she had done several years teaching as an uncertificated teacher before coming to college. She proved a very wise, kind proxy 'mother' although I think I caused her as many anxious moments as I did my own mother.

The regime in college was very strict indeed. All students had to be back in college by 8.00 pm on week nights and by 10.00 pm on Saturdays and Sundays. As lectures went on until 8.00 pm, there was hardly need for a weeknight curfew. The Saturday night 10.00 pm curfew was another matter entirely. Supper was optional but we had to sign ourselves out and sign ourselves in again at 10.00 pm. Defeating the Saturday night curfew gave rise to fertile imaginations. Most of us managed to escape to the outside world to meet our boyfriends, if we had one, and not many came in through the front door at 10.00 pm. One or two volunteers signed the book for us while those still out came in via a conveniently open window in the wash room. We then had to crawl up the back stairs to our dormitories, our hearts thudding in case we were caught. We had a very young mistress in charge of our dormitory who must have been deaf and blind. She could not have missed the gales of giggles that nervous tension gave rise to.

My cubicle in the dormitory was the only space I had to call my own. Each dormitory had about twenty cubicles. I had a narrow bed, a dressing table, chair and a single wardrobe. This was 'home' for the coming year. Each student was responsible for cleaning their own cubicle. It had to be done every morning, dusted, swept and the windows opened. Woe betide you if your bed was not as neat and tidy as Matron wanted it. Nothing was to be kept on top of our wardrobes. No laundry, towels, or bathing costumes were to be hung out of the dormitory windows. Most important of all, no man was to be taken to your cubicle under any circumstances, at any time. Interestingly, we did not even question such petty rules and regulations.

Despite the restrictions, life in college settled down. Work was hard and long. Lectures started at 9.00 am and ended at 8.00 pm with breaks for lunch and tea. The hardest thing for me to bear was the homesickness. No one had prepared me for the lump of misery I carried about with me that first term. It was the longest period of my life and I was so miserable. We were not allowed home for a visit until half term. It seemed harsh then. Looking back, Miss Ellen Evans was probably very wise. She would have lost some of her students if they had been allowed home earlier. Gradually, of course, I learnt to manage my homesickness. I have never cured it.

Sex, of course, reared its ugly head. We were woefully ignorant of the subject. Not for us sex education in schools. We learnt from those girls willing and able to enlighten us. We hung on their every word. Could you become pregnant by kissing? We were not sure. My fourteen-year-old grandson knows more about where babies come from than we did then. Miss Ellen Evans lectured all the students herself on a Monday morning. This was called 'Ethics'. We were exhorted not to go with boys unless we had met them in church or chapel. I complied with this in every degree. It came about in this way.

My best friend in college was a Methodist, while I was an Anglican. Her father, Garfield, had a powerful bass voice. The Methodists were doing 'Elijah' and Garfield was engaged to sing the bass lead. My friend Marion had a late pass to go to the performance and she could take a friend. She took me. The choir stalls were stuffed full of forbidden fruits: boys. After supper one of them chatted me up. He had a friend who was already courting a college girl. Through them I had my first date with the man who was to become my husband. In a year or two, we will be celebrating our golden wedding.

Boys were allowed into college to the end of year dance. What excitement that caused. My first long ball gown. The boys in evening dress or smart suits. It was magical. Consternation was caused when one couple were caught 'necking' in the bushes. If it had not been so near the end of term, the girl would probably have been expelled. Boys were also allowed in to see the St David's Day concert. I have never been so embarrassed. When my dear husband-to-be saw Miss Ellen Evans in her full Welsh costume – frilly hat and all – he fell about laughing. He could not contain himself.

Teaching practice was something we were introduced to in the third term of our first year. Grins and giggles usually greeted our appearance in the classroom. The children could not take us seriously. How could they, when we had to wear ankle socks to school? No make-up was tolerated. In fact, Miss Evans lay in wait each morning as we walked through the main gates to board our buses taking us to our schools. Any sign of lipstick and we were sent back to scrub it off in the washroom. We became cunning, however, and put our make-up on during the journey. When the lecturers called, they usually turned a blind eye. We suspected that they were ruled by an iron rod too, especially the younger ones. The teachers usually greeted us with open arms. Especially when it came to P.E. It is amazing how many teachers will do anything to avoid doing P.E.

We, as junior or infant school trainees, had to cover all subjects, including P.E.

We were given a grounding in all subjects on the school curriculum from the 'three Rs' to Nature Study, Craft, P.E., R.E., Science. You name it, we were taught how to teach it. So much so that students coming out of Barry were in great demand. The local authorities knew that our training had been first class by excellent lecturers. We took two or three specialised subjects. Mine were History, Maths, and Needlework. After two years of intensive training, we sat our final exams. Our one priority was to pass the exams, gain our Teaching Diploma and find a job. Only then would the sacrifices made on our behalf have been worth while.

Our dearest wish would have been to find a teaching post near home. Alas, for most of us from Glamorgan this was out of the question. There was a great shortage of teachers so soon after the war. Those authorities, such as Glamorgan, who were training many teachers, both male and female, had to exercise a quota system whereby they could only employ a limited number of newly trained teachers. You had to be an exceptional student and be able to speak Welsh in order to stand a chance of getting a post in Glamorgan. As I did not qualify on either point, I had to cast my net wider. Most girls who qualified the same year as me applied to places like London, Birmingham, and Dudley, where the need for teachers was a bottomless pit. I applied to all three. London was the first to offer me an interview and once again my father accompanied me on this very important occasion. Whereas he had visited London before the war, I had never been further than Cardiff. I went to the head-quarters of the London County Council. I must have done quite well because I was offered a post, which I accepted that day. It was only later that I found my brother had a post in Dudley and my college friend had one in Birmingham. Once again I had a lonely beginning.

The school I was assigned to – Malmesbury Road School – was in the East End of London, just off the Mile End Road. It was a tall Victorian building with four floors: the staff room was in the attic so we were always fit. On street corners round the school stood piles of rubble, silent witnesses to the terrible bombing the East End had endured. Here and there tower blocks of flats were beginning to rise out of the devastation. The children I taught were cockneys and I was broad valleys Welsh. They did not understand me and I did not understand them. Not much teaching was done or received that first term.

I spent two momentous years teaching in London. During this time we had the Queen's Coronation, with all the excitement that brought. My husband-to-be was doing his National Service in the army and was on duty lining the route the Queen would take to Westminster Abbey. The evangelist Billy Graham came to London at this time too, with his crusade to save the nation. His meetings at Harringay Arena and the White City Stadium were packed to capacity. I have never seen or been part of gatherings of so many Christians since.

I cannot say the two years sped by, but they did pass. My fiancé was coming to the end of his National Service and it was now possible for us to get married. This we did in 1954. Fortunately, there was no bar to the number of married teachers Glamorgan could take and I was offered a choice of two schools. I began my teaching career in Barry at Gladstone Road School under the headship of Miss Florence Sharpe. I felt I had come home.

# CHAPTER 3

# TEENAGERS

# Coming Out

~

*Marianne Jones*

**Marianne Jones** was born in a Bangor hospital towards the end of 1944 and brought up on Ynys Môn, Anglesey. Her first sniff of teenage liberation came with the discovery of Shelley's *Prometheus Unbound* in a second-hand bookshop and hearing rock and roll for the first time. She went to university and did teacher training, which took her to Japan and Canada. She came back to Wales, working as a Project Manager for the Welsh Office providing Japanese lessons in Welsh schools, and then back to Anglesey, where she lives with her partner. Several of her poems have been published in *New Welsh Review* and other magazines, her translations of Japanese poetry have been published in *Scintilla* and she has had a short story in *Cambrensis*.

I grew up in a world of puritan chapels, whitewashed cottages, smallholdings and farms made derelict by the 1930s, the dinosaurs of farm equipment rotting near wet haystacks. The air was full of rain. We seemed to inhabit an underwater kingdom – surrounded by water, dyked up on its western edge, saturated in the $H_2O$ of showers, downpours, mists and fog. A hard silver light reflected off wet slate roofs, puddled fields and ponds with colonies of alder and ducks.

Across the water, or the Telford bridge, were the mountains – an even more remote and harsher region with a recent history of slate quarrying and lock-outs, now opening cafes and museums for tourists. Moch Môn – Anglesey Pigs – they called us over there when we went to play rounders with them, while we called them Apaches. Then we had a great time ganging up with them after the flicks in Bangor on Saturday afternoons and poring over names like 'Gypsy

Red' and 'Pink Passion' at the lipstick section in Woolworths. If my life, with its litany of school, homework and church, sometimes seemed to be coloured grey, there were golden oases in it like that, and the beaches in summer, the smell of oak woods and bluebells after rain, my father's sense of humour.

My father. He was learning to play the tuba for the town band at that time and woke us up each morning with dreadful squawking from the foot of the stairs. Mistar Trydan – Mr Electricity – they called him.

In the 1950s and early 1960s there was no electricity supply to several of the villages on Anglesey. Farms had their own generators. The town of Llangefni, where we lived, and other towns were connected to the mains, but I was used to visiting relatives in the countryside with boxes of Christmas goodies and seeing paraffin lamps lit at dusk. My father's job, and that of his boss, was to bring light and other electrical splendours to the inhabitants of Anglesey, who lived in this outer darkness. His boss had a flair for publicity. Every time they put a village 'on stream', he organised a grand opening with light bulbs, kettles, washing machines and cookers all coming on at once to gasps of admiration from everyone present. Then he read a poem he had written in honour of the occasion. These grand events were reported in the papers, much to the embarrassment of the big bosses in Liverpool, who did not want anyone to know that electricity had only just reached parts of their region.

My father had stories to tell: how a few people were scared of electricity and only used it to put on a light to find a match to light a candle or lamp; how one woman had foisted a goose on them in payment of a bill and how they had hidden it in the stationery cupboard during a meeting with one of the big bosses, while hoping that its smell would not get even more powerful.

My great auntie Blodwen sat by the coal fire with us sometimes, listening to these tales, laughing and checking that there were no electric lights on in any other room before she left. 'You're burning money in here!' she said if she found one. In her seventies, dark-eyed and straight-backed, she had a mysterious egg-shaped bump on her forehead and a nervous mouth, always moving, and she was as honest in one day as most of us get in a lifetime.

But I was talking about oases and one of them was about to appear in my life in the second week of December, 1960: there was to be a Christmas dance in the Town Hall. At first there was a great family debate about it. I was too young to go, only fifteen. On the other hand, I had all my O levels on me, was in the first form sixth and all my friends were going. At last, permission came: I could go in the company of a small group of young women from my neighbourhood; the older brother of one would escort us down the street and into the dance.

I was in a state of agitated excitement all the week leading up to the dance. The only thing I was unsure of was the dress that my mother had bought me for the occasion; what an ingrate I must have been! It was a floaty, romantic, lilac ball gown with a rose on its collar and I liked it until an older girl in our class, Helen, said, 'Of course, a black number for me – nothing unsophisticated.' I remember that she was plastering her kiss-curls into shape with water from the drinking fountain at the time and combing her eyebrows into arches. The idea of not being sophisticated threw me into turmoil.

My younger sister put her head on one side when I tried on the dance dress for her inspection and said, 'Hmm. Yes. The waist's great but the skirt should be fuller.' Then she helped me pour a two pound bag of Tate and Lyle's granulated sugar into an inch of cold water in the bathtub to make the strong solution that would stiffen up my layered petticoat. We left the petticoat to soak overnight and, on the following morning, carried it out into the back garden like a drowned cat and hung it on the line with wooden dolly pegs. If this fashion of full skirts and tiny waists ever resurfaces, by the way, let me pass this skill on to you. It worked a treat. By the time we had come home from school, we could stand the petticoat upright on the parlour floor.

My next worry was dancing. We had been taught how to do it by the biology teacher. It was done methodically. First the boys were lined up at one end of the school assembly hall, which had been cleared of chairs for the occasion. Then the biology teacher shouted out, 'And – one, two three; one, two, three,' and the boys proceeded woodenly down the hall. 'Quicken the pace now, boys!' the biology teacher called out, once she was confident they had memorized the steps. This was the nearest we got to a sex education at school. After the boys, the girls learned their steps, only they had to go backwards.

Then, and most embarrassing of all, the boys had to pick a girl to dance with and if the wrong one got to you first, you had to learn how to deal politely with body odour and pimples while your partner grasped your arm and waist with sweaty palms.

Even worse, if possible, was 'ladies' choice' when you had to get up, cross the entire length of the hall and ask a boy to dance with you, all the time fearing that he might say, 'No, I'm dancing this with someone else. Thanks, anyway,' or maybe not even thanks anyway. Ballroom dancing: I was not sure about it at all. But there was bound to be at least one rock and roll number and possibly more and there was going to be a live band. At that time, I was passionate about rock and roll, and nineteenth century romantic poetry.

The other thing I wondered about was boys. To date, my most exciting experiences with them were being asked for my hand in marriage at the age of eight and being seized by my arm during playtime by a boy with sandy hair and exciting green eyes from the upper sixth, who wanted me to run away from home with him. However, since my upbringing was Catholic and since the priest was now saying dark things like kissing could be a mortal sin, I was very unsure of myself around them. And yet the myth of Cinderella going to the ball was alive in my heart.

On the night of the dance, you can imagine how excited and nervous I was in the lilac dress, as I twirled around for my mother's inspection. My father was working overtime but due back to see me before I set off for the Town Hall. My sister was pulling at her lip and saying, 'When will it be my turn to go?' over and over until my mother nearly lost all patience with her.

'I'll tell you all about it!' I said, as if that was any help.

At that point, the doorbell rang.

'It's them!' I said.

'Calm down,' my mother said. 'And go and open the door in a ladylike manner!'

But when I rushed to the door it was my father, his briefcase under one arm. 'You look nice!' he said. 'But I'm afraid I've got something to ask you.'

'What?' I said, leading the way back into the parlour.

'Your Auntie Blod is in a bit of a state tonight and she's asked if you could go and sit with her. She asked specifically for you – her oldest and favourite niece, I suppose. She doesn't have children of her own, after all.'

'What?' my mother said. 'You can't ask that of the poor girl. What on earth is the matter with Blodwen?'

'I popped in to see her after work and she seemed quite agitated.'

'Trust her to be inconsiderate!' my mother said. I gathered that, 'You're-burning-money-in-here' was not appreciated by her.

'Well, I'm going back there after supper. I've never seen her like this.'

My mother gave one of her angriest martyred sighs.

The doorbell rang out again.

I took a deep breath. 'That has to be them,' I said. 'I'll go down and see her after the dance, Dad.'

'It'll be too late for a visit then.'

'Well, tomorrow?'

I flung my coat on, ducked past a barrage of 'don't catch cold, don't drink, when you get old . . ., where's your scarf?' and opened the door to smell face powder and eau de cologne and see the radiant faces of a small group of people somewhat older than me. The man in charge, Llew, looked handsome in his suit. His coat was sitting on his shoulders and his winklepickers were polished to a high shine.

'Yes, sir,' he said to my father. 'I'll look after everybody. No, sir, I won't let them out of my sight,' and we set off down the street past the flat-roofed comprehensive school, the deserted county grammar school with its high Victorian windows glinting in orange lamplight, past the station and down the hill to the Town Hall. I felt my spirit grow taller than all the buildings as we walked along. It was expanding with a heady sense of freedom I had never imagined before, not even when I read Shelley's *Prometheus Unbound* in my back bedroom overlooking the school fields.

There were a few snowflakes in the air but none of us noticed the cold. We went laughing and chattering past all the closed shops – Dicks, the Emporium, the Golden Eagle. We were almost there. I felt sick. This was it! As Llew handed in our tickets at the door, I thought about the 'coming out' parties I had read about in novels and suddenly realised this was mine.

As soon as we handed in our coats at the cloakroom, Llew disappeared in the direction of the drinks table and did not come back.

'Come on, let's check our make-up,' one of the women said and I followed her and the others into the Ladies, sticking close to them for company.

There was quite a squeeze around the mirrors in there and hairspray and loose face powder were flying everywhere. A woman with blonde curls was taking a swig out of a bottle half-hidden in a brown paper bag.

'Steadies the nerves, girls,' she bellowed.

Helen was there, looking dismissively at everyone, mascara brush in one hand. Her fat arms reminded me of a goose I helped pluck the Christmas before.

'Who've you got your sights on tonight?' the woman with the bottle shouted.

'Give us a swig of that Dutch courage, girl,' Helen said.

Everything around me was too frantic and stifling and I left and walked towards the dance hall, stopping near the door. I peered inside at paper and tinsel hanging from the walls, bare boards and a trestle table with bottles on it. The band seemed to be warming up and was practising the last waltz but there were one or two dancing couples. As they circled round, a fragile-looking girl was leaning against Big John, the sixth-former with a reputation for James Dean-style defiant silence.

'Pathetic, isn't it?' Helen said, as she walked past me and into the dance. 'If he said, "Jump off that cliff," she'd probably do it for him.' She marched towards the trestle table.

I followed her, thinking I would look as if I knew what I was doing and someone's brother asked me for a dance as I crossed the floor. Then I chatted with some friends from school and began to feel that I was getting used to this and possibly slightly bored, when the band, now in full swing, began to play, 'Rock around the Clock'. Several couples got on the floor and began to jive. My toes twitched. I wanted to dance. A man – handsome rather than ordinary but with slightly booze-bleary eyes – was at my elbow asking 'for the pleasure of'. We twirled on to the floor and swirled to the rhythms of rock and roll. The band was playing a set. We carried on dancing. This was fun!

Suddenly, in the interval between one rock number and the next, a woman marched across the floor towards us. 'I'm leaving!' she yelled at the man. 'And you'd better come with me.'

'Hey, girl,' Helen shouted out from near the trestle table, her attention drawn to me by the woman's shouting. 'Fair's fair. He's a married man, after all.'

Everyone nearby seemed to swing around and stare at me.

'Oh,' I said, 'I didn't realize.' I excused myself and started to walk towards Helen.

The man followed me. 'Here. Lemme walk you home,' he said. 'Angel in this hell hole.'

'We're bloody getting out of here now,' his wife shrieked.

The man was hauled off, only to return. 'I wanna take you home, darlin',' he blubbered, grasping my arm.

A group of people began to gather around us. I tried to break free, managed it at last and ran out of the hall. I had enough presence of mind to grab my coat from the cloakroom and then I rushed out into the street. I hardly noticed the town clock or the time but began running in the direction of my great aunt's house. As I passed the cattle auction grounds and the dairy, I slowed down, partly because I felt winded. I looked behind me: there was no one there. I pulled my coat on and began to walk onwards, over the wooden bridge across the Cefni, up the hill towards Dolafon. I felt cold and wet: it was snowing.

When I reached my aunt's house, and just as I was about to ring the bell, the door opened and our doctor came out carrying his black bag.

'Well, young lady!' he said as I dived past him and then past my father in search of my aunt. 'I'll be back tomorrow.'

My aunt was tucked up in blankets and lying on her sofa in front of a coal fire. She opened her eyes, raised her head and said, 'O, cariad bach – oh, little love,' before sinking back on to her pillow.

'Your aunt's had a heart attack, I'm afraid,' my father whispered to me.

I would have flung myself on to my knees in front of her like some Dostoevsky heroine, if I hadn't realised that such dramatics would exhaust her even more. Instead, I turned the Welsh word for aunt over and over in my mind as if it were a pebble in my pocket:

*modryb*. There's a Welsh proverb that says that a good aunt is a second mother and she had always been that for me.

'Have you walked through Llangefni on your own in the dark?' my father demanded. 'I'll have words with you later, young lady – and with that Llew.'

'Read . . . from the Psalms,' my aunt whispered, her lips quivering. 'Where God leads his people ... out of the wilderness.'

'Don't exhaust yourself,' my father said. 'You know what the doctor said.'

I rushed to get the great Bible from its place of honour. My aunt had brought this with her down from 'the mountain' when her health and other people persuaded her to move into town. The mountain was Mynydd Bodafon, 591 feet above sea level.

Like a fool, I read the psalm I was sure of, *'The Lord is my Shepherd.'*

'Green pastures,' my aunt whispered after me and then I faltered, realising that the valley of the shadow of death was in it.

My aunt opened her eyes again and smiled at me. The stubborn expression around her mouth and chin told me that she was going to fight. How much I wished that I could join forces and fight with her. She lay there on her sofa like the spirit of Wales, determined to rise again. And God forgave me and brightened the Spring of 1961: my aunt survived.

# The Rock and Roll Years

~

*M. Muriel Hughes*

**M. Muriel Hughes** was born in Llanrhystud in 1943, went to Aberaeron Bilateral School and did teacher training at Trinity College, Carmarthen. She taught in Shropshire and Birmingham, before returning to Llanrhystud with her young family in 1972. She has had poetry published by Arrival Press and *Pennine Ink* magazine, among others. She attended a creative writing class held by R. Gerallt

Jones in the 1990s and completed a creative writing course with OCA.

I was a child of the fifties. I was seventeen when 1960 burst on the scene. In those days you were legally a child until you reached the age of twenty-one, and the only privileges that brought you were the key of the door and the vote. I didn't automatically have the key of the door as there was nearly always someone at home. Until the mid-fifties, my mother ran a family business and was out driving the delivery van every day, but she was always there to see that I was washed and ready for school. Until I went to secondary school she plaited my pigtails, tied ribbons in them and off I went to primary school, on my own or meeting friends on the way. No need to worry about the danger of strangers in those days. Cars were few and far between and most people were far too occupied to worry about a girl on her own. Children were children then, at least until they left school. We had to do as we were told and were reminded of our immaturity whenever we wanted to do anything bold. Then, if we acted childishly, we were told to 'grow up, act your age'. If we kicked against the traces we were told 'you're only fifteen' or whatever age we were at the time.

There must have been a particular time when I stopped wearing clothes which my mother chose for me. She would drag me into traditional outfitters or ladies' fashion shops and persuade me to have something that would last for years. All that I wanted to last for years was my love of pop music, rock and roll, dancing, films and boys. At Aberaeron Secondary School a small select group of my friends and I would spend our lunch hours hiding behind the domestic science block, away from overbearing prefects. We talked about pop and film stars. Our idols were Bill Haley and the Comets of 'Rock around the Clock' fame, Buddy Holly and the Crickets, and of course, Elvis – The King! In between doodling their names on the paper covers of our exercise books, we would ponder as to what we would do if . . . if one of our idols came round the corner *that* minute? We would probably have been stunned into complete silence.

That would have been a miracle in itself as we never stopped talking while we had the chance, for when we went back into the classrooms we would be forced to be quiet or risk the wrath of a stern teacher who would either keep us in after school or give us lines to do. We had to write out one hundred lines of the most boring memoranda, such as, 'I must not talk in class.' It had no benefit at all as we all copied each letter in turn to the bottom of the page: I, I, I, I . . . soon lost its meaning when repeated thirty times.

My family did not acquire a television until 1958, just before I took my O levels. At first it was snobbish to have a television, then it became another kind of snobbery not to have one. Before the television came to our house, my brother and I spent far too much time watching our neighbour's set. It was a revelation to me to see my pop and film idols in the living room, as it were. Until then, we had to be satisfied with regular visits to the cinema.

Apart from various village discos, going to the cinema was the most exciting a Saturday night could get. Chip shops stayed open long enough for cinema-goers to have a sit-down meal and a chat about the film or a take-away in newspaper, whilst walking fairly quickly to get the last bus home at between ten-thirty and eleven o'clock.

Freedom from direct parental control did not come until you left school and went to college. If you left school to go to work locally, you would still be living under the same roof as your parents. As had been the tradition in Wales for many years, young people had to go away to college or to work. There was the usual exodus of teachers to London and the Midlands. Most young people had never been away from home before. If you lived in the country or near the coast, you didn't go on holiday. We had it all there any-time we wanted. Living on the west Wales coast around Cardigan Bay, we had the added pleasure of getting to know holiday-makers' children, who had different backgrounds from us. They played on the beach, chatted over sand-loaded sandwiches and pop. They reluctantly left on the last day of their holiday promising to keep in touch. They never did. The next year would bring either the same set of children or a new lot. It gave us country children a different outlook on the world, if only for a short time.

My father was a sea captain, one of many who set off from Wales to seek pastures new. He found it difficult to come to terms with the changing youth scene. He still had the idea that children should be seen and not heard. Luckily, he was not home often enough to press the point. He tried to be a 'cool' dad but as with all teenagers, we greeted his efforts with hoots of laughter. He picked up 'See you later, alligator, in a while crocodile' in America. It was completely out of date by the time he came home! However, he did bring back new-fangled transistor radios for my brother and me from Japan. There were so well used, in the end they literally fell apart. I carried mine in the saddle-bag of my bike as I went to my holiday job at the caravan park. 'Speedy Gonzales' was top of the pops then, blaring from my saddle-bag as I rode along. I was known from then on as Speedy Gonzales to everyone at the park.

I did not have a record player until I met my husband but for my twenty-first birthday I did have a tape recorder, a hefty thing that felt the weight of half a sack of potatoes. The idea was that, as my friend had a Dansetta record player, I could record all her LPs and singles onto my tape recorder. I hadn't bargained on her turntable having a wobble, so all the Jim Reeves' songs would 'blip' throughout the recordings.

Along with the noisy beat of American rock and roll, there exploded on to our ears the Mersey Sound – the Beatles, Jerry and the Pacemakers, Herman's Hermits, Freddie and the Dreamers – all home-grown boys with enough audacious energy to set the world alight. The uncontrolled sound systems in dances then may have contributed to hearing loss on a massive scale. Conversation was impossible. Boys didn't come to the dance hall till the pubs had turned them out. Waiting would be rows of girls in flared skirts and winklepicker high-heeled shoes. They would coolly pretend to be unaware of a certain boy's arrival, but by the last waltz they would have found each other. Lucky couples would walk a short distance to the nearest dark corner for some serious snogging before walking home or, if they lived in another area, piling into a battered old van, full of inebriated young men. The don't drink and drive laws were unheard of then. It was easier to avoid trouble on the roads because most vehicles were going the same way and there were fewer anyway. It was a miracle that some drivers avoided ending up in a ditch. If they did they would sleep in the car or walk home, collecting their cars in the morning.

Sophistication came in the sixties with my move to work in Birmingham. There, Mecca Dancing was the normal weekend venue. Port and lemon and student-priced cider gave way to vodka and lime or lager and lime, depending on your finances. Beehive hairdos made the girls look like galleons in full sale on the dance floor. Huge handbags full of hair preparations and cosmetics lined up along the vanity units in the ladies' cloakrooms. Late buses arrived, filled up and disappeared, leaving desperate girls who had lagged behind looking for taxis. Taxis were a great luxury in those days and a last resort.

We had yet to see the effects of drugs on our close-knit society. We saw flower power and pop festivals on TV, but my friends and I would not have recognised a cannabis reefer if it had been waved under our noses. We were a fun-loving generation who had more money to spend on clothes and cosmetics than our wartime mothers ever had. We even had a meal out now and again, in a Chinese or Italian restaurant. Such sophistication was secretly envied by our mothers. From time to time, they felt obliged to say, 'Of course, in my day, we didn't . . .'

No, they didn't, did they. But we did.

# How High the Moon

~

*Pam Clatworthy*

**Pam Clatworthy** was born in Rumney, Cardiff, in 1933 and educated in the village school and then Gowerton Girls' Grammar School in Swansea (the best school in the world). After Swansea Training College, she married, had two children and moved to Cumbria, where she now lives. She concentrated on writing after retiring as headmistress from Gosforth Primary School, Cumbria. She has written for *Yours*, the *Daily Telegraph* and *The Countryman* and had poetry and short stories broadcast on regional radio. She is currently writing her first novel and a radio play. She loves listening to other people's conversations and train journeys from Carlisle to Swansea are particularly rewarding.

My first grown-up party, my first special boyfriend, my first journey into unknown sexual territory: the year 1950, the place Cardiff, the atmosphere explosive. I was seventeen years old, studying for A levels at a Swansea grammar school and was as innocent as a little lamb. Brought up by God-fearing parents, with a father who thought that letting me catch the last bus back from town at 10.30 pm was stretching things a bit far, I had no idea of what went on at 'adult' parties.

My boyfriend, Dave, was a science student from the Swansea Valley, studying at Cardiff University, and lodging with a kindly widowed lady and her son Aled, near college. When she went to visit her sister in Aberystwyth the house was in the hands of Aled and the three students who lived there. It was too good an opportunity to miss; they rolled back the carpet, stuck a couple of candles in Chianti bottles, bought in the cider and sent out invitations.

My grandparents lived in Cardiff and I was able to stay with them for the weekend. It took two hours on the N and C Express coaches to get from Swansea to Cardiff, and I was stuck with sitting next to a rubicund, middle-aged vicar with a warty chin, who quoted Omar Khyam's *Rubyiat* between Aberavon and Bridgend, then proceeded to tell me how much he regretted his past innocent life and wished he had lived more for the rest of the journey. In the suburbs of Ely he squeezed my knee and told me I was a nice girl. Hypnotized, I promised to sit with him on the return coach on Sunday night, making a mental note to return early on Monday morning instead.

It took me hours to get ready for the party. I bathed in a dismal, green-painted bathroom, filling the cold air with the smell of Yardley's lavender bath cubes. I squeezed my black-heads and applied Nivea Crème, as I gazed into the small, yellowed mirror on the cracked tiled wall. Austerity was still the key word of the early fifties: it was considered quite sinful in our circles to want to stand and look into a mirror for too long. My bra strap twanged and snapped as I tried to pull it ever tighter to make my boobs look bigger, so I had to use a safety pin to secure it. My dress was beige jersey wool, and had accordion pleats. It was pleasant, lady-like and boring, but I only had one good frock and that was it. I borrowed my Grandma's enamelled blue-bird brooch with the diamond eyes, to tart it up a bit.

Dave came and called for me that evening, and we walked to the party. After the cold dampness of the autumn air, it was pleasant to get into a warm, cosy suburban semi and hang up my navy school gabardine mac, which, because of clothes rationing, was the only decent coat I owned. The sitting room was almost in darkness, just a few guttering, white household candles in wine bottles lit up huddled shapes on the sofa and easy chairs. The sluggish fire in the mottled tiled fireplace was almost out. A record of Stan Kenton 'How High the Moon' blared from the walnut veneered radiogram, shaking the cut-glass vases on the utility sideboard.

Aled came forward. 'Here's a glass of cider, Pam. Nice to see you. We're starting off by sitting on our partner's knees, then we'll move around later to get to know each other.'

My heart turned to ice and my stomach churned. I didn't fancy sitting on anyone's knee at all. Nice girls didn't do that sort of thing. Still, what did I know about the real world? If that's what people did at 'adult' parties, I had to be game for it. Dave looked as sick as I felt; he was an innocent abroad too. I sat on Dave's knee like a guy at a firework party, then trembled as I thought of what my father would say if he knew what was going on in that darkened room. Dave and I didn't say a word to each other, we were both lost for words. He tentatively nibbled my ear. The cider was sweet and sickly. I took little sips at first, followed by gulps to fortify myself for what was to come.

'Everyone change partners.'

Reluctantly I moved on to the next pair of knees. A spotty face stared at me. I don't think the bloke was keen on what he saw.

'I'm John.'

'I'm Pam.'

John's knees were knobbly and his grey, flannel trousers felt rough on the back of my shins. To my horror, I felt a cold, skinny hand unbutton my dress and feel around the back of my shoulders to unhook my bra. With a sudden ping the safety pin snapped open and a cry of pain screamed from John's thin lips. He was impaled on my emergency bra securer. We disentangled from each other, and in complete disarray I sped off to be violently sick, the cider contributing to my downfall.

Dave was waiting for me when I eventually stopped retching and staggered weakly out of the loo.

'Shall we go? It's not really my cup of tea.'

I would have kissed him, if I hadn't been completely off that sort of thing at the time. We got back to my grandparents' hours before curfew. Dave spent the rest of the evening playing chess with my Uncle Reg. I curled up on the sofa with a hot water bottle and a glass of warm water and bicarbonate of soda, Grandma's sure fire answer to a sickly stomach. It would be a long time before I would go to an *adult* party again.

# Periods

~

*Gillian Morgan*

**Gillian Morgan** was a war baby, born in Cwmffrwd, Carmarthen in 1943, when her mother was twenty and her father fighting abroad. For the last forty-three years, she has lived in Pembrokeshire. After bringing up her daughters fulltime for ten years, she trained as a teacher. While teaching, she had a book of postcards published and self-published a novel. She has written regular articles for the local papers and had poetry published in Britain and the USA. Since retirement she has gained an MA in Creative Writing. She is now concentrating on being a Welsh 'Mam' with her daughters and four grandchildren living on her road.

On my eleventh birthday, March 1954, I had my first period. In those days women referred to periods as being 'unwell', a reflection of inherited attitudes, probably. My mother warned me not to wash my feet or hair during menstruation, as it could lead to madness.

I already knew something about this messy business from a friend, who had the advantage of a bedroom window overlooking the house next door's washing line. Not a month would go by without the pair of us dashing upstairs to see twenty homemade sanitary towels hanging on the line, like a row of clinical bunting, celebrating the arrival of 'the curse'. One day, as we were leaning out of the window, counting them loudly, the friend's father warned us we would fall and break our necks; this led to a fit of uncontrollable giggling.

When I stayed in the country with my Auntie Hannah in Cwmffrwd, Carmarthen, she always aired the sanitary towels before I used them. On my visits I was accompanied by a pack of shop bought sanitary towels, 'just in case', because she lived in the country. A sanitary belt, through which the towels were looped, was also included.

Despite the cumbersome 'hygiene' necessities, I was quite interested in the whole process and Auntie Hannah sent for a booklet from a sanitary towel company for me to read. It was written in a friendly tone by 'Sister' and combined technical details of the monthly cycle with line drawings of a young girl engaged in very active pursuits, such as walking, cycling and climbing mountains. The message was to exercise, sleep with the window open and eat plenty of fresh fruit and vegetables. Cool baths were also recommended. I took it very seriously but, once I became used to the business of the monthly bleed, I wanted to try internal sanitary protection. Auntie Hannah, who was then in her late sixties, did not wholly approve, fearing one of them might get 'lost' inside me and would require a doctor to remove it, surgically. However, I was allowed to buy a box of Tampax and after much fiddling, was able to use them.

# Sweet Sixteen

~

*Joan Hilditch*

**Joan Hilditch** was a teenager in the fifties, born and raised at the head of the Rhymney Valley in south Wales, where her father was a policeman. She was educated in the local grammar school, then trained as a nurse in Cardiff. Her first love was writing and she moved to Manchester to be a Community Arts Worker, where she taught creative writing, visited schools and prisons, and organized writing groups. She has toured America reading her work. She returned to Wales after her divorce. Three times divorced, she has four children and eighteen grandchildren and great-grandchildren. She believes strongly in recording her life to preserve the past, for her children and for Wales, and also writes fiction and has been published in educational books and anthologies.

Mam burst like a banshee into the bedroom I shared with two smaller sisters in our home in the large village of Rhymney at the head of the valley, south Wales. She was holding my navy school knickers at arm's length between her forefinger and thumb. I had been in that pre-sleep stage where I was drifting in thoughts of what other fifteen-year-old girls have dreamed about throughout the ages – clothes, shoes, natural lipstick so Dad would not notice, and what IT would feel like. It being a French kiss, which is as far as I had got in sex education learnt in the school grounds.

When we all sat up in bed, bleary-eyed and confused, I made out the words Mam was shouting. In fact, I guessed the whole village by then knew that I had started my first period without noticing and left my school knickers on the back of the kitchen chair to be seen by Dad and his mate when they got back from the pub, and, horror of horrors, I had washed my hair and rinsed it in cold water before bed, and so ruined my insides for ever more. However much I told myself that this was nonsense, her words terrified me. Now too it seemed I could 'catch babies'. Oh God!

Mam had calmed down by the next day and led me to the toilet to teach me how to pin on these folded cotton pads, and I had to wash them myself, retching as I did so and needing to make sure no one was about to come in and catch me at this. Not being allowed to bath, or wash my hair or even put my hands in cold water frustrated me utterly, as did feeling hot and smelly and dirty. Perhaps worse still was the woman to woman talk my mother had planned. Blushing red, she held my hand and patted it while she asked if I knew how babies were born.

'Of course I do,' I blustered, shaking with embarrassment and fear.

'Good, love,' she said. 'Now be sure not to let any man touch you down there!' God, I thought, why would he want to?

It seemed the whole village was informed of my new status. 'I hear you're a woman now,' said Auntie Betty, the grocer lady. A man at the back of the queue sniggered and I fled without the butter!

'Growing up now, aren't you?' said Dai the Fish.

It seemed I could go nowhere my womanhood hadn't already been discussed. Even callers to the door, nudge, nudge, said, 'Woman now she is', and Mam would wink. I could not stand this till the dreaded change of life at God knows what age.

Suddenly too, I noticed the buds of my breasts swelling. Not more signs of womanhood, I thought, please God, I'm only fifteen. They itched at the most public places, and hurt and burned. If a man touched my arm, let alone anywhere else, I jumped out of my skin. I started sniffing beneath my arms and, to my horror, I had begun to bush out there and between my legs too. I wanted to die. So many rules. I would never be happy as a woman.

I nagged and pleaded but finally fainted at school and the doctor demanded that my hip length hair be cut short, which is what I had wanted. My head felt light, my body swollen, my fingers seemed to pick up everything as if they were egg shells. I began to walk with slower steps, mainly for fear the pad would drop out. Boys turned to watch me in the street, so that I fell over my feet and dropped things. I blushed and developed a lisp, to my horror, as well as the breasts. My sisters unmercifully teased my new singing voice and said I was 'putting it on'. I was confused about this and laughed with a nervous giggle.

My mother made me a dress to sing in the chapel anniversary. It was a beautiful blue, but with a babyish sash. But she had ruined her eyes and bloodied her fingers working far into the night to embroider the hem and bodice. Now finally on me, with my big grown-up straw hat and slip-on shoes without socks, I was horrified. Wreaths of flowers circled each of my little budding breasts like frames. I couldn't wear it. I could not. Finally I stood to sing in my wavering voice, holding my old hand-knitted cardigan across my chest like a security blanket. I never sang again in chapel before the congregation. I heard the whispers: 'Ahh! Growing up she is . . . shy . . .' and, 'She will be proud of them soon enough.' I stumbled on, near to tears.

On the whole, the fifties was an innocent era of Teddy Boys and rock and roll, of bouffant hair styles and putting on your make-up in the crowded ladies' toilets at the dance hall, of quick fumbles and holding a boy's wrists so that he did not go too far. No one went 'down there', though, in time, I opened my mouth to bumping, passionate kisses and my body arched to hands which moved like spiders beneath my jumper and stirred strange feelings of delight within.

Not that I had much opportunity for this. At the time I was allowed out just two nights a week – to the mid-week dance and to the pictures on the weekend. I always went with a girl friend and we wore no make-up, stockings or high heels. Dad would meet me and walk me home and then, as time went by, I was allowed to walk home with boys, with Dad following close behind. That certainly put them off, those spotty, innocent mini-men. My father was a policeman and being interviewed or followed home by him was enough to make them beat a quick retreat. Suddenly they remembered, 'I told Mam I'd be home early like. Be worried she will.' They dashed off, all of them, until I met Dan.

Dan was drunk when I met him at the first weekend dance I had been allowed to for my sixteenth birthday. He literally fell into my lap and up came the bouncer and tried to drag him off. 'Is he with you?' he growled.

'Yesh, s'am,' the boy slurred.

'Well, keep him under control.'

And I was left. I wasn't sure what to do about him. I could hardly ignore him when his head was resting on my new suspender belt clasp, driving it into my thigh. I looked down as he looked up and my astonished dark brown eyes met his laughing blue ones. 'Shorry,' he said, and smiled. He staggered me to my bus and said he would be there the next week. I tingled all over. Next week could not come quickly enough, but when it did, I was terrified. Did I have a date or did I not?

I stood outside the Queen's dance hall in Tredegar Square, hearing the bom bom of the big band. I was hot. I was cold. I was scared stiff. For once I had come alone, though Dad did not know that. With Lipsyl on my mouth and a touch of brown shadow on my eyelids, I needed nothing else. I had gone through agonies over a spot that had come up overnight on my chin, and I had pinched Mam's *Evening in Paris* perfume; *Wild Fire* had seemed too bold and *Californian Poppy* too sick-making. He was already there. My eyes widened even more. No spotty boy this, but a man in black leather with studs and tight jeans, a James Dean look-alike. Dad would definitely not approve. I felt like crossing the hall swaying my circular skirt made of felt with its layers of flouncy underskirts. I wished I had pointy-toed high heels and not the bopper slippers I wore. But he looked up and held my gaze. The evening was a great success – so much so that Dan lasted nearly two years and was my first experience with 'IT'. But I am rushing it. I won't be rushed now, nor would I then.

First Dan had to run the gauntlet with Dad. I broke the news that Dad was a policeman. 'A Rozzer,' he said wonderingly. Then told me each slang word for policemen. It hadn't seemed to put him off.

Dan was nearly four years older than me. To Dad's eyes, he was a man to my child. I had to break the news first to Mum, then get her to soften Dad up and then casually mention it: she didn't get a chance.

The next weekend I had a head cold so I'd failed to turn up at the Saturday night dance. On Sunday evening, I was at home with my hair in curlers, and my oldest clothes on, playing cards with Dad and the girls. Mum got up to answer a knock at the door and there was dead silence. A long silence. Then the kitchen door opened and in walked an ashen-faced Mum and Dan in the full dress of a Teddy Boy, the brothel creepers, DA hairstyle, midnight blue drapes with navy velvet collar and cuffs, pink shirt, shoelace tie. My mouth dropped – I hadn't even known he was a Teddy Boy. Then I flew upstairs and in five minutes flat was down again dressed in red, skin-tight sweater, black pencil skirt and the boppers, hair back-combed and mouth pink and shining. Dad still had his mouth open. I introduced them and Dan shook Dad's limp hand and greeted my Mum. We left. And walked silently.

'Do you like the gear?' he asked.

'Very nice,' I said faintly.

'Not scared of Rozzers,' he said. 'Had a lot to do with Rozzers in my time.'

Oh God! I thought. We walked on.

'Are you a virgin?' he suddenly asked out of the blue. I nearly choked on the gum he had given me.

'Yes,' I whispered.

You would have thought that I had given him the key to the world. Which I suppose I had, in a way. He was overjoyed. 'You have made me so happy!' he gasped and kissed me. I was too busy trying to work out how to keep the gum from his exploring tongue to wonder more. His hands moved beneath my sweater. 'Let me see them,' he whispered. So, by the light of the moon, and the satanic backdrop of mountains, I shyly, and yes proudly, bared my up-thrusting, small, firm breasts for their first male eyes. He gently touched the nipples with his mouth then firmly pulled down the sweater. 'Not yet,' he whispered. 'It must be special first time.' I admired his self-control, me – I wanted to part my legs and allow him to have his wicked way with me, catching babies or not!

Dad did not speak to me for a blissful three days. But when he did, I was surprised how understanding he seemed. How much he seemed to know about feelings, girls' as well as boys'. I was well impressed.

I was allowed to see Dan every Saturday. I met his parents. He had met mine. We went to the dance. Then the pictures each mid-week together. He told me he loved me and sang 'Sweet Sixteen' to me. We danced cheek to cheek and jived. My dreams were confused and I was over-emotional, bursting into sudden tears or tempers. After a year we went to stay on holiday at my grandma's house in the Forest of Dean. It had been my seventeenth birthday a few days before and Dan had given me an engagement ring. I was now working in a factory, waiting to be old enough to start my nurse's training. I told him we would have to wait at least three years before we could marry.

September has always been my favourite month. Autumn, golden leaves and silver moons, the air growing icy on the body sweat. And I lay on the dry leaves with my dress open and, at last, his hands and mouth moved over my body until neither of us had any breath to spare. It was wondrously exciting. I eased my panties over my pointy-toed high heels, and fell his tongue and fingers touching me 'down there'. 'Not all the way, sweetheart,' he whispered. 'I want my virgin bride.' My stomach churned and I was wet. I could see my body long and slim and silver under the moon. I could see the want in his eyes. We could not marry for three years or more. I wound my long legs about his waist and lifted my hips. It was that easy. Searing pain, so that I all but swooned, then so much pleasure my heart was beating and I could no longer see the trees.

When I looked at him, he was crying. 'I wanted it to be special, darling,' he said. 'Your first time.' But it was. Oh God it was.

# CHAPTER 4
# CHAPEL

# The First Stone

~

*Lorna Pope*

**Lorna Pope** was born in 1928, in Cwmaman, Aberdare. The family moved to Mountain Ash where she spent her formative years during the war. She has lived in Ogmore-by-sea for the past forty-four years and began writing seriously ten years ago. She has had stories in local publications and articles in magazines. Married to Harry for over fifty years, they have one son and four grandchildren.

I was fifteen at the time, but I remember the details as if it were yesterday. I was sitting in our chapel in Mountain Ash. The whole congregation was silent. 'Like the grave it was,' my mother said later over supper. The young couple stood at the front of the chapel, in the big seat, or *Sêt fawr*, where the deacons – black-clad like crows – gathered, sagely nodding approval of some phrase in the sermon or muttering 'Amens' when the spirit moved them. The congregation waited. I looked across at the girl, pale under her Sunday hat, her thick dark hair falling over her slim shoulders, and shifted my gaze to the good-looking young man who stood beside her, his eyes lowered.

The hands of the old chapel clock slowly turned and at six o'clock precisely, one of the deacons stood up, his bald head glistening in the evening light, his bull-neck red above his stiff collar. His voice thundered, echoing around the chapel walls. 'We are gathered here tonight to take back into our fold this young couple, who have grievously sinned.'

Now the girl was weeping quietly, tears streaking her pretty face. The boy put his arm around her.

As the light caught the glint of gold on the deacon's watch chain, I didn't want to look at the weeping girl and I tried to fix my eyes on the gold chain straining across his fat belly. The buttons on his waistcoat strained too and I thought of the pigs I had seen that morning in the farmyard at the top of the hill. I tried hard to concentrate on his gold watch, large and fat, burnished through years of rubbing against cloth. But his voice intruded and I was forced to listen. 'Shall we forgive them? Shall we pray for them?'

There was a murmur of assent, a nodding of heads. I bent my head, looked at the shiny, smooth wood on the shelf in front of my pew, ran my finger over the grain, smelt the mustiness of the old hymn books resting there, turned to look at my mother. But my mother stared straight ahead and avoided my gaze. On and on he droned. Their guilt, my mother had explained to me earlier, was that their little son had been born just five months after they were married. This was their night of atonement, when they asked for public forgiveness so that they might once more attend chapel.

I had been accepted, only three weeks earlier, as a member of this chapel. I had listened proudly as the minister told the congregation what a good girl I was, how I visited the elderly, how I took part in the life of the chapel, always had a smile for everybody and how happy they all were to welcome me into the congregation as one of them. God's blessing was upon me that night. I walked home arm in arm with my mother, my new membership card clutched proudly in my hand. Tonight, as a member of this community, I would be expected to put up my hand as a recognition of forgiveness.

The deacon was smiling benignly at the sorry pair; all the time his pudgy hand straying to his watch, stroking it, running a fat finger across its smooth surface.

The sweet smell of my mother's perfume filled my nostrils. Lilac. Gall rose in my throat. Last Sunday, the sun warm on my back, the smell of lilac heavy on the still afternoon, I had turned the corner into the back lane. Voices murmured, a girl giggled. Underneath the lilac bush, his heavy body pressed against the body of a young girl who worked in his shop, searching hands fondling young breasts – our deacon.

I pushed past my mother, hymn books hurtling, and ran outside to be sick on the chapel steps.

# Fitzclarence Forward Movement
# Presbyterian Church

~

*Lynne Rees*

**Lynne Rees** was born on the Sandfields Estate, Port Talbot, in 1958 and lived there till she moved for work to Jersey in 1978. She has lived in Florida and Barcelona, but is now based in Kent, where she teaches creative writing for the University of Kent, Canterbury. She is a graduate of the University of Glamorgan's Masters writing programme and her poems and prose have won prizes and been published widely in the literary journals. Recent work has appeared in the anthologies *Teaching a Chicken to Swim* (Seren 2000), *Reactions 2* (UEA 2001), *The Woman Who Loved Cucumbers* (Honno 2002) and *The Pterodactyl's Wing* (Parthian 2003).

By quarter past eleven the threepenny bit would be sweating brassily in the palm of my hand. My sister, because she was older, had sixpence. The wooden collection plate was passed around during the main service, handed from seat to seat to the end of the row, where it was passed to the one behind by men you could trust. I was always excited to see a half crown smothering the smaller coins and, once, a brown ten shilling note, unfolded, crisp, seemed to hover above the scatterings of change. 'Stop looking,' my sister said. When my mother didn't have any change she sent my sister with a shilling between us, or sometimes just the sixpence, and my stomach churned itself into a sea of shame as I walked through Port Talbot's Sandfields Estate, up Chrome Avenue, along Marine Drive and into Western Avenue – I was convinced that people would despise me, would think I had to be riddled with badness to come to church and not put even a penny in the collection. I practised clenching my fist, then quickly loosened my fingers low over the plate as it passed, hoping a cough would disguise the absence of a clink.

The church was a belly of light with long skinny windows reaching up to the pitch of the roof at one end and a wide pulpit at the other, where the beetley figure of Reverend Steed hunched over the pale wood. There were more windows along the sides of the hall, which were partitioned off with vinyl concertina doors for the Sunday school groups afterwards. There, a steely-haired woman in glasses told us the Devil would try and tempt us, and taught us the hand movements to 'Get Thee Behind Me, Satan'. There, Mr Cumstone, a thin man with shadows in his cheeks, who never looked happy, handed out *Sunny Smiles* booklets with pictures of babies for us to sell, and told us about Hell. I thought that God probably looked like Reverend Steed – big teeth, a black suit, a briefcase holding all his notes – and that the Devil looked like Mr Cumstone. In picture books Jesus looked like a hippie – long kinky hair, a sleepy smile that said 'Peace'. You would probably feel better just by being around Jesus, but there was no one like Jesus in our church.

At Easter we wore our suits – blue and peach Courtelle, three-quarter sleeved button-up jackets, and skirts with thick elasticated waists. And hats – mine was blue straw embroidered with red cherries, my sister's a white cloche like the one Julie Andrews wore in *Thoroughly Modern Millie*. And shoes – white, pointy-toed sling-backs over white ankle socks.

We wore them again on Whitsunday when we were sent back to the church at two o'clock to be rallied into lines on the grass outside by the Reverend Steed, ready to march for Jesus. He helped carry the banner at the front and we followed him singing 'Onward Christian Soldiers' down Western Avenue, where people stood in their front gardens and waved and smiled at us, and around the roundabout, up Fairway, past the Post Office and the Co-op to the skipping rhythms of 'Jesus Wants Me For A Sunbeam'. The rough kids on the estate, hanging around outside McCarthy's, drinking from bottles of dandelion and burdock and chewing Bazooka Joes, sniggered at our scrubbed faces and clean shoes and yelled, 'Jesus wants me for a bumbeam.' I was troubled enough by rough boys – threatening to throw me down the sand-dunes, or hitting me in the face with loaves of Mother's Pride – and I didn't want to attract any more attention, so I stuck the hymn sheet against my face, kept level with my sister's elbows and followed the heels of the person in front. We were back at the church at ten to three with the second verse of 'Mine Eyes Have Seen The Glory Of The Coming Of The Lord', but before we were allowed in for our free tea of luncheon meat sandwiches, red jelly, a Garibaldi biscuit and weak orange squash, Mr Cumstone stood at the only open door and stamped our hands from a pad of indelible ink to make sure we couldn't get in a second time.

I remember it as always being hot then. The straw hat itched my head, the sun prickled through the double knit of Courtelle to my petticoat and white vest. Cloudless blue skies beamed through the Sunday school window while Daniel stared down the lions and the beach was just streets away. It was hot when me and Anne next door walked home without my sister and practised variations on the swear words we knew – *bloody buggers, bloody buggering buggers, buggering bloody buggers.* But we always stopped at the bend in the top of our street and let our mouths be washed out by the fresh air, worried that our mothers would somehow detect our sin, that even though they hadn't heard us or even seen our lips move, they would be able to tell what we had been saying by the colour of our tongues, by our breath.

Mostly I was a good girl. I memorized Bible verses. I once read a psalm from the pulpit. I could recite all the books of the Bible by heart, from Genesis through to Revelations. But one Sunday I refused to go. I didn't know why except there was a terrible weight in my chest that stopped me from getting washed. My sister waited, perched on the edge of the settee in the living room, while my mother walked up and down the stairs warning me I'd be sorry and eventually sent my father to sort me out. I was still in my nightie, hoping if I hung around in the bathroom long enough it would be too late for them to make me go.

'Are you going to get dressed?'

'I can't,' I cried. The idea of putting on my best clothes seemed as difficult as him asking me to sprout wings.

'Get dressed now!' he shouted and his voice crumpled me over the sink.

'I can't.' My voice broke into squeaks and I knew absolutely that it was an impossible thing for me to do.

'Damn you,' he said. 'You're upsetting your mother.' And he smacked my backside and marched downstairs.

I threw myself onto the tumble twist rug, breathing in grains of talcum powder with each great sob. My father had smacked me. I cried until my face was raw and knew that he would never go to heaven now.

# The Turning Point

~

*Gaynor Cohen*

**Gaynor Cohen** was born in 1938 in Llansamlet. She went to Manchester University to study social anthropology, where she met and married her husband, a professional anthropologist from Israel. They had three children, five grandchildren and had carried out field research across the world, including in West Africa. Her husband had carried out research on her old chapel in Llansamlet, but sadly died before the book he was writing could be completed. Gaynor was a senior lecturer at the Civil Service College in London and Sunningdale and worked as an advisor for the Department of Education and Employment. She has published articles on education, anthropology and social policy and a book, *Social Change and the Life Cycle*. She now lives in Oxford, participates in seminars on Women and Development and is a member of a writing group, Oxford Voices.

I am standing on the steps of Bethesda Chapel, Llansamlet, that granite mountain, my head still reeling. I have just seen HIM. The man of my dreams, and in Bethesda's pulpit, of all places! It was the monthly children's service. To please my father, I read aloud Psalm 51. Ridiculous, a fourteen-year-old young woman being asked to 'perform' alongside some of the little ones! Had I known HE would be there I would have spent time practising the Welsh reading beforehand. As it was, he came as a bolt from the blue; very different from the usual breed of ancient ministers. When the service began, the chapel secretary, who happens to be my father, announced a young man, still training for the pulpit, Doctor Gwyn ap Gruffydd. Like a young Greek god he climbed up to the pulpit. I didn't take in much of his message. My gaze was fixed on his large blue eyes and blond waves piled high above his forehead, like a halo of light.

When the service ends all I want is to wallow in that vision. My Sunday ritual, however, determines that I visit my aunts. My father's three sisters are large and formidable presences in the chapel. They live close to each other, in houses built in the twenties. Modern and yet near the old farm where they were brought up.

The first house is Mary Annie's. It's only a year ago that I learnt that *both* these names belonged to her. I had assumed that her name was Merryannie. It sounded that way when others said it. Three men live in her house. Her father, my grandfather, with pale, almost transparent skin, showing his dark blue veins, inherited from mining. Her husband, Dai, dark and wiry, like a Spaniard, and her brother Gwilym.

'*Sut wyt ti heddiw*?' Mary Annie asks me.

'Fine, thank you, Nanny,' I reply in English, as I always do. Mary Annie's thin, fine hair curls pathetically on the top of her head. Her cheeks, rouged as those of a china doll, tremble loosely when she talks, while her broad back is so curved that her breasts seem joined to her stomach.

'Too proud to speak Welsh, is it, since you've been to that school?' Mary Annie spits fiercely at me. Her dentures are loose. She doesn't realize that I'm too nervous now to reply in Welsh. I don't want to show them how much of the language I've already lost.

'Pity.' That is my uncle Gwilym.

My grandfather says nothing.

Next is Maggie's house. Some say she was a beauty when young. I find it difficult to visualise any of them as young. Maggie looks worn out. She's had four children, her husband's been off sick for some time and money is tight. Wearing her usual floral overall, she looks closely at my new style, straight haircut.

'Well, well, hairdressers these days have an easy time of it!'

Although quieter than her sisters, she excels at the stinging, backward swipe.

The last house is Morfydd's. She's the eldest. Her jokes embarrass me, and she laughs so loud that everyone looks at her. Molly, as I call her, is large and well built. With a good bra, her posture can be regal. Her strong face has a large straight nose, its deep furrows forming a triangle with her wide mouth.

'Handsome fellow, isn't he?'

Such a direct approach leaves me unprepared.

'Who?'

'No need to be coy with me. Blushing, is it? Look at her, Is.'

Characteristically her nose twitches and her mouth puckers before she throws back her head and laughs. A deep laugh coming more from her belly than her throat. My uncle Islwyn, himself red-faced with embarrassment, says nothing. Why do so many single men live with their mothers or sisters, even into old age? Is it something peculiarly Welsh, or do the women make them too comfortable?

I take stock on my three mile walk home. I don't want to be laughed at, so I must avoid showing any reaction to Doctor Gwyn. My aunts still think of me as a child! Back in our kitchen my mother asks, 'What did you think of the minister? Your father says he's a bit of a heart throb.'

My emotions under control, I reply, coolly, 'I suppose so, if you like that sort of thing,' but I see 'a look' passing between my mother and father.

Occasionally Bethesda's visiting minister joins us for Sunday lunch. Today the newspapers have been left, lying openly on the chairs. Usually they're hidden under the cushions, to show respect for the Almighty. So no minister has been invited.

I didn't ask my father whether Doctor Gwyn was taking the evening service. I would not give him that satisfaction, but I dressed carefully, wearing my new, swing-back, red and black tweed coat. It's got the latest puff sleeves, fastening at the wrists with a matching small, lined beret. It makes me look – at least nineteen!

My coat swings regally as I walk down the aisle to our family pew. People are looking at me. My parents are important in the chapel. My father, the chapel secretary, is highly respected while my mother, the chapel organist, is an accomplished musician. Morfydd is already sitting in the pew. Difficult to believe that the dignified figure, in a smart black suit, a diamond brooch in its lapel, and the hard snout and beady eyes of a fox fur emerging from her neck, is the same woman I saw this morning. Morfydd is well groomed when she comes to chapel, but I can still smell her uncle's farm and the cows she milks every morning. Tonight I reject her boiled sweets, brought to keep me quiet. She raises her eyebrows, but says nothing as Betty Owens has just walked into the seat in front of us. I don't listen to the sermon. The Welsh is too demanding. I am drinking in HIS presence, and floating on HIS voice. My father gets up to make the weekly announcements. He says we are fortunate that Doctor Gwyn will be returning to Bethesda at the end of November, to complete three months of his training. Why didn't he tell me? In bed that night I dream about 'my Gwyn', as I already think of him. How can I get him to notice me? I am a keen actress and he will be with us over Christmas; an excuse for a nativity play. I'll volunteer to put one on. If I move quickly we can start rehearsals in a week's time.

My father's support wins me the goodwill of the congregation. I concentrate on my task and finish it after a week. It will take too long to make special costumes, so, very boldly, I set the theme in modern times.

'Funny ideas they've got now,' Morfydd says at the casting meeting.

'It's that school of hers. Everything English is modern and must be good!' Mary Annie tells everyone and reduces me to two feet high.

'Not for us though,' Maggie says, 'You can't have angels in modern dress.'

The week before Christmas my mother remarks, 'Seems our new minister's been walking out with Betty Owens.'

'She's a very pretty girl but her mother's very strict,' my father says.

'Not strict enough,' is my mother's view. 'That girl's been flashing her favours in front of any man in the village.'

It can't be true, not my Gwyn! No, Betty Owens hasn't got what it takes to trap a serious, well-educated man like Gwyn.

The final rehearsal goes well. Gwyn turns up for it. I feel so excited at the weight of his arm over my shoulders that my tongue sticks to the roof of my mouth. I can't reply when he tells me, '*Da iawn, cariad*.' But only I know that 'very good, dear' really means 'I'll wait for you, darling.'

At last it's Christmas Eve, 1952. So far, my ploy has succeeded. Gwyn has noticed me. I am a person. By the end of tonight I'll not be a tongue-tied adolescent, but a woman of poise, talent and sophistication. I've persuaded my mother to let me wear her Christmas present to me, a slim-fitting, red velvet shift. I dress carefully and perfect my make-up. I need to appear a mixture of saint and sinner.

The cast of six is waiting for me when I arrive. Chairs for the audience have been set up in the empty vestry. The stage curtains are down and behind them we sit, checking our lines and the props, and waiting for the arrival of the 'angels'. Everything is in order, but where are the 'angels'? My leading lady tells me, soothingly, 'Don't you worry about them. They'll turn up, they're old troupers.'

Old, yes, but troupers?

The seats start to fill. Still no 'angels'. With one minute to go before seven, my main actress gestures towards the curtain.

'No, give them a little longer. They *must* come.'

A commotion outside; Morfydd's resonant and Mary Annie's high pitched tones carry to where we sit. I peep through the curtain. Yes, the three angels are filling the aisle, chatting and laughing with everyone they pass. At that moment, I hate them. Now the performance *has* to be so impressive that everyone will forget this unfortunate prelude.

Backstage, eventually, Morfydd's voice booms, 'Sorry, *cariad*. We couldn't get near our wedding dresses. We've brought sheets. We'll hold them together with safety pins. It'll be all right. Don't you worry. Wouldn't let you down, would we?'

The play goes off without a hitch. The cast are word perfect. Beryl Jenkins, an angelic Mary, Joe John, a protective Joseph, Ivy Davies, a stern hotel owner, and even the boys, the wealthy Arab businessmen from the East, are all right. Finally, the baby is born and the heavenly chorus arrives. My three aunts, like pregnant polar bears, wrapped in white sheets. The titters, which had started quietly, ripple and grow as the singing starts. Each angel balances two pairs of spectacles on her nose, until a distinct, '*Diawl*,' comes from Morfydd, followed by a loud, 'Hush,' from the other two, as one of Morfydd's spectacles slips on to the floor. A roar of laughter follows. I look at Doctor Gwyn. He's laughing so much he's using a handkerchief to mop up his tears. The audience, uninvited, join the angels in singing the last carol.

The applause goes on and on, but I cringe and hold back until someone drags me to the front. 'Please let me die right now,' I pray to myself. Doctor Gwyn is on his feet thanking the cast and the '*young*' producer and scriptwriter, for a delightful and memorable evening. I can't look at him. It has been a disaster! People will remember it for ever. I know they will. I barely take in my father's final announcement. He is congratulating Doctor Gwyn ap Gruffydd on his engagement to a beautiful young member of Bethesda's congregation, Miss Betty Owens, and wishing them every success with their forthcoming marriage.

# House of the Rising Sun

~

*Jude Brigley*

**Jude Brigley** (née Roach) was born, brought up and educated in Maesteg. She is Head of English and Media Studies at Cardiff High School and is Chief Examiner for A level Media Studies. She has written on education and edited two poetry books. Teaching remains her vocation and her passion, although she hopes to write more in the next track of her life.

Jesus bids us shine with a pure, clear light. The chapel was in the centre of Maesteg and at the centre of my early life, enclosing the patterns of family life in a circle of births, marriages and deaths. This was inevitable since my forefathers had helped found Bethel Baptist Church and my great aunts were pillars of that matriarchal society, organising prayer meetings and jumble sales, flower arrangements and hospital visits.

I liked chapel, especially Sunday school. As a child, I never resented going there, because I enjoyed the stories, the songs and the landmarks which broke open the year. The anniversary service was something we rehearsed for weeks and on the day, with new dress or costume and brand new shiny shoes, I recited the newly-learnt lines of verse in front of the matriarchs of the family, who nodded approval and dabbed their eyes with handkerchiefs, reliving their own past glories. And then the treat. Off to the beach or field for organized games, singing the songs we had resented learning at the top of our voices and clutching our packed lunches, compliments of Tuckers' Bakery, stalwarts of the chapel, giving out luxuries like ham sandwiches and bought cake!

Later, it was with pride that I was Sunday school teacher and lay preacher, touring the Llynfi Valley for one night stands. Taking on religion like a cause and preaching love and forgiveness to my elders and betters. Once, I heard Dietrich Bonhoeffer speak of his cemented prison and how the grass through the cracks gave him the miracle of hope. On Sundays the streets were silent as no children played except for those of the disreputable or the damned. At chapel, we learnt to understand narrative, to dispute and deconstruct the text, to disagree yet act with formality and restraint. From hymns came poetry, from sermons came speech, from textual study came awareness of language. I can still smell the sweet smells of polish and pollen, standing in the pulpit of my mind with an audience listening to the rhythms of speech and the old and obvious rhetoric of religion.

There is nostalgia in it for I would have made a good preacher, but somewhere in the valley of self-congratulation I lost God. It was the sixties and we wanted liberty not tradition and I had a real feeling that the House had been the ruin of many a poor girl, and on the day I saw the grey blind eyes and the grey bars of its railings, the Cyclops was left stranded on the island of my youth.

# Zoar Baptists

~

*Marian Tawe Davies*

**Marian Thomas** (née Davies) was born in Ystalyfera, at the top of the Swansea valley, in 1930. Her memories of her childhood are of being part of a limitless extended family, as most of the residents of Cyfyng Road seemed to be related to her. As a young girl, under her competition name Marian Tawe Davies, she competed in local and national eisteddfodau and won many cups and medals for recitation. In 1953, she married Gerald Thomas, whose autobiography *Growing up in the Varteg – A Trip Down Memory Lane* was a sell out success in Wales and abroad. Sadly, Gerald died in 2002 after forty-nine happy years together and Marian now lives in a converted police station in Ystalyfera, visited regularly by her four children, eight grandchildren and two (soon to be three) great grandchildren.

I was baptized along with ten other girls at Zoar Chapel, in Ystalyfera, by Reverend Ivor Jones. It took place in the area known as the '*Sêt fawr*' where the chapel deacons sat, just below the pulpit. The floorboards would be removed to reveal the 'baptism chamber', which would then be filled with water. We were dressed in long white dresses with coins sewn into the hems, which ensured that the dresses remained in place when we entered the water, thus safeguarding our dignity. The baptism ceremony involved each of us in turn being ducked below the water by the minister, which gave you a strange feeling, though at the time we were too young to fully realize the importance of the event, a significant factor being that we were now fully fledged members of the chapel.

That little chapel was the centre of our social and religious life. Each Tuesday evening there would be 'Cymdeithas', 'Cwrdd Gweddi' on Thursday, 'Band of Hope' on Friday and attendance at chapel three times on a Sunday – morning service, 'Ysgol Sul' in the afternoon and evening service at 6 o'clock. The gallery would be full of us girls 'dressed to kill' in our Sunday best clothes. So different today, where the chapels have an aging and declining membership.

It is difficult to explain the atmosphere on a Sunday evening as we listened intently to Mr Jones' sermon. It was as if we were 'at peace with the world'. Maybe it was because we were young, with our future before us, and anything was possible. All that remains today is the derelict vestry, but if only those ruins could talk, what a wealth of memories would be revealed, not only for me, but also for quite a number of my generation. Alas, another chapter has come to an end.

Another precious memory is of the Sunday school trips that we all looked forward to each year. The venue was either Porthcawl,

Barry Island or Ogmore Vale. The outing took place on a Saturday in the summer and on the Friday night we would go along to Zoar Chapel to collect the tickets from Mr Jones, our minister, who always had a broad smile on his face and a cheery remark, such as, 'I hope you have packed your swimming costume and don't forget to bring plenty of sandwiches and pop.' On our arrival at the seaside, deckchairs would be hired and we would all sit in a circle and have a laugh and a chat. Then after a while we would play on the beach, make sandcastles, eat our sandwiches, drink our pop and then, clad in our bathing suits, run down to the sea.

Meanwhile, our parents would have a good chinwag about village life. There were some real characters amongst the women and as the day progressed, some would grab hold of the minister, who was by then also clad in his bathing costume, carry him down to the sea and pretend to baptize him. He took it all in good spirit, and would say, 'Never mind, ladies, I'll get my own back one of these days.' For him to permit this showed, in a way, how much they all admired and respected him. He was in every way a prac-tising Christian, who didn't just sermonize, but would by any means possible go out of his way to help you. Tragically, a few years later, he suffered a massive heart attack and died. His wife was incon-solable and talking about it a few weeks later, she burst into tears. For not only had she lost a husband, whom she dearly loved, but he had also been her best friend.

This reminds me of another time, years ago, when a local woman told me, 'Marian, fach, it is never the same when your partner has gone.'

When I was a child, I used to recite 'Cloch y Llan', and there is a line in the poem that has always stuck in my mind, 'Fe fyddai'n drugaredd, Siân, pe galwai'r "hen gloch" ni'r un pryd' (It would be a blessing, Siân, if the "old bell" called us at the same time).

# CHAPTER 5

# COURTSHIP, MARRIAGE AND DIVORCE

# Managing on a Budget

~

*Gillian Morgan*

**Gillian Morgan** was a war baby, born in Cwmffrwd, Carmarthen in 1943, when her mother was twenty and her father fighting abroad. For the last forty-three years, she has lived in Pembrokeshire. After bringing up her daughters fulltime for ten years, she trained as a teacher. While teaching, she had a book of postcards published and self-published a novel. She has written regular articles for the local papers and had poetry published in Britain and the USA. Since retirement she has gained an MA in Creative Writing. She is now concentrating on being a Welsh 'Mam' with her daughters and four grandchildren living on her road.

Despite attending Gowerton Grammar School, staffed by fiery feminists who preached that every woman should have a training, I left school at sixteen and, on the last day of summer that year, 3 October 1959, I married. My husband, who was nine years older than me, was a teacher. We had intended marrying the following year, but when the chance of furnished rooms occurred, we took the opportunity to bring the date forward.

For our wedding, which took place in St. Michael's Church, Loughor, I wore a simply styled white satin dress, interlined with silk, made by a tailoress in Hendy. It had long sleeves, which came to a point and tiny, satin-covered buttons fastening down the back. In my hair, I had three gardenias, very fashionable at the time, with a short veil and I carried a spray of gardenias on a wide ribbon. My only jewellery was a pair of mother-of-pearl earrings. A tiny suspender belt held up my fine, seamed stockings and my feet were clad in brocade high heels.

My husband and the male guests wore morning suits. My mother was resplendent in a dark green satin dress with gold embroidery, a hat of black and green feathers, grey, sheer stockings and gunmetal shoes. Like some of the other women guests, she carried a fur stole. The wedding reception, for thirty relatives and friends, was held in the Stepney Hotel, Llanelli. We began with a vegetable soup, followed by a hot roast turkey dinner, finishing with sherry trifle and an iced cake, accompanied by coffee and champagne.

We had no honeymoon, for there was school for my husband the following Monday, so we travelled to Fishguard immediately after the reception. My husband, thoughtfully, bought me a copy of the magazine *Good Housekeeping* to read on the train. One of the recipes featured jugged hare, which recommended using the hare's blood in the gravy; there were also suggestions on how to make leftover turkey interesting. Sad to say, a teacher's salary did not stretch to turkey, even at Christmas time, in those days.

I adjusted easily to my new role, being used to cooking and cleaning as, following the divorce of my parents, my mother worked as an insurance agent, which meant I had plenty of experience baking sponge cakes, cooking Saturday's lunch and tidying the house. I could not wait to have my own home and be a proper housewife.

My husband's pay amounted to thirty five pounds a month; in a five week month we had seven pounds a week to spend and just over eight pounds ten shillings on four week months. I kept an itemized book of all expenditure. We paid two pounds a week for our furnished accommodation and ten shillings for coal. Food cost three pounds a week and I put ten shillings aside for the gas cooker, for which we had a meter. We saved part of the remaining pound for the electricity bill, bought a daily newspaper and had something left for Sunday's church collection. Anything over was put in a tin and kept until it amounted to seventeen shillings, which covered the return train journey to Llanelli for the two of us. We could not visit relatives on a regular basis, which I found difficult at first. New clothes were expensive (almost impossible on our income) and I wore the same winter coat for three years or more. Shoes, including my stiletto heels (kept for special occasions), were mended regularly by the cobbler.

To ensure we were properly fed, I read an old Ministry of Food publication which explained basic nutritional requirements. We had a joint of meat on a Sunday, which lasted until Wednesday, the butcher always managing to sell me a larger piece than we needed. To add some variety, I used the remains of the meat in pies and pasties. I cooked sausages, liver and mince on other days, but on a Thursday, I went to Fishguard market. Here I bought faggots, bacon, eggs and Carmarthenshire butter from Will Davy Rees, who travelled from Pontantwn. Sometimes I made fish pie on a Friday or a Fray Bentos steak and kidney pie, baked in its own tin, accompanied by dried peas, or frozen peas when we could afford them. Each day we ate fresh vegetables, such as carrots, swedes, parsnips or cabbage, depending on availability and the time of year, plus an apple or maybe an orange. My mother thought I was extravagant buying ready-washed potatoes in a plastic bag. I also liked Danish bacon, dearer than the one the butcher sliced, but often sweeter tasting. Twice a week I baked a fruit tart and scones, but on Sundays we had a Bird's Eye Dairy Cream Sponge as a treat. Most of my shopping came from George Mason's shop; a delivery boy brought the weekly order on his bicycle, but I also shopped every day for meat, bread and vegetables.

The first Christmas we were married, I made the pudding and boiled it in a muslin cloth, to get the round shape. However, it had little taste and most of the flavour was lost in the water. Disappointing though this was, the chicken, free-range from the Gwaun Valley, was delicious.

I decided to look for a job to ease the financial situation and also because I felt isolated living in Fishguard. There were very few jobs of any sort in the area and unemployment statistics were high. I attended evening classes, thinking typewriting and shorthand skills would be useful. We bought a typewriter on the 'never never' to enable me to practise my homework. A few months later, I obtained a post as a wages clerk in Trecwn, a nearby government office, where I stayed for three years. My starting pay was five pounds a week, later rising to three hundred and fifty pounds a year. I was very pleased to have my job, for I knew that many firms, including the major banks, did not allow women employees who married to keep their jobs. I joined one of the large Civil Service Unions that had gained equal pay and employment for women. I paid the married woman's stamp, at that time four pence a week; the Civil Service provided sick pay, whichever stamp a woman chose. Eventually, I hoped to have a family, but had no intention of working while pregnant or afterwards, so this was another reason for paying the smaller stamp.

Since my husband might want to change schools and move to another area, we decided not to buy a house until we felt settled. Instead, we rented a large old house. Unable to buy a great deal of furniture, we went to Pugh's, Llanelli, and bought a bed, two easy chairs, a dining table and chairs, chosen from the Ercol range, which we still use today. The house was very large and our furniture did little to fill it, but it was wonderful to have new things around us, after the previous drabness of furnished rooms. We chose lime and orange covers for the chairs and yellow curtains in the dining room. Television sets were not reliable in the sixties so, at first, we rented a black and white set, watching programmes like *The Man From Uncle, Double Your Money* (with Hughie Green) and *University Challenge*.

Cars were a luxury, even in 1961, but we bought a six-month-old Triumph Herald (which we kept for thirteen years) and this added a new dimension to our lives. Our house was in a terrace and we rented a garage from the local chemist. The car was used only at weekends. We did not need it during the week, as I had subsidized travel to work and the bus stopped, conveniently, outside our door.

When I was twenty, my husband became a head teacher and the extra money meant I could resign from my job. Soon after (the first month we tried, in fact), I became pregnant. During the first three months, I suffered constant sickness and after giving birth I was a stone lighter than I was before I conceived. Fortunately, our elder daughter weighed a healthy seven and a half pounds when she was born. (Cases of thalidomide were prevalent at this time and women were frightened of taking any medicines during pregnancy.)

I would have liked a home birth, but the doctor persuaded me to book a bed in the County Hospital, Haverfordwest, which was fifteen miles away. I stayed in hospital for ten days, which was normal at the time. At first, I breast fed, but later changed to a bottle. My Auntie Hannah recalled covering her breasts with a paste of flour and water, in an attempt to stop the milk leaking, when she wanted to finish breast feeding.

She also remembered how women worried about conceiving too soon following childbirth. Her advice was to 'be careful', though she did not say how. (Many couples bought condoms through the post, which was convenient and discreet.) But times were changing, and reading the local paper, I saw a 'Family Planning' clinic had been opened in Haverfordwest. The woman reporter's account was glowing. Apart from traditional barrier methods such as the condom and the cap, the revolutionary 'Pill' was available (this was 1964). Although my pregnancy was planned, I arranged a consultation. I was advised to try the 'Pill' and took it for two years. When I wanted another child, I stopped. This time it took me six months to conceive. Later, I decided not to go back on the 'Pill' because I had heard too many stories of women dying from blood clots as a result of taking it.

In 1968, Auntie Hannah died and her funeral took place on a blazing day in July. I wore a thick jacket over a dress because I was breast feeding and feared the milk might leak through my clothes.

Remembering the times I had spent sewing with my aunt as a teenager, I bought a sewing machine to make garments for my daughters and myself. There were few clothes shops in Fishguard and they were all expensive.

Gradually, I realised my children would soon be in school. I was asked to return to the Civil Service, where hours were becoming more flexible, but I did not want to work during the school holidays. Wondering if I might gain some qualifications through a correspondence course, I sent for a brochure to the National Extension College. The courses were not cheap but I enrolled for two O levels and an A level. Passing the first examinations spurred me on and between 1966 and 1970 I gained six O levels and an A level.

In 1970, my husband's job took us to Haverfordwest. My children, aged nine and five, were both in school and, for the first time in nine years, I had some free time during the day. I enrolled on a teacher training course in a college thirty miles away, which meant travelling back and fore each day. At the end of the four-year course I gained a BEd degree. I taught for twenty one years before taking early retirement from my final post as the Head teacher of a nursery school.

Marrying at such a young age was limiting in many ways, though I did not see it like that at the time. Living in an isolated area also restricted the opportunities available to women. I was fortunate in having a job in the Civil Service and gaining qualifications which enabled me to go on to higher education.

When I first married a woman's place was in the home. During my lifetime a silent revolution has occurred and women are expected to work, have children, plus everything else that entails. I am not sure whether we have created a more equal society or not.


# From East to West

~

*Judith Maro*


**Judith Maro** was born in Jerusalem, in the first suburb outside the city walls, in 1927. The years covered in her piece were spent mostly in Lleyn, with frequent forays to Israel. She married Jonah Jones, the artist and writer, in 1948, and they have three children and grand-children. They now live in Llandâf. She has published *Atgofion Hagana*, a memoir (Y Brython, 1972 and 1973), *Y Porth Nid A'n Angof* (Y Brython, 1974), *Cleddyf a Swch*, a novel translated from Hebrew (Cwmni Menter, 1974), *The Remembered Gate*, a novel (Christopher Davies, 1975), *Hen Wlad Newydd*, essays (Y Lolfa, 1974), *Y Carlwm*, a novel (Y Lolfa, 1986) and numerous articles and contributions to anthologies in Welsh, Hebrew and English.

In the green and stony wilderness that climbs behind our home in Lleyn to the craggy heights of Snowdon, I feel as far removed from my native Israel as if I were treading an unknown moonscape. This is the Occident, the last stretch of land into the Atlantic before America. Unless there is a long heatwave, the uncertain summers and mild wet winters are remote from the predictable heat of my early years, perpetually 'blue' (as they say in Wales) and renewed.

Here in the summer, the long lush evenings die so late as to be unbelievable; in winter the dark is upon us shortly after lunch. Summer or winter, the locals exchange gossip outside my window in a strange language of which even Israel's wide philological range is innocent. From the darkness of prehistory, the hordes pressed ever westwards across the steppes and ridges of Asia and Europe, down into the toes of Greece and Italy, Spain and Scandinavia, thinning out and settling and driving their predecessors further and further until, on this westernmost Celtic fringe the hardiest remnants settled and took root. The Celtic fringe, the unknown country beyond two seas.

Nothing in my early life had prepared me for Wales. Would I ever see it, let alone make it my home? Highly unlikely in the compelling reality of the battle-torn Middle East. Cader Idris had imprinted itself on my imagination in primary school, after reading a children's book describing the majestic scene. Then there was the heart-rending *How Green Was My Valley*, depicting the tragic life of a mining community in south Wales. Could the two belong in the same country?

Suddenly, in the wake of Israel's Independence War in 1950, I found myself resident in Lleyn. And so we came to Wales to make our home in a fourteenth-century ruin halfway up Moel-Y-Gest. Like our whirlwind courtship and marriage across hostile barricades between our two peoples, at the end of the British Mandate on Palestine, the decision to settle in Wales had not been planned. Although Jonah had seen Wales only from afar, he had always nurtured a dream to return to the Land of his Fathers, *his* 'promised land'. The long train journey from Newcastle-on-Tyne (Jonah's birth-place) was grey and uninspiring. I was too preoccupied with our seven-week-old son to notice it. Then, *Croeso i Gymru!* At once we were in another country.

The evening sun setting over the sea welcomed us, brilliantly if not warmly, for it was winter. A clean landscape, open spaces, granite chapels, an undisturbed pastoral scene after the industrial landscape of northern England. The people alighting at rural stations were different from the English, darker, stockier. And the language! I felt an immediate sense of kinship with those strangers, responding to the sound, the 'll' and 'dd', '*bach*', '*coed*' and '*mawr*'. It was like music in my ears.

It was a very wild February and our mediaeval 'castle', in spite of Jonah's efforts to make Bron-y-Foel habitable and weatherproof, was hard put to it to keep out the elements. To be sure, he had done wonders, but the place had been empty for thirty years and much the worse for it. Indeed, the last tenant had committed suicide. Not a promising beginning, but we had no choice: there were no houses available unless you were a wealthy industrialist from the Midlands opting for a second home. The malaise had made its appearance already. We weren't anywhere near that class of customer! Our annual rent, including rates, was twelve pounds.

Siberian weather notwithstanding (and it lasted weeks), we loved the peace and isolation of Bron-y-Foel. Doors and windows were propped up with homemade sandbags; we had no car – nor road, had we had one – no electricity, gas or telephone. We did have running water, however, thanks to my husband's ingenuity: Jonah had connected a well above the house, got hold of some old pipes from a field, and laid on water. With the help of a second-hand back-boiler, we had plenty of hot water. We may have been as poor as church mice, but at least we were clean! Coming from mining stock as he does, a sizeable tin bath was decreed a must by Jonah. David, our firstborn, describes the 1950s as the 'decade of grind and deprivation'. Not a bit of it. We were happy in our old ruin, took hardships in our stride, loved the magnificent view of Lleyn, with Ynys Enlli on the far horizon. We climbed Moel-y-Gest of an evening to glory in our rich domain.

We never tired of our splendid isolation. The loft boasted a colony of bats hanging upside-down on the roof beams by day, then darting about in the wilderness that passed for our garden by night. There were powder-closets adjoining the bedroom, the odd friendly owl, a heavenly panorama of sea and mountains reminiscent of the scene I had left behind on Mount Carmel. There were thick walls complete with arrow slits, should we be called upon to defend our home, a mountain rising steeply behind our kitchen, a Turkish carpet (purchased in Port Said before embarkation) in the restored living room, bookshelves complete with classics to peruse by night, an adorable baby, a tabby cat answering to the name of *Pyosik* ('little dog' in Russian) and the friendliest of ghosts to visit us. What more could a young family ask for? We ate simply, if wholesomely, tried unsuccessfully to cultivate strawberries, were entertained by the locals, had friends to stay. Curious neighbours would drop in with offers of help, as did mountain sheep and once a very surprised bushy-tailed fox. I was homesick, but I did not fret, and counted my blessings.

Three years later, in 1953, we had to leave our mountain paradise. Jonah was in a sanatorium with TB, fighting to regain his health. We left our ruin with sadness, determined to make a fresh start. We would stay on in Wales. I had travelled a long way from East to West – next stop Pentrefelin.

And what of our nocturnal visitor at Bron-y-Foel?

Bron-y-Foel was the ancestral home of Hywel y Fwyall (Hywel of the Axe), famous for his bravery at the battle of Poitiers, when he cut off the head of a French charger with one blow of his axe, thus assisting at the victory of the Welsh Black Prince. Hywel was made Constable of Caernarfon Castle as a reward, but was too restless to settle down, and soon sought refuge in Bron-y-Foel, though not for long. He quarrelled with his cousins and had to flee when they threatened to burn him out of his farmstead – not that Hywel was much of a farmer! He vanished, very likely finding his end in some foreign battle. As to his spirit, legend has it that he would haunt Bron-y-Foel. That is where we came in.

End of November: David is eleven months old. Jonah is climbing on Snowdon. A dull evening, no wind. The path near Bron-y-Foel is like a carpet of fallen leaves. Fire glowing, Aladdin lamp hissing on the kitchen table. David is in his bath near the fire; the cat snoozes on the hearth. A distant sound. The night is moonless, eerily still. I listen. No, it is not Jonah's tread. Who then? Am I imagining it? Perhaps the wind is rising? A pheasant, maybe? I *do* hear footsteps, heavy, slow, hob-nailed boots. I can only wait. Why am I not frightened? Probably because I don't believe in ghosts. The backdoor to the washroom opens, creaking in the dark. Why does Hywel hesitate? He shuts the door. His footsteps echo as he approaches. Very gingerly, Hywel opens the kitchen door, letting in the chill November air. I know it's Hywel. I can feel his presence.

Suddenly enraged, I turn to the invisible visitor. 'Oh, do close the door!' I snap. By what right does he come to disturb our evening? The door is drawn to, the raised handle comes down. What does he want? Surely not to chase us out? I turn to the hearth. David has stopped playing and stares at the door. What does he see? The cat, quite relaxed, looks in the same direction. We are suspended in mid-air, a mime, a silent pantomime. The fire is burning low now, the bath water has gone cold. How long have we been 'entertaining' our uninvited guest?

I too turn to the door. 'If you're not going to show your face, will you please leave?' I make my voice stern. Enough nonsense.

A faint chuckle. Hywel is amused, takes his time.

I take a deep breath: it *is* his home after all. 'We really love Bron-y-Foel,' I try to reassure him, 'and we don't mind when you come at night, just now . . . well, it's the wrong time, don't you see?' Talking to ghosts!

Slowly, as if reluctantly, Hywel retraces his steps. Silence. I put a shovelful of coal on the fire, put hot water in the bath. We relax. Jonah returns, looks askance at me. 'Did you have a visitor?' he asks.

Two years after we had left Bron-y-Foel, a Dominican priest exorcised Hywel's ghost, thus banishing him for good.

Pentrefelin was a friendly, sprawling village on the Cricieth to Porthmadog road, still fairly quiet when we lived there in the 1950s, though getting ever busier by the month with tourists, weekenders, and above all Butlinites. Our new home was Plas Afon, a three-storey Victorian house, arguably once a glorified inn or a vicarage: old timers could not agree. We liked its character and distinctive features; a sort of gin-palace portico with darkly stained glass, inwardly curving double doors to the living room (our 'retreat' where the children were admitted as a treat only), a secret priest-hole, and an 'oubliette' in the middle of the kitchen floor which opened to reveal the fast flowing stream of the Cidron. A spacious house, but needing much attention and renovation.

We got it for a song, courtesy of Clough Williams-Ellis, who gave us a mortgage, interest to be paid in artwork by Jonah for his beloved Portmeirion. Recovering from a nasty bout of TB, getting back to work slowly, there was no chance for Jonah to secure a building society loan. Our gratitude to Clough was boundless, for his generosity as for his graciousness. A good friend always.

While we were happy in Pentrefelin, we secretly craved for the peace of our mountain house on Moel-y-Gest, not unlike Cézanne's Mt. St. Victoire. We would achieve our cherished dreams in the 1960s.

After the frenetic, ever-crowded life in Israel, constantly fraught with danger, the sheer peace of Wales's strangely Biblical *cwms* and rivers was very special when we first came to live here. After fifty years, I still remember the sensation of peace with wonder; utter peace, absence of threat, of war, of perpetual danger, fear for life and limb. Unless you have lived through the never-ceasing tension, you may find it difficult to grasp the unbelievable contrast.

Our three children attended primary school in Pentrefelin. Enter the redoubtable Miss Williams, a real treasure, the school's dedicated teacher – at first, the only teacher. I had already established my credentials in Pentrefelin (where, to quote the then Minister's wife, 'everyone is related to everyone, so watch your step!'), thanks to my being *not* English, while being fluent in the language, plus possessing a typewriter. I had become, through the village bush telegraph, the accepted Ombudsman, unpaid and unofficial, of course, but a useful member of society if someone had trouble at school, the Labour Exchange, with the NHS, with a neighbour, a builder, all authority of any kind. So a delegation of parents called on me when David was about to start school, to organise a petition, asking Miss Williams to stop the teaching of Welsh.

'It's no use in business,' they proclaimed, 'it only holds the children back.' I was appalled. Their own mother tongue, the language of their forebears! Speechless, I could only stare at the assembled faces, very earnest, hopeful. I had to say something.

'A child's mind is elastic,' I tried to explain, 'the more the child learns, the more the child takes in.' They were not impressed. I had to play my trump card. 'If we in Israel thought so little of our languages, Hebrew would never have been revived!' My words fell on deaf ears.

Miss Williams, my first Plaid Cymru contact, impressed me at once. She informed me that since David's language at home was English, he would learn through the medium of English. I wouldn't have it. 'Oh, no, Miss Williams,' I retorted, 'please teach him in Welsh. I can teach him English!' Thus the deal was struck. In turn, Pedr and Naomi too would start their schooling in Welsh. A triumph for commonsense at a time when the old tongue was not in vogue in its traditional heartland. But then, nearby Cricieth was always more English than Welsh.

Miss Williams was a perfectionist, strict without being unkind. Some thought her formidable. She was an excellent teacher and a firm believer in discipline and standards. Seeing the shambles of much of today's education, her pedantry was not excessive. 'If a job is worth doing,' I hear her vibrant voice, 'it is worth doing well!' Miss Williams taught our three well, laying the foundation for future study. She also taught them how to *work*.

By the time our children were at school, I had become a regular contributor to BBC Radio Wales. The programmes, going out at 9 am, were listened to by the whole school, courtesy of Miss Williams. The children were treated to my homilies on the Holy Places of Wales, named after the original sites in the Holy Land, like Jerusalem, Moriah, Galilee, Acre, the Dead Sea, Bethel, and various other locations and Biblical associations. These talks led to a literary stint at the behest of the Welsh Book Council. No wonder I felt at home in Wales. By way of gratitude, and as a matter of principle, I resolved that my work be published in Welsh rather than in English. I never regretted the decision. Journalism followed suit, and continues to this day.

Our years in Pentrefelin brought me into an open conflict with the Welsh Sunday. This was new to me. For all the prevailing images in the media, Israel was, and still largely is, a secular society. My own upbringing was not in the least religiously orientated; we studied the Bible and its sequel as part of Hebrew literature, of course. Pentrefelin, on the other hand, boasted two chapels, Tabor and Cidron, attended three times each Sunday by young and old alike. No child would dare being seen playing out-of-doors on the Sabbath. When David was given his first tricycle for Christmas at four, it stood by the door for three weeks, waiting to be 'inaugurated'. The weather had turned nasty, it poured day after day. Then, on a Sunday morning, the sun shone. 'Can we go out, please?' David asked. He had been very patient. What should I do?

I hesitated, but only for a moment. 'Of course,' I replied brightly, 'but we'd better hurry before chapel . . .' The child loved his first outing, while I kept looking over my shoulder for a forbidding figure to chastise us.

We did not have to wait long – first one, then another. 'Playing on the Sabbath?'

I lost patience. 'Would God begrudge a small child his treat after weeks of bad weather?' I asked, as sweetly as I knew how. They seemed lost for words. This would not have pleased the sticklers for the undiluted Sabbath. But before long, other children, emboldened by our example, followed suit. We had set a pattern.

There was more to come. In autumn 1961, the first referendum on Sunday opening of pubs was upon us. It coincided with the campaign initiated and run by Women against Nuclear Testing in the Atmosphere. It was the first such feminist activity on a global scale. We were busy collecting signatures for petitions to be presented to the leaders of USA, Britain, France and USSR, the then four nuclear powers, by women everywhere. An activist in the anti-drinking lobby (a woman) took me to task. 'Ours is far more important,' she chided me. 'We're fighting for the soul of future generations.'

'Maybe you're right,' I replied, 'but if we don't stop this lethal fall-out in the atmosphere, there'll be no future generations to save.' I doubt if I convinced the good lady any more than she convinced me.

I may add that three decades later, shortly before we left north Wales for Cardiff, I voted for the first time *against* Sunday opening in and around Porthmadog, by way of protesting about the erosion of Wales's traditional way of life. It was the last of the referenda and too late to save what once there had been. Time had moved on, and perhaps in my small way I had contributed. Wales's 'dry' Sunday was much in keeping with the Jerusalem *Shabbat* by the undiluted Orthodox Jews from eastern Europe, as observed in my student days. We young disapproved of their intolerance then, no less than most of us abhor the religiosity now infiltrating Israel's body-politic. Why I regret the passing of religious mores in Wales, when I deplore their presence in my native land, is a moot question.

We left Pentrefelin in 1966, for another heavenly location presented on a platter, a tiny old cottage overlooking Traeth Bach in Meirion-nydd, with Ynys Gifftan and Harlech Castle across the water and the mountains of Ardudwy rising on the other side. Too blissful for words! The cottage had to be demolished, but the new Tyddyn Heulyn, planned and executed by Jonah with the help of his small workforce, three or four men, rose from the ruin to grace the scene and provide us with a perfect family home. After more than ten years' 'exile' from our Shangri-la on Moel-y-Gest, we returned to our rightful habitat, in the company of grazing sheep, migrating birds and a resident robin. We had come home indeed.

# Living at the End of the World

~

*Elaine Morgan*

**Elaine Morgan** was born in Pontypridd in 1920, educated in the girls' school in Treforest and at Oxford and married in 1945. The events described in 'Living at the end of the world' took place in 1952 and lasted for about a twelvemonth. Since returning to Wales, she has lived in the Cynon Valley, first in Aberdare and for the last thirty years in Mountain Ash. She spent a couple of decades as a television scriptwriter, mostly for the BBC. She published *The Descent of Woman* in 1972, followed by four other books on human evolution.

It was at the beginning of the 1950s that we moved with our two very young sons into the Birches. It was a farmhouse with thick stone walls, built high on a mountainside a few miles from the village of Michaelchurch Eskley in Radnorshire. In many respects it might as well have been the 1850s as far as the standard of amenities was concerned. There was no electricity, no gas, no piped water, no mains drainage. There was a lane leading up to the house but it led no further: we were at the end of the line. There was no other human habitation within sight, but far away on the opposite side of the valley you could sometimes see the smoke rising from the chimney of our nearest neighbour. The bus stop – to Hereford – was three miles away and the bus went twice a week. (I was on it three times in the course of the year we spent there.)

Our arrival was not a matter of leafing through an estate agent's catalogues and choosing our dream house. My husband Morien had begun teaching in the grammar school in Abertillery, but teachers' pay at that date was at rock bottom, and owing to a couple of pieces of bad luck we had nothing in the kitty. So the amount we could afford to pay for housing was roughly zero. By a happy coincidence that was precisely the rent being charged for the Birches. It had been empty for four years, and the farmer who owned it wanted someone to live in it and keep it warm until his eldest son should marry and take it over. During term time Morien lived in lodgings in Abertillery for five nights a week, coming home up the mountain on his motor-bike at weekends.

I have very happy memories of the place. Of course I was only playing at being a countrywoman. Like most of the townies who move into Wales's rural areas, our lifestyle was subsidized. There was enough money coming in to pay for essentials. We didn't have to plant and plough and hoe and shear and worry about the weather and the vet's bills and the harvest and the fat stock prices. Free of these burdens, I could play at living the simple life and enjoy the idyllic side of it – the home baked bread, the new-laid eggs, fresh milk from Flake, our British Saanen goat. And then there was the landscape – hawthorn blossom and the lark in the clear air and the sunsets –

'Yet shall your ragged moor receive

The incomparable pomp of eve' – and all that jazz. The realities are grimmer if you have to live off the land as well as on it.

Water came from a stream that flowed past the house. Within the first few weeks, Morien installed a tank in the dairy equipped with a tap and filled it at weekends. The lavatory was at the end of the garden under a plum tree. There was a wooden seat with a round hole in it and underneath a deep drop. There were no arrangements for the removal of night soil. So we redirected the course of the stream to flow underneath the deep drop and away down the mountain side as seemed to have been originally intended. In the spring you could sit there happily enough and watch the petals drifting down, but on a stormy winter's night, accompanying a small boy down the wet slippery path by the light of a Tilley lamp was not so much fun.

Everything took longer than it does in town. All the hot water for dishes, bathing and laundry had to be boiled in a bucket over the little grate. Instead of switching on a light, there was a gadget that had to be soaked in methylated spirits to warm up the oil before lighting the Aladdin lamp. The mountain mists got into everything. Before dressing the boys in the morning I would light the fire and hold each garment in front of it until the steam stopped rising from it. A grocery van came up from the village once a week with basic essentials like flour and butter and soap and coffee. After a few weeks of silence, a second-hand battery-powered wireless put us back in touch with the outside world and played music to us and felt like the last word in modern technology. We grew our own potatoes and gathered the rural freebies like blackberries, whin-berries, hazelnuts, boletuses (woodland mushrooms), and wild watercress.

It was a great place to bring up very young children in. There was no traffic outside, only wild ponies. There were no visitors to drop in unexpectedly and wonder why the place was in such a mess. Children can drive you round the bend if there are other things that have to be attended to at fixed times, if a disturbed night cannot be slept off next morning, or if their noise offends the people in the flat upstairs. But on the equivalent of a desert island, it is far more relaxed. I have no answer when people ask me why I wasn't bored. But think how long Jane Goodall spent alone in the jungle observing chimpanzees without getting bored. I had a pair of young primates of my own to observe and I found them fascinating.

For working farmers' wives, the life was very hard. Some of them ran their own little marketable sidelines – raising ducks or making cheese – to ensure getting at least a little hard cash into their own pockets. Already in the fifties, young women were starting to vote with their feet and heading for the town. They were sorely missed. A wife is as indispensable to a hill farmer as a horse, and not nearly so easy to find. So news of a young farmer's forthcoming marriage would be greeted with a buzz of excitement and envy. 'Where did he get hold of *her*, then?'

For several months I thought that we were living at the end of the world – but there were people living deeper in the hinterland, with lifestyles reaching even further back in time. We exchanged visits with one couple who had heard that the Birches was now inhabited and invited us over, leading two staid carthorses for us to ride, each with one child in front, since it was too far to walk. Their farmhouse had a huge open fireplace with one end of a felled tree blazing merrily under the chimney. The rest of this log reached far out into the room and was just ignored and stepped over, and when the lit end was almost burned away to ash, they lifted the outer end of the log and pushed it further in. I imagine this method of space heating was probably as old as the hills, much less laborious than chopping the thing up into firewood, and it probably lasted longer that way too.

They had a mentally retarded son of about fifteen, who if they had lived in town might well have been taken away from them and put into an institution. When he showed signs of agitated behaviour, his mother simply sat down and took him onto her lap and wrapped her strong arms tightly around him until he calmed down.

Not long afterwards she came to the Birches on her own, on horseback, bringing a Toni Home Perm kit which she had been given a year or two earlier as a present, but hadn't had the confidence to try to use it on her own. We spent an interesting afternoon, memorable for cups of tea and girl talk and the smell of ammonia. Then she rode away, curly-headed and happy, and that was the last we saw of any of them. I would not have been able to find their place again even if I had tried, without the aid of a map and a compass.

One thing never in short supply at the Birches was time. Every weekend, reading matter would be brought up on the bike from Abertillery, including the *New Statesman* and the previous Sunday's *Observer*, and I had all the week to browse over them. I several times won a guinea by entering the literary competition in the back pages of the *New Statesman*. The postbox was a long way off, but I persuaded my kith and kin to write to me often, even if only to say 'Hi,' because when the postman called he would take away letters as well as delivering them. Towards the end of the year, I amused myself by sending off an entry for the *Observer* essay competition.

Then suddenly the rural saga was over. Morien had got a new job in Pontypridd grammar school and raised a mortgage on a bungalow in Aberdare with a paddock attached, which we felt was essential for the livestock. The bungalow was one of five dwellings at the back of the Abernant coal tip and we found we were still minus a few mod cons. The council's sanitary department had declared some years earlier that the approach was too narrow and rough to allow access to their new vehicles, so there could be no more refuse collection for the residents of Little Row. The site where their rubbish had been tipped over the years was across the lane from our bungalow and provided sustenance for a thriving population of rats. However, the authorities were induced to change their policy after a little friendly discussion; I gathered that one of the arguments that seemed to carry weight with them was the proposal to empty some of the refuse and some dead rats at the entrance to the council chamber, with a photographer from the *Aberdare Leader* invited along as witness.

Once inside our new home, the twentieth century welcomed us with open arms. Especially for the two boys, who had little experience of such things, the first few days were gilded with the wonder of being able to switch on a light, flush the lavatory, and climb into a bath with two taps, a cold one and a hot one.

But it was not all rejoicing. Three things happened within the first ten days. The bad news was that a fox got into the shed and wantonly slaughtered all six brown hens. I had never learned to lock them up securely at night and nothing had ever happened to them; perhaps the uplands around the Birches were too bleak to offer good hunting-ground for foxes. The worse news was that Flake began to shiver and run a temperature and died within twenty-four hours. Pedigree goats can be delicate and nervous and perhaps the journey and the strange surroundings had upset her. She was a beautiful creature and I was very sad.

The third thing was the arrival of a telegram. In those days telegrams were a rare event. It arrived early on a Saturday morning before we were up, and I remember taking it in and climbing back into bed with it before opening it in some trepidation. Telegrams came in small, bright yellow envelopes and usually consisted of a small piece of paper with two or three printed lines of terse telegraphese pasted onto it. This one was extraordinary in that it contained three sheets stapled together. It informed me that I had won third prize in the *Observer* essay competition. It was fifty pounds. It was also a great confidence-booster, because it attracted letters from three different literary agents offering to represent me if I had any novels hidden away in a drawer. If not, they advised me, there was a flourishing market for budding authors who would write short stories for women's magazines – which featured a lot more fiction in those days than they do today.

I naively imagined that with the high-tech advantages of life in town, I would have more spare time to embark on a career as a writer. But it wasn't quite like that. Parkinson's Law – that 'work expands to fill the time available' – seems to apply with special force to women, and it has the corollary that the standards you are expected to live up to promptly expand with every increase in amenities. Once you have carpets on the floor, you have to keep vacuuming them. Once you have acquired a twin tub washing machine, because it is less laborious, the sheets and everything else get changed much more often and that makes more ironing. Because there were shops within walking distance, I felt a compulsion to get the kids washed and dressed and hang a shopping bag on the handle of the pushchair and set off to buy things and carry them home – no longer three times a year but, in the days before the fridge, three or four times a week.

However, I managed to write and sell some stories, and when I ventured to write a play (destined in my fevered imagination for the West End) it was finally sold to the weird new medium of 'television'. That was in 1952. Television sets were small, with twelve inch screens; the pictures were grey, drizzly and unstable; the drama producers were learning their trade by trial and error. Every bloomer or mishap, that would now end up on the cutting room floor or in a Denis Norden collection of out-takes, then went out live on the screen. The only consolation was that hardly anybody was watching, because so few sets had been sold, certainly in the Cynon Valley. In the event, I sold three plays to television before we got around to buying a set of our own.

I was very lucky to get in on the ground floor of a new kind of career right at the beginning. The door was wide open to beginners at that time, because no writers of any stature wanted to squander their precious plays on a one-night run under such hazardous conditions, and no established actors were keen to risk their reputations on it either. But it was everything I wanted. It was a job that I could do from home in my own good time, and pop the script into the Abernant Post Office the next time I went over to the Co-op. Later it became more competitive and deadlines began to be introduced. But by then I had got a head start and I knew the ropes, and the children were both in school, and I knew I could cope. We were sensibly putting the money into a special account because we were saving up to buy a car. I don't know why it is, but when you get older and look back over your life, it is usually the beginnings of things that are the most fun to remember.

# Back to the Land

~

*Eirwen Gwynn*

**Eirwen Gwynn** was born in Liverpool in 1916. Her family moved back to Wales in 1927, first to Abersoch and then to Llangefni. She was educated at Llangefni County School and University College of North Wales, Bangor, where she got a BSc in Physics and a PhD for research into X-ray crystallography in 1940. She taught Physics at Rhyl Grammar School and married Harri Gwynn in 1942. Harri was in the Ministry of Supply, evacuated to Warwick. Eirwen, having failed to get employment in her own field due to male prejudice, became an auditor in the Exchequer and Audit Department. All returned to London in 1943 and Eirwen's son, Iolo, was born in 1944. In 1950 the family moved to Tyddyn Cwcallt, Cricieth, to farm, and also to write, lecture and give frequent broadcasts. In 1962, they moved to Bangor, where Eirwen worked in radio and television, until appointed tutor-organiser for the WEA in Gwynedd, where she worked till she retired in 1979. They moved to Llanrug in 1970. Harri died there in 1985. She has written 1,400 articles and is the author of eleven books in Welsh. In 1987 she moved to Talybont, to be near her son.

Spring in London – as elsewhere – was rather pleasant. The weather was improving so that we could look forward to weekends cruising up the Thames in our small cabin cruiser, which was moored at Putney. My husband, Harri, our six-year-old son, Iolo, and myself loved spending weekends up river in the open country beyond Richmond and Teddington. Our boat had two bunks, a hammock we had rigged up for Iolo, a galley and a toilet.

We lived in Clapham Park, convenient enough for Harri to come home for lunch every day from his office at the Board of Trade. Since the end of the war our social life had burgeoned, particularly amongst the London Welsh; we had established a new Welsh society and a Welsh drama company, Harri producing and myself acting. And some of our MP friends used to invite us to concerts and first night film performances in the West End. Local friends were always ready to stay with Iolo, so that we could accept. All in all, ours was quite a comfortable, interesting life. To say the least, life was far from dull.

So imagine my surprise when Harri came home for lunch one day, in spring 1950, and casually announced that he would give up everything if we could get a small farm in Wales! Everything? A permanent job with promotion prospects and pension; educational opportunities for Iolo; employment prospects for me; our friends and our social life. And yet both Harri and myself had a craving for life in the country and, for Iolo, a Welsh education. But I was so shaken by Harri's unexpected announcement that I started pouring gravy over the desert, much to Iolo's dismay!

I had for some time been trying to persuade Harri to apply for educational posts in Wales. But farming? I knew nothing about farming. Harri didn't know much. I was not averse to the idea, and perhaps I had rather romantic notions about such a life and agreed too readily to Harri's suggestion, not realising what an enormous change it would mean. We bought books on farming and the following summer we spent the best part of our three weeks' vacation searching for a small farm that we could afford in Wales.

We tried Anglesey first, since my parents lived on the island, but there wasn't a farm on sale which even had water on the land, let alone in the farm house. So we tried the mainland and eventually came upon a thirty-four acre holding in Rhoslan, three miles from Cricieth, and lying between two rivers, the Dwyfach and Dwyfawr, well known to lovers of the Welsh poetry of R. Williams Parry. It was a delightful spot and there was a deep well and pump near the house. That clinched it. True, Tyddyn Cwcallt (Cuckold's Croft) was small but good land and we assumed that we would be able to buy more land in the future; after all had we not been advised to start small? And this was within our means. We would of course

147

have to spend a great deal more than just the price of the farm on stocking farm animals, implements, tractor, and other essentials. The boat would have to go as well as our house in London.

After counting the cost, we reckoned we would have £150 on which to live for the first year, and that was very little even then; we had been living on £1,000 a year. But we took the plunge and returned to London to sell up. Harri gave notice of his resignation and arranged to take evening classes on history and Welsh literature for the Workers' Educational Association in Wales the following winter, work with which he was familiar, to supplement our income on our return.

It was November when we arrived in Wales and the countryside looked rather different by then. But the weather was bright and clear and we had the consolation of having left the dense London fogs behind – forever. My father had managed to get us a small car – cars were not easy to come by in the post-war years. This was a renovated 1934 Austin 7 and it looked like new. It was awaiting us at my father's house in Llangefni. A few days later, as we drove through the wooded countryside to our new home in Rhoslan, I imagined that the rustling, dancing autumn leaves were welcoming us.

But my fanciful, romantic ideas were soon dispelled by the harsh reality of a house with no water, electricity or sanitation and no heat until we started a fire in the ancient grate. The removal van got lost, so we had a long wait with no furniture, kitchen equipment, plates or cutlery. But there was a Calor gas stove and the potato crop had not been harvested. So we dug up some potatoes with our bare hands, washed them under the pump, baked them in the gas stove and spread some butter on them with our fingers!

It was dark when the furniture arrived and we only had candles for lighting. The first priority was to air the mattresses, which had been in store for some time. So we stoked up the fire and arranged the mattresses around it. We had no time to unpack anything else because Harri had to go to his first evening class about ten miles away, and as he had only a learner's driving licence I had to accompany him. (I had kept my licence throughout the war although we had no car in London.) There was no problem regarding leaving Iolo behind as Tom, a teenage cousin of Harri's, had moved in with us to give us a helping hand, and very welcome it was. But our trials were only beginning; on leaving, the empty furniture van got stuck in our narrow lane, blocking our way. Eventually we got to the class, though several minutes late. We arrived home about 10.00 pm and started unpacking. The following morning I dashed down to Cricieth for supplies and particularly to buy paraffin lamps; filling these was one of my daily chores for the next seven years.

It took several weeks to stock up on animals, implements and a second-hand tractor – and a lot of money. Harri had insisted that I be responsible for our finances since I was the mathematician! But it took a great deal more than mathematics to keep us solvent. We ran up a huge bill at a local merchant's and for the first time in my life I had the unpleasant experience of having to ask the proprietor to wait for his money. They say it takes five years from scratch for a farm to get going financially. Anyway, the kindly proprietor was very patient and he got his money.

We started off with seven milking cows, increasing the number over the years to about twelve. And of course, at first we had to milk by hand. We had been practising beforehand in London. To that end, Harri had bought a pair of thick rubber gloves. After piercing the tip of each of four fingers, he then filled the glove with water and hung it up; it made a good imitation of a cow's udder. But milking cows was quite a different proposition – some would kick or lash out with their tails. However, we became very fond of them all and their behaviour improved as they got to know us. Later on, we acquired a milking machine which we connected to an ancient paraffin engine, which had been found in one of the buildings and which we managed to coax into operating. It would splutter and snort and produce explosions, frightening all the birds and cats in the vicinity. This went on until we got electricity in 1957.

In the same building as the snorter, we used to store animal feed and soon found all the sacks ripped open by rats. We tried using Dak, a nasty sticky substance which we spread on cardboard sheets in their paths, and sure enough, we caught some, but then had the odious task of having to kill them. Eventually we found there was only one sensible answer to our problem – an army of cats. We had twenty at one time.

Cows we found to be very intelligent. The cow who made herself leader we called Siân. She was gentle and easy to milk, though very definitely the boss of the others. One day, she unexpectedly kicked while being milked and we found her udder was bleeding. Sian had spent an adventurous night! We found that she had escaped from the meadow where she and the others had been confined for the night, had climbed over a barbed wire fence and, ignoring a field of juicy vegetables, had made for another field of corn more to her liking; she had eaten her fill and had made her way back to the meadow before we came to fetch the cows for milking – but obviously not carefully enough. She had torn herself on the fence. It was not the only time Siân demonstrated her ability to plan. Cows are intelligent creatures. Not so hens.

Early on we had bought seventy pullets almost at point of lay and housed them in three fold units on one of the fields. A fold unit consisted of a hut with a sizeable enclosed run; the hens could not be allowed a free run because of the menace of foxes. Each hut had a roosting platform about a foot from the ground with a hole for the hens to jump through from below. By now it was winter with about three inches of snow on the ground. So the first night we thought it would be as well to check on the hens. We found the stupid creatures piled on top of each other in the snow at the far end under the roosting platform. This would never do; they would not survive the night. Someone had to get under the platform to get them out and that had to be me since Harri was too big. I have never sworn so much in my life as I did that night, squeezed under the platform in the snow, snatching each hen out individually with the curved handle of an old umbrella and pushing it up through the hole – all seventy of them! Harri couldn't help in any way – he was convulsed with laughter. I laughed about it later but not at the time.

We had a lot of fun but much trouble as well as, for instance, when one valuable £100 cow got mastitis and wasn't treated properly by a local man. She deteriorated and we had to get her into a sling in order to lift her with pulleys every day to avoid 'bedsores'. After six weeks of this and treatment by a proper vet, she died. We got ten shillings for her skin and a £20 bill from the vet. To this day I have a great deal of sympathy for farmers. At the time we were consoled by our wise old neighbour, Hugh Williams, who said philosophically that it was never too bad if the loss was outside the house.

Another philosopher friend of ours was Wil Sam Jones who had a second-hand car business at his home in Llanystumdwy. He has since become one of our best known playwrights in Welsh. He would visit us often as a friend and as a car and tractor mechanic. His comment, when we were in the throes of one of our many tribulations, was that too easy a life can be very boring. As a mechanic he was, to say the least, unconventional. On one occasion the radiator of one of the jalopies we had bought from him sprang a leak. When Wil responded to our S.O.S. he asked for six eggs and went to search for a sizeable thorn. This he pushed into the small hole in the radiator and then broke six whites of eggs into the water. 'There you are, it will hold now,' he said. And it did! I was able to drive to Cricieth to do my shopping. No wonder Harri named him 'Y Dewin' (The Magician).

Harri gave every animal and machine a name. We bought three young sows, Nia, Julia and Eirian, which used to follow us around the farm like dogs, getting up to all sorts of mischief, their curly tails waggling with glee. That was all very well while they were young, but became a problem when it was time to load them into the trailer Harri had built to take them on a visit to the boar on a neighbouring farm. We tried every subterfuge, from prodding them with the electric fence to enticing them into the trailer with a juicy turnip on the end of a string.

Our family increased in other ways too. We reared many calves – delightful creatures with beautiful film star eyes with long lashes. Having reared them it wrung my heart to see them taken away to be killed. But such is farming; such is life. Gradually I even learnt to kill chickens and feather and dress them for sale in the village.

We also sold peas in the summer months and mushrooms which we grew on racks which Harri had rigged up in the dark cart-house. I made yoghurt (very new in the district at the time) which I sold to a shop in Cricieth. And we took on some goats which friends wanted to be rid of. I wasn't surprised, for the goats used to push us around at great speed – they had been thoroughly spoiled. Added to all this activity, we overwintered a flock of sheep from a hill farm, but they were not much trouble.

Iolo loved our new life, despite having to walk to and from school nearly two miles distant. He would be joined part of the way by children from other farms and on his way home he would usually be met by our sheepdog. He loved all the animals. When he got to secondary school age, he would catch a bus to Cricieth and from there a train to Porthmadog. At Eifionydd School he made many new friends. As he grew older he would roam the hills with a special friend from a neighbouring farm, or go on the river in the canoe he had built for himself, or hide in the branches of a tree for hours to photograph a family of badgers which lived in burrows near the river. It was a grand life for a youngster.

We too made many new friends and found most people very helpful and neighbourly, though most of our neighbouring farmers were very doubtful that these two academics (Harri an MA in History and myself a PhD in Physics) could possibly make a success of farming. But we managed not to go bankrupt, though it was difficult at times. And some of our activities shocked our neighbours as when we were seen carrying wet grass for making silage, which was unknown in the district at the time. We got some publicity in the press, with the result that sometimes, and always when we were at our busiest, complete strangers would turn up to see these peculiar creatures who had revolted against Welsh traditional behaviour by throwing over promising careers and security in order to settle on the land.

On the domestic scene, things were very difficult to begin with. Every drop of water for ourselves and the animals had to be carried from the well. We had two huge iron kettles on the hobs either side of the open fire for a constant, though not plentiful, supply of hot water. And these kettles had to be carried to a small building near the house for washing milking utensils as well as our often very dirty clothes. I used a scrubbing board for this chore. Baths were taken in a tub in the kitchen and toilet arrangements were primitive. The kitchen fire was the only source of heat in the house. It was amazing, really, how well we got everything organised with such primitive arrangements, once we got used to thinking differently.

After about eighteen months of this, things improved. We had an extension built to the house. This included a bigger kitchen with a modern stove, a bathroom and toilet. A drain had been laid for the sewerage and the house was piped for hot and cold water, this being pumped from the well into a tank in the loft by the aforementioned spluttering engine. In later years an electric pump was used.

The money Harri earned by taking evening classes was not much but very welcome, mainly to pay for the feedstock bills, never for luxuries. In about 1953, I too was invited to take classes. I was in a quandary about accepting, because I thought that my specialist subject, physics, would not be acceptable. So I devised a course entitled 'Today's Problems' and treated subjects such as diet, health, overpopulation, power production and pollution (very new then) from a scientific point of view. The course went down quite well. As this work developed, we were both out every weekday evening and had to employ a man to do the evening milking.

We were both writing weekly articles for a Welsh newspaper and being paid the princely sum of £3.00 per article. Later we started broadcasting, on radio to begin with and, in later years, on television. I got £10.00 for my first radio broadcast and used it to buy an electric clothes boiler which was a great boon – of course, this was after electricity was installed. Another year elapsed before we acquired a telephone – before that we had to cycle over a mile to a kiosk whenever we needed a vet, an artificial inseminator or there was an urgent domestic need. Things were really looking up – in one way.

But our lives had been vastly complicated when, in 1954, we took in an old widowed uncle of Harri's; and a few months later my mother, father and epileptic brother. Life was difficult – there were many tensions. Added to this, Harri had been persuaded to become General Secretary of the National Eisteddfod at Pwllheli. It was a two year job and towards the end, in August 1955, he would work late into the night. We had to employ a man to help me on the farm.

Eventually my brother became too difficult for us to handle and had to be taken to the mental hospital in Denbigh. A little later Harri's uncle was taken to hospital in Pwllheli, where he remained until he died. And then my father became ill with cancer of the lung and was taken to Llangwyfan Hospital near Denbigh. All the visiting took up a great deal of time. Mother was not a well woman either and I was finding it increasingly difficult to cope with everything, as I was suffering the after-effects of radiation sickness from working with X-rays for over three years in the thirties, when we were appallingly ignorant of the dangers. There was really no end to trouble.

Towards the end of the fifties, after Harri had finished with the

Eisteddfod, our lives seemed to be getting busier all the time, although we had by then acquired most of the modern conveniences we had been without for so long. But we had learned that such conveniences were not the making of happiness. And despite them we never seemed to have a moment to ourselves.

We cut back on our range of farming activities and concentrated for a time on just poultry and sheep, but even then our broadcasting and lecturing activities were gradually taking over and promising to be more profitable than farming on so small a farm. It was time to make a choice. Harri had undertaken to travel to Manchester twice a week to present items from north Wales on the Welsh television programme 'Heddiw'. And later he was invited to go into television fulltime. What a quandary! It was 1962 and we had to consider that Iolo was going to college that year and we would want to be in a position to support him. And Harri, being an astute student of international affairs, could see trouble brewing for farming, especially for small farms such as ours; they were not considered economic units and never received any grants as big farms did, although they had supported families for generations.

We reluctantly decided to give up farming and accept the BBC's offer; this entailed moving to Bangor to be within easy reach of the studios. Iolo was disappointed. I was heartbroken, although I knew life would be easier. Indeed a new and exciting phase of our lives was opening up – but that is another story.


# When the Honeymoon is Over

~

*Pamela Cockerill*


**Pamela Mary Cockerill** was born in 1935, married in 1958 aged twenty-two and has three children and five grandchildren. She started telling stories to her sisters as soon as she could speak. She joined a creative writing class in Penarth thinking it was a calligraphy class. She sold her first article to *Woman's Own*, wrote regularly for the *Western Mail*, and has had stories on BBC Radio 4 and in various magazines, before concentrating on children's books. She has published seven books for 8-12 year olds, including *Donkey Rescue* (Canongate), *Winter Ponies* (Hodder & Stoughton and Canongate) and *Finders Keepers* (Pont), and had books translated into five other languages. She has been a runner-up for the Mathew Prichard short story award three times. She is presently writing a novel and an autobiography.

We both stared at the little brown book. 'Well, we've done it now,' Mac said, turning the first page, 'one thousand pounds advanced on the property situated 70 Kings Rd, Cardiff. Monthly repayments eight pounds, eight shillings and ten pence, for fifteen years at five and three quarters per cent.'

I didn't answer, fighting nausea that owed nothing directly to mortgage repayments. When I returned from the bathroom, I said, 'At least we've got a roof over our heads.'

'Not much of one according to your parents.'

'They've always rented. They think of mortgage as a debt.'

'Which it is.'

'Don't start. We'll manage.'

Mac brightened. 'We'll start straight away. The sooner we get a couple of rooms fit to live in, the sooner we can be on our own again.'

Since we'd spent the first six months of our marriage working in a holiday camp with over six hundred other people and then two months living with my parents, I thought the 'again' rather inaccurate. 'Where do we start?' I looked around at dingy cream and brown walls, stained ceilings, flaking plaster and filthy windows, overwhelmed by the chaos.

Five months later, I put my paint brush carefully in a jar of turps. I was ten months pregnant. Perhaps it had fossilized, pickled in fumes of paint and white spirit. In the relaxation classes – an innovation of the 1950s run by Mary, a radical midwife determined to replace every old wives' tale with inside knowledge – I often fell asleep during the exercises, a landed whale on the hard wood-block floor. Personally I could have done without all this gory information and I had more than enough exercise crawling around painting skirting boards, probably inhaling lead-loaded paint – we were an ignorant lot about external effects on foetuses in the fifties.

'Soup?' Mac asked hopefully from up his ladder where he was painting the coving. I heaved. The gas board were proving elusive and the second-hand cooker was not yet connected. I opened a tin of mushroom soup and balanced it on a pile of bricks, then lit the paraffin blow lamp that we used to burn off paint. Heating soup by playing the blue flame on the outside of the tin gave the soup an odd scorched flavour only marginally better than drinking it cold. I poured it into a mug and handed it up. He went on working and whistling.

'I think the baby's coming,' I said, trying to sound casual.

The whistling stopped but the brush did not waver. 'You sure?'

'Yes. A show.' I used, self-consciously, one of Mary's technical terms.

'Well, can you hang on till I reach the corner?'

I stared up at him. In all the books I'd read, the films I'd seen, first time husbands-soon-to-be-fathers invariably panicked. They put their trousers on backwards and tripped over furniture while shouting to the little woman to keep calm. Why was mine still up his ladder? There wasn't any furniture to trip over anyway, so I sat on the floor, back against the wall, trying to ignore the niggles of pain around my spine. Above my head the Wedgwood blue tide crept corner-wards.

The nursing home was ten miles away. Five minutes to the phone box, ten minutes for the taxi to arrive, thirty minutes for the journey . . . forty-five minutes. Babies sometimes arrived quite quickly, Mary said, even first babies. Perhaps this baby would be anxious to make up for lost time. I got up and wandered round the room, avoiding the scorched tin of soup.

Mac descended and I sighed with relief. Then he dragged the ladder along the bare boards and climbed back up to finish the last few feet. I looked out of the bay window down into the crowded, cosmopolitan, terraced street where my child would spend its first few years. Children belonged in the country.

Mac descended again and began to wash his brush in a jar of turps. I gagged at the smell. The world was full of smells I'd never noticed before and all of them were nauseating. The sickness hadn't ceased in nearly ten months and now I was a shuffling stick insect with a swollen belly. He disappeared into the bathroom. Perhaps three minutes to phone, five minutes waiting for the taxi . . .?

'What time is the next bus?' he shouted above energetic splashing.

'Bus? Bus!' I shrieked. 'Aren't we having a taxi?'

He came in, towelling his muscular torso, looking deeply handsome, deeply tanned and deeply shocked. 'A taxi?'

'Yes, a taxi. Anyone would think I was suggesting a helicopter. A bus will take ages. What if this baby is in a hurry?'

'Hasn't shown much sign of it so far. It's three and a half weeks late. First babies are rarely in a hurry,' he added with all the authority of one who was once a baby himself.

'You don't need to tell *me* it's late. I'm the one who's been carrying it round in a heatwave.'

'We've only got five pounds left. A taxi to Barry would cost a fortune.'

'We could go as far as my parents, then Dad would take us the rest of the way.' Suddenly I wanted my mother – well, a mother. Anybody's mother. I wasn't grown up enough to become a mother myself yet. Cree on high ground.

Mac's jaw tightened. He hadn't forgiven my father for describing our crumbling three-storied bargain as 'a millstone round our necks'.

'They'll be out. It's Sunday.'

That was true. Other people went for drives and had picnics on Sundays. I'd forgotten there was a world out there beyond painting and plastering, panting and puffing, shovelling up rubble. The pains went away as we argued. This child was obviously non-confrontational. 'I'll get the time table,' I said resignedly.

There was only one bus an hour on Sundays. Our progress down the road was slow. 'Hang on, there's a pain coming.' I leaned against a wall.

'Not pains, contractions.' He had attended just one of those innovative childbirth classes before more important male demands claimed him.

'You can call it what you like. It's bloody painful.'

He looked worried. 'Perhaps we *should* get a taxi.'

So I turned stubborn. 'First babies are rarely in a hurry . . .'

We made it to the bus stop. When the bus came the conductor looked from me to the small case Mac was carrying. 'Better not go on top,' he said.

I collapsed on the nearest seat. There were twelve bus stops between our stop and the nursing home and at every one arthritic pensioners with artificial legs were waiting to get on and off. I gripped the silver rail, sweating in the hot May sunshine and in between waves of pain, wrote and re-wrote the headlines. 'Baby Boy Born on Bus'. Yes, nice alliteration that. 'Driver's Desperate Dash after Delivering Delayed Daughter'. Overdoing it a bit? If it was born on the bus, would the company give it a free bus pass for life?

At the nursing home a nurse checked me in. 'Mrs Pamela Cockerill?' Mac gave me a reassuring hug and went. I wasn't reassured. I was terrified. The minute he disappeared so did every vestige of pain. I started to tell the nurse I'd changed my mind, but she took my arm firmly and led me into a ward full of mothers. They all stopped talking and some smiled sympathetically. They were lying there with flattish stomachs, all safely over the bar except me.

'There's your bed, dear. I'll run you a bath and then we'll examine you. Get undressed.' She pulled a screen round the bed.

I undressed and got my wash bag and a book out of my case. Books were to me what pills or cigarettes were to other people and I wasn't going anywhere without one. There was six inches of tepid water in the bath. I clambered in and started reading, a weepy, where strong women supported weak men. I was busily identifying with the heroine when the nurse reappeared and pulled the plug out. 'My, we've a cool one here,' she laughed, indicating the book. I didn't try to explain it was a shield to hide my chattering teeth.

Back in bed the blonde next to me said, 'Much pain, love?' She was manicuring her nails, massaging cream into perfect half moons.

'Not much,' I lied, hiding my workman's hands under the sheet. I hadn't been able to get all the paint off. A back-combed redhead wandered over and started to tell me details about her recent labour. I was a rotten audience. A chasm separated me from all these women and until I too had given birth I couldn't be one of them. As soon as I could, I hid again behind my book and tested out phrases like, 'This is my son . . . my daughter . . . I am a mother . . .' None of this was real. Eighteen months ago I hadn't known Mac existed. He was a stranger, living a life unconnected with mine. How come I was lying here giving birth to his child?

We had met at a Saturday night dance like hundreds of others, at Cardiff City Hall, marriage market of the 1950s. I was twenty-two and liberated, having just thrown up a promising office job after nearly four years of boredom. I'd taken a job as a sales rep with a firm selling motor accessories. I didn't know a petrol pump from a carburettor and I couldn't have sold a tin-opener to a castaway surrounded by tins of baked beans but there was a plain green van going with the job and available for personal use. No one my age that I knew had their own transport. I had learned to drive when I worked on a farm at seventeen, though I'd had little chance to practise since. Being mobile meant I would no longer have to leave Saturday night dances in time to catch the 10.30 bus home to Barry. I had never before ventured to a dance alone. In between boyfriends, I usually went with 'the girls' but this Saturday no one was available and, restless and miserable after yet another disastrous love affair, I drove alone to Cardiff and joined the group of girls cattle-marketed on one side of the ballroom. The lads were crowded near the entrance for a quick getaway.

I did not lack partners. Probably standing alone made me less intimidating for nervous hopefuls. At ten o'clock I was dodging a persistent walrus-mustachioed teacher who was trying to persuade me to join him and twenty twelve-year-olds on a school trip to France. I wasn't too sure about the existence of the boys. Feeling a tap on my shoulder, I turned, hoping it was a girl friend and there was Mac, six feet of lean muscle, tawny gold hair that matched his beard and moustache. He was a fair swop for the walrus, with or without twenty boys. It was a lively quickstep and he was more interested in dancing than talking. Three dances later, he announced, 'I'm off now to Sophia Gardens' dance or maybe I'll go to the dogs.' I was entranced. I'd never met anyone who'd gone to the dogs. Was this an invitation or an excuse? Sometimes a girl has to take chances, so, for better for worse, for richer for poorer, I said, 'I'll come. Have you got transport?'

He shook his head. 'Only feet.'

'I've got a firm's van,' I boasted, and we left, stepping without a backward glance into the cool night air and into our future. That night I won thirty shillings on a greyhound called Templeton Hero at the track at Cardiff Arms Park . . . and a husband.

'You okay, dear?' I rode another wave of pain to find a sympathetic nurse by my bed. 'Doctor's coming to examine you, then we'll take you to the labour ward.' To my surprise I was expected to walk and immediately felt better. In those days, childbirth and bed were synonymous. I would have been far better left walking about, but fashion is fashion in maternity as in everything else. The delivery bed was high and hard for the convenience of the midwife's back. Behind a thin partition, another mother was struggling to produce a baby determined not to be born. I sensed panic underneath the noises behind the screen. A harassed nurse examined me briefly, said, 'While to go yet, love. Yell if you need us,' and disappeared. I was on my own.

Two hours later, I was still on my own, a listening audience to the ongoing drama behind the screen. 'Now then, darlin', you want this baby out, don't you? Then you're going to have to push harder.' I lay there, terrified, listening to the other girl's yells. I had been brought up not to 'make a fuss', 'don't draw attention to yourself', so I didn't. The next few hours blurred. No book could save me from this. Occasionally someone popped round and checked on me. Once, our family doctor came in and told me everything was normal. Normal? Typical bloody man. My mental language deteriorated hourly but training held and I kept quiet. I was afraid of falling off the bed which was only inches wider than me so I clutched the edge of it with one hand and the gas and air mask with the other and became obsessed with time, begging anyone who passed, 'What time is it?'

'Why, got an appointment, love?' nurses joked, sweeping by without telling me. Why I wanted to know the time I've no idea. At 5.30 that afternoon, my neighbour finally produced a daughter whose cry was strong and lusty. I could hear her mother laughing with hysterical relief as she received the midwife's congratulations. 'Well done, dear! My word, she looks at least ten pounds.' The

Jo Mazelis (left) with sister Gillian, 1961.

Hazel Farr on Swansea sands, 1948.

Carolyn Lewis, age 4, in 1951.

Rachel Nevin (Treadwell) front row centre
with sister Lucy and back row – mother,
uncle Michael, twin brother Simon and father.

Rachel Treadwell
in Holy Communion dress.

Gowerton Girls' Grammar School, 1963 – Gill Fisher, Lynette Parry,
Beth (Evans) Clarke, Marion Roberts, Elizabeth West, Diane Smith.

Carys Richards.　　　　Ann Rodgers in college scarf at 19.

Barry Training College – Ann Rodgers standing far left.

Pam Clatworthy with David, June 1950.

Swansea Training College, 1952 – this group were mostly smokers, banished to their 'special room'. Pam Clatworthy, middle row, second left.

Muriel Hughes (centre) on Sunday School trip, 1958.

Rag Ball, 1964, at The Ritz Ballroom,Llanelli.
Muriel Hughes, left.

Lynne Rees (left) with brother and sister in Sunday best, 1966.

## SIX YEARS OLD

### YSTALYFERA GIRL'S CUPS AND MEDALS

Marion (Tawe) Davies, daughter of Mr. and Mrs. Ivor Davies, 65 Cyfyng Road, Ystalyfera, has during the last four weeks won two Silver Cups and four Silver Medals as an elocutionist at West Wales Eisteddfodau. One of the cups was won at Llandebie. Soon after she took the first award at Morriston for children under 8 and under 10. On the same day, travelling to Cwmamman, she took first prize, making three in one day. Later in the week the second cup was won at Gwynfe, and another first prize at Gwrhyd. Marion is only six years old.

Gaynor Cohen with her parents, 1952.

Marian Tawe Davies
in local paper at six.

Gillian Morgan as a bridesmaid in 1954 . . .

. . . and Gillian at her own wedding in 1959.

Judith Maro, 1950.

Judith Maro with husband and son outside farmhouse.

Elaine Morgan with Dylan
in 1946.

Eirwen Gwynn –
Fflwj receives her reward.

Eirwen Gwynn, Harri and Iolo, 1950.

Sally Gough and Rob, 1959.

'A very candid photograph of the Ellis family, 1954'.

Dot Clancy in New Look, walking with her father, 1951.

Dot Clancy's mother Hilda with her son Richard (aged 4).

Eirlys Ogwen Ellis (left) with her son David,
sister Enid and their mother, 1962.

Margaret Smith with David,
aged 3 weeks.

Margaret Smith's father with David.

Heulwen Williams, back row, second from left – Ysgol Fore Sadwrn, 1950-54.

Ysgol Gymraeg Rhymni, in the 1960s.

Percival Pott Ward, 1953. Brenda Curtis second from right.

Jude Brigley with Santa at Leslies Stores.

Molly Parkin.

Jen Evans (Wilson) aged 16 in 1960.

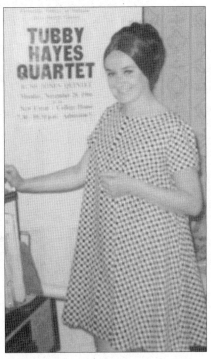

Jen Wilson in Streatham in 1967.

Margaret Lloyd with her younger son and parents, 1966
(note knees *not* exposed).

Stella Schiller Levey (right) with
Marilyn Schiller Corne in Israel, 1956.

Stella Schiller Levey
dancing with Gerald, 1956.

baby's cries drowned out my feeble call that something was happening. When they finally came, one said, 'Oh Lordy, you're well advanced, head presented nicely,' and at six o'clock I gave birth to a weakly five-pound-odd boy who didn't cry at all. I was allowed a brief glimpse of perfect doll-like features then they whisked him away. Bonding hadn't been invented in the 1950s. He looked too small for the world – half the weight of the amazon still bawling on the other side of the partition.

I could hear good-natured laughter, then the cries of the baby faded as presumably she was taken to the nursery. Everywhere was bustle. Not, as I discovered later, to save the life of my child, who I imagined was now in an incubator, but to wash and restore us to our beds for the sacred visiting hour of seven o'clock.

Husbands stood in the corridor waving through the glass doors, clutching bouquets and waiting for the clock to strike seven. I lay, sore and frantic. Every time a nurse passed my bed I asked, 'Is my baby all right? Is he in an incubator?'

'Bless you no, he's fine. A bit small. He's in the nursery with the others. Quiet little mite.'

I knew she was lying. Mothers know these things. The clock struck. The doors opened. A stream of self-conscious men poured through. Best suited, collars and ties, clutching flowers, chocolates, cards, they scattered one to a bed. No Mac. A screen had been placed around the bed opposite. I lay in bed staring at it. That occupant, too, had no visitor.

Ten past seven. No Mac. I knew he knew, because someone in the confusion had remembered to tell me he had phoned and was on his way. He was riding his bike from Cardiff to save the bus fare. He had been knocked off it by a lorry and we had no insurance because we were young and couldn't afford the premiums and anyway we were immortal. Was I widowed as I faced the death of my first child? My febrile imagination supplied the morbid details as I lay waiting for him or the bad news to arrive.

On the stroke of eight, my blonde neighbour told me, everyone would be thrown out. Then the glass doors swung open and everyone looked round. Mac galloped down the ward, carrying a bicycle pump, wearing crumpled khaki shorts and an open-necked shirt. He collapsed on my bed, breathing heavily. 'Sorry I'm late, love. Saw this advert. Swopped the bike for a tandem. Spent our last fiver, but you should see it! It's a Claude Butler. Holds the track record for Maindy Stadium. Best of all –' pause for effect – 'it's got a little side-car for the baby! I've seen him by the way. A nurse took me up to the nursery. He's lovely, isn't he? Clever you.' He bent and kissed me, breathing hard, but more from lack of breath than passion.

I lay, too shocked to speak, trying to adjust to not being a widow, to my baby riding in the side-car of a tandem rather than expiring in an incubator and feeling ridiculously jealous because they'd shown him to Mac before I'd seen him properly myself.

I said the first thing that came into my head. 'Where's my present?'

He reached into the pocket of his shorts and pulled out a bag. 'Picked you these from the garden. First ones.' He put a dozen squashed strawberries onto my outstretched hand. Drops of juice ran through my fingers, pinky-red on the white sheet. 'Sorry they're squashed. It must have been the cycling. Oh, and something else . . .' He put two pound notes and one ten shilling note on my locker top, grinning triumphantly. 'John and Julie have finally moved in downstairs. That's the first week's rent. Hey, d'you realize what that makes you? A landlady!'

I stared at the strawberries and then at the money and burst into tears. 'I'm not a landlady, I'm a mother, so tell that bloody nurse I want my baby.'

# A Young Wife in the Fifties

~

*Sally Gough*

**Sarah (Sally) Noyle Gough** (née Thomas) was born in Ponty-cymer in 1929. She spent her childhood partly in the Garw Valley and partly in London, where her parents had moved. She married in 1952 and set up home in Barry, where she still lives. She obtained her A level in Art at fifty and is now a full-time painter. She also attends creative writing workshops and has written drama for local productions. Sally's sister, Molly Parkin, writes about her life on page 239.

Nineteen fifty marked a turning point in my life. It was the year in which I celebrated my twenty-first birthday and became legally entitled to vote, which I did later that year, self-importantly marking my cross against the Liberal candidate and convinced that I was changing the course of history. It was the year in which my Welsh-born parents moved from London to Brighton, leaving my sister and I to live alone in a flat, she to complete her term at Goldsmiths Art School and I to work out my notice in a publishing house: we loved that flat even though we had to share a kitchen with other tenants and there were some pretty weird smells. But most important of all, 1950 was the year in which I met my future husband. What began as just a holiday flirtation soon turned into a deeper, serious relationship.

My sister and I usually spent our summer holidays at Pontycymer in the Garw Valley, where the rest of our family lived and where we'd been born. After our grandparents died, we stayed with one of our cosy aunties in her house, with deep feather mattresses and a china-pot under the bed for the night: the alternative was the outside toilet and a candle. There was a bright coal fire in the kitchen, cups of tea and lots of gossip, with their knitting on the go all the time. We listened to the latest records with our very special cousin, the only one with a record-player, and renewed old friendships, catching up on who was 'going' with who – 'She never is, who'd have thought!' There were walks up the mountain to favourite places and ice cream in Joe's Italian cafe.

Then came travelling on the coach to the seaside pavilion at Porthcawl for the Saturday evening dance. The twinkling ceiling-ball and live dance band – I had a weakness for the drummer in any band. Girls in pretty full-skirted dresses, permed hair, high heels, make-up and perfume (Muguet-des-Bois for me), just like the Hollywood stars. Boys in sports jackets or blazers, ties and Bryl-cream. Quicksteps, waltzes, jiving, latin-american, congas. Strictly no alcohol on the premises. The lads usually visited the pub before descending on the dance-hall but no one was drunk at that stage. Girls didn't generally go into pubs.

It was always a gamble on how good a dancer the chap was. The female had to wait and be invited to dance and your heart sank when you had a lousy, plodding partner – and no conversation. What joy when he was good and this redhead was. The chat was lively, too. In between dances, it was back to the friends and third degrees about the partners you'd just had, avoidance tactics on those regarded as boring and territories laid out between us. That was for the 'ladies' invitation' dance, the only chance for the lass to ask the lad she particularly liked. Of course, I asked the redhead.

Great disappointment when I learnt he'd not be at next week's dance. He worked in Barry along the coast and had just come home for the weekend. Turned out, though, that he lived further up the same valley and would be on our return coach. He asked if he could walk me home from the bus but I pointed out I was with my sister and friends.

He looked crestfallen so we met the next day to say goodbye to each other. The end of another short holiday romance. But during the week, I knew I wanted to see him again before my return to London so I wrote him a letter and took it to the post office for a stamp. Whilst at the counter, the postmaster called from his office that there was a telegram coming through for me. It was from the redhead, asking me to meet him at Bridgend bus station, Saturday afternoon. My letter was already sealed so I simply wrote 'Yes' on the back and posted it. The postmaster winked at me and I grinned back. He knew my grandfather, who'd also been a postman.

So for a few hours we walked and talked and laughed a lot. We had so many similar tastes, but he was horrified that I'd be voting Liberal, being a fervent Labour man himself. So there were also fierce arguments and I said how much I hated Brylcream. Then he told me of his future prospects at work and what he earned. All serious stuff – no one had spoken to me on such long-term subjects before. Holiday affairs weren't like that and were supposed to be light and frothy.

Of course, there was a strong physical attraction. Those were the days when to become pregnant before marriage was regarded as a disaster, so the terror of that happening was a spur to the enormous self-control necessary. The rule was anything above the belt but nothing below! We promised to write and kissed goodbye yet again at the bus station. We did write, haphazardly, he in Barry and I in London. The Korean war started so I was very worried he'd be called up, as he was a reserve after his National Service, following his time at university. But that didn't happen. Eventually, my sister and I moved to Brighton. Many months and only a few letters later, he wrote to say he was going on holiday to Ireland and on the way would drop in and see me for a few days. My father didn't think much of his sense of direction and couldn't stop laughing.

When I met him at the station, his bright copper head blazed from the far end of the platform and I noticed there was no Brylcream. After my parents' shop closed, we all had a meal together and my mother and I were alone in the kitchen. She hissed she could not believe I would like someone like him because of the awful colour of that hair! So much for parental approval. That year was the start of a relationship that would last fifty years.

We married in Brighton. We had a wonderful white wedding and after the hotel reception, we travelled by Pullman to London for our honeymoon. Rationing was still in force and if you were away from home for longer than three nights, you had to take your ration book with you. What embarrassment at the reception desk of the posh hotel as I handed over the ration book. My single name was still on the cover. Now everyone would know we were a honeymoon couple. We were still trailing confetti, too, stuffed down our backs by friends and relations as we'd boarded the train.

We seemed to settle into our new lives and were very happy. There were, however, numerous misunderstandings as this was the first time we'd lived together. Punctuality was a problem and would remain so. He would prefer to be on the platform at least an hour before the train was due, whereas I regarded this as a complete waste of time and, anyhow, there'd be another along a bit later. Having been brought up in London, this was true, especially with buses. I had to learn it wasn't the case in Wales. We both did try hard to compromise. We also came to terms with our temperaments, me with my sulky moods and he with his volatile short fuse!

Married life in Barry started off in a few furnished upstairs rooms of a large house, overlooking the sea and harbour entrance. It was idyllic. Our wedding presents were mostly connected with laying a 'good table' – china, glasses, cutlery, tablecloths, tray-cloths, napkins.

We'd been given a trendy pressure-cooker and a bright yellow electric iron, but I was forbidden to use this as the landlady said it would take too much electricity. She gave me two flat-irons to heat up on the gas stove – my husband's white collars had to be starched so ironing was a nightmare. There were other irksome rules and we moved to another flat later on.

If you married just before the tax year ended, there was a substantial rebate and with ours we bought a large brown Bakelite radio. This was powerful enough to tune into Radio Luxembourg and the American Forces Network with their great music programmes. We were part of a busy social life, involving rugby club friends and newly-weds from work and dances at Bindles ballroom. We were always on the lookout for a better flat and ultimately, a whole house, all of the rooms furnished, of course. These were like gold and found only by word of mouth. We were all in the same boat.

We were both working but my new office job didn't pay as much as I'd earned as a medical secretary in Brighton. Saving was hard and slow. The cheapest sandwich fillings I could buy were either cheese or brawn and I still heave at the thought of brawn. We even contemplated self-build but my husband had no building skills at all. Then we all heard of a small, new development which might just be within our financial reach, especially the bungalows. With an extra hand-out of cash from my parents and the go-ahead from the mortgage company, we put down the first deposit on our very own place. Only the husband's salary was taken into account. It was assumed that babies would arrive sooner or later and the mother could no longer be a wage-earner. After marriage, it was accepted the wife would no longer have to work, though, in fact, all my friends did. In due course, our first daughter was born and certainly she was the most beautiful baby in the world, with a mop of black hair. Not even a hint of ginger at that stage, which pleased my mother when she came to see us in hospital.

Some months later we moved into our two-bedroomed bungalow, around the corner from our friends, who had already moved there with their new son. In the kitchen was one fitted sink-unit and gas stove, a table and two chairs; the main bedroom had a double bed, small wardrobe and chest and an airing cupboard; small bedroom, one cot, tea trolley with moses basket; lounge with all-night coal fire, dresser, table and four chairs, two armchairs; one large black pram in the hall (present from my parents). The bedroom furniture was bought on hire purchase – again only the husband's income was allowed in setting up the agreement. We felt that we owned the world. At last in our own home as a little family. We were so lucky!

It was tough each month paying the mortgage and money was very, very tight. But most of our friends were in the same situation and certainly there was no thought of keeping up with the Joneses. We walked most places but there were good bus services. Milk and bread were delivered daily, and vegetables and fruit bought from the smallholder who came around in a horse and cart. Meat and fish were sold in shops down the road. Bedding was collected and delivered by a laundry. Other washing was hand done at home and terry nappies were boiled in a metal bucket on the stove. Yes, my hands were a problem and were very chapped in the winter because of hanging washing outside on the line.

The development had been built on fields, so there was a bumper crop of produce that first summer. My husband thought he was the prize gardener. But how much we enjoyed the taste of those new potatoes and kidney beans. I was very pleased with my design for the lawn and curving flower-beds and we were both grateful for the advice given us by our older neighbours.

Electrical goods were too expensive for us at that point but we did have the yellow iron and an antique Electrolux cleaner that had belonged to my grandmother. We'd finished paying for our bedroom furniture and then bought two easy chairs instead of the old ones we'd been donated. Before our second baby was due, we had just finished our hire-purchase on the chairs so we decided a washing machine was the next priority, instead of a fridge. It had been our policy to have only one big item at a time on hire-purchase. That's the way it was for us in the 'Never Had It So Good' days.

My in-laws came to stay with us as our visits to them diminished. Travel was difficult with a baby as it involved three bus changes. Their visits usually coincided with our requests for overnight babysitting for special dances, as normal babysitting was traded amongst our friends. My sister was now working in London and my parents saw no point in staying in Brighton, so they moved and bought a guest-house overlooking the sea in Barry. To be near their granddaughter, really. It made babysitting easier for us, too.

Our family continued to grow and there was great excitement when our son arrived, also with a mass of black hair. He was blue when born and, after I'd held him briefly, he was whisked away to the nursery and brought back to me a few days later. I thought him wonderful, much heavier than his sister but so thin. He soon put on weight and was such a placid baby, not at all like our daughter. Weeks later, my husband and my father said that when they'd seen him through the nursery window, they'd both agreed if you had to choose your baby then he'd probably be the last one left, he was so scrawny. I was furious and deeply upset. But my father couldn't wait to buy him a Meccano set and my husband could already see him playing rugby, for Wales, of course.

Life changed dramatically some months later. My father suffered a coronary and was in hospital a week before he died. I'd been used to my grandparents dying and seeing them in their coffins, but that had been in the order of things. They were old and that's what happened and we greatly mourned them. But my father's death at fifty-seven was all wrong and I felt a huge anger. I had more rapport with my father than with my mother. I would never again take anything for granted and saw calamity around every corner, and still have difficulty in projecting and planning for the future.

My mother was so shell-shocked that she, literally, took to her bed. After my sister returned to London, I called on mother daily, pushing the big, black pram up and down the steep hills, the baby inside and the little girl in a pram-seat on top. Soon my mother moved in with us, to help with the children and to ease her finances by letting her flat for a short while. Her house had been altered to make three flats as she could no longer manage it as a guest house. Our bungalow really was bursting at the seams and we had to look for a house.

We'd started looking for a new house before our third baby was born but nothing had been settled. Then he became seriously ill after we returned home. It was normal to be in hospital for at least ten days after the birth. Our GP was calling twice a day and recommending kaolin poultices for the lung congestion. Very gradually, the baby improved and we could put our minds to house-hunting.

We moved to a ten-year-old, semi-detached, three-bedroomed house with garage at the end of a cul-de-sac. Our GP insisted on visiting us that moving day, to make sure we had a fire going and it was warm enough for the baby. There was a long garden, french-windows opening on to it from a dining room and a front lounge. The kitchen was compact but had fitted sink and cupboards with a larder under the stairs. Just enough room for the all-important washing-machine and our gas stove. We bought a bed-settee and smart electric fire for the lounge and I made new curtains for the extra windows.

The road was safe for bike and trike riding and there were a lot more young families with children. I joined a Wednesday coffee group which met in the members' houses on a rota basis, which saved our sanity while our children played and squabbled in the garden. The only nurseries were for mothers who had to work and playgroups were unheard of. We wondered how families in high-rise flats coped in their situations; we found it exhausting coping with the incessant demands of very young babies and children, delightful though they were.

Some time later we had a phone installed, on the insistence of, and with financial help from, my husband's workplace. I was able to order goods from the local shops, which they delivered. This was especially helpful when the children were ill, which seemed to be frequently after they'd started school. It was at this move that we were able to buy a car. After the children were in bed, we'd go into the garage and just sit, breathing in the smell of the leather seats of the old second-hand car. Neither of us could drive but before too long my husband passed his test, with the help of friends and neighbours. Our horizons widened. He took our daughter to school each morning and brought her home to lunch, then returned to work and dropped her off at school. I would then meet her with the baby and her brother. When he started school, he too joined the routine.

But another calamity was around the corner. My father-in-law became very ill and weeks later died. It seemed a pattern, a new baby and then months later, a death in the family. My mother-in-law had the support of her three other sons and their families, who lived near her, so we weren't as involved then as I'd had to become with my mother.

There were no other babies for a long time. Was it because I wasn't completely happy in our new home or that there was more than enough to do – who knows? We made good, lasting friendships at this time and all our neighbours were very supportive during the trauma of our daughter's meningitis. Parents were not encouraged to be in hospital with their children and the same was true the following year when our son had to be admitted. Thankfully, they both made full recoveries.

When they started school, we became absorbed in helping them to read and write and were in awe of their ability to lap up knowledge. We were very anti-television but the children were disappearing at tea-time and we realized they were off to watch in friends' houses. So we succumbed to a second-hand set and it was then that we found out our eldest son had a sight problem. At the age of three he was fitted with glasses and we worried how to persuade him to wear them. No problem, first thing on in the morning and last off at night – and he stopped walking into walls!

I became a member of the NSPCC, which I still support, and helped found the Ladies Circle in Barry – my husband had been a member of the Round Table for some time. He had been brought up in the Church in Wales and the two older children had been christened there. The Noncomformists was my background and I took the children to morning Sunday school, held at the same time as the service, and the baby was christened there. As time progressed, my husband left the Church, preferring the Noncomformist service. As Liberal fortunes waned, I voted Labour and my husband thought I'd matured politically. But I still remembered my grandfather telling me about being thrown out of the tied cottage if you didn't vote Conservative, when the only alternative was Liberal.

The end of the fifties? I suppose by then we were getting on our feet. There was never quite enough money but my husband's salary was increasing – so were the demands of our growing family. I made many clothes for myself and the children, also curtains and upholstery too, but shoes were always expensive items. We did have a washing-machine and the yellow iron was still going strong! Because of the car, we'd had our first holiday – a few days on the Gower. But we did live at the seaside, so we were lucky. After initially being convinced we'd never have children, we had a daughter and two sons!

'Never Had It So Good', eh? But a lot of people were getting it much, much better and always would. Some folk were getting nothing at all.

# 1954: Excerpts from a Diary

~

*Mari Ellis*
translated from Welsh by Elin ap Hywel

**Mari Ellis** was born at Dylife, Montgomeryshire; has lived in Meirionnydd and Caernarfonshire and in Aberystwyth since 1944. She graduated BA Hons in Welsh in 1936 at the then University College of North Wales, MA in 1938. Having worked in public libraries in Colwyn Bay, Llandudno and Kingston-on-Thames, she was appointed to the National Library of Wales, Aberystwyth in 1944. She married T. I. Ellis in 1949, and has a son and a daughter. She edited 'Tŷ Ni', a woman's section of *Y Cymro,* for 9 years and published *Ffenest y Gegin* in 1965. She also had a column in *Y Llan* for many years. She has published three novels and *Y Golau Gwan*, the love letters of T. E. Ellis. With her daughter Marged Dafydd, she published *Eglumpi Cymru.* She has contributed to many periodicals and edited *Y Angor* for 2½ years.

*5 October, Tuesday*
[At Murmur y Don, Taid and Nain's house, in Llanfair, Harlech. They are my parents.]

The very time I long to write a diary is when I'm extremely busy, and have all kinds of work to do. I can think of a hundred and one interesting, funny little details to record: the things the children say, the things they get up to, things I've heard on the radio, and so on. But when I get a bit of leisure at the end of the day, I'm too tired to find a piece of paper to write on, never mind thinking of something to put on it.

Here I am in bed, having meant since the beginning of the month to start on a fuller kind of diary than my little one, but with neither the time nor the energy. We came here, T., myself, and the two little ones, to look after Taid so that Nain could go to Liverpool to my sister's, but by the time we arrived Taid was in bed. [He's a great deal older than Nain.]

T. took the service at Llanfair church at 5 on Sunday afternoon, and then returned home [to Aberystwyth]. The weather is cold and dismal, and enough to depress anybody. Yesterday, Monday, Nain went to Liverpool on the 2 o'clock train, and the weather is still so wet I can't dry clothes.

We fed the hens before tea. The Little One is very lively, but cries and screams if I am out of sight. By about 6 o'clock I feel very tired.

*6 October, Wednesday*

It's wonderful to see a fine day! The first thing that occurred to me was that I'd be able to dry the clothes and to start on another, bigger wash. The children can play out in the sun while I pick black-berries in the garden, cut cabbage leaves for the hens, and pick French beans and apples. The Little One is cutting his teeth, which is why he's so cross. He wouldn't let me put his overcoat on him, and screamed when I put on an old coat to go out to the hens.

I'm afraid I was rather abrupt with some man from the District Council who called here with a *Survey*. I was cold, and in a hurry, and had no patience to answer questions.

*7 October, Thursday*

T. arrived quite early while I was trying to bandage the Little One's knee after a fall. T. himself was in terrible pain, as he'd tripped and fallen in Pier Street, Aberystwyth, and twisted his ankle. As I understood it later, he almost fainted, but was given glucose and *sal volatile* in Miss Ballard's shop nearby [Miss Ballard is a pharmacist]. This didn't prevent him from driving the car to Llandrindod Wells to see Ll. Hooson-Owen, and then on to Knighton where he was to sing with the Aberystwyth Madrigal Singers.

When he arrived he sat in the kitchen nearly all the morning, while I made an apple and blackberry pudding, stuffed a marrow and prepared potatoes and French beans. It was lovely to have him here with us, and neither I nor the Little One was quite as cross as usual. Pwt and he love being in each other's company.

After lunch we went to Harlech in the car for messages, but I couldn't for the life of me remember what I wanted and came home without the yeast. I forgot to give T. bacon and eggs to take home with him. His patience amazes me.

The Little One makes less of a fuss about his food if I recite rhymes to him while he's eating. This is what we had tonight,

> Hen ŵr oedd fy nhaid yn byw yn y Borth,
> A'i gwch ar y don i ennill ei dorth.
> Afiechyd oedd ei waeledd a marw wnaeth o'r diwedd,
> A phridd ar ei draws a phridd ar ei hyd
> A dyna lle bydd tan ddiwedd y byd.

[My grandfather was an old man/who lived in Y Borth/To earn bread and butter/He sailed the sea foam/His illness was sickness/He died at the last/ With earth all across him/And earth all along him/And that's where he'll stay/Until Judgement Day.]

Tonight I wrote four letters I should have written at the beginning of the week.

*9 October, Saturday*

When I woke this morning, late, it was a glorious day and the sea and the beach looked indescribably wonderful. I gazed at the view while drinking my tea, knowing that I should have no time to look at it later. And I was right.

As I was late, I had to curtail my timetable to get lunch ready by one o'clock. I managed it, and we had lobscouse, lemonade and semolina pudding with a meringue topping.

Herbert was here working in the garden and Pwt chatted to him while he worked; I could see her yellow head and red jersey from the kitchen.

Nain came home from the station in William Jones's car. Pwt was allowed to ride in the car as far as the gate with him on his way back. She poured the whole story out when I went to meet her.

'Red trousers for Rolant, and a paint brush for me.'

She was carrying pink flowers. They had a cake with pink icing on it for tea.

T. telephoned tonight; he is not in as much pain.

*10 October, Sunday*

A sunny day; it was a pleasure to stand by the kitchen window peeling potatoes and carrots, with the sun hot on me. At breakfast time I was looking over towards Mochras, and saw white and grey sheep in a green field. In the sunshine they looked huge.

Picked potatoes, and felt I could stay in the soil all morning. In the afternoon I let the children run on the lawn in the sunshine.

I went to the service at Llanfair church at 5.30; everyone had appreciated T.'s comments the previous Sunday.

Tonight I looked through tree and flower catalogues, and planned what to plant in our garden at home. There are so many lovely things to be had, but time is short. What about all the stories waiting to be written? So far, I'm devoid of inspiration.

*11 October, Monday*

We're expecting Alsie and Glyn [my sister and her husband], so we were busy tidying and preparing food. There were boats and a little ship in the bay and a crowd of people on the beach watching the ship being moved.

*12 October, Tuesday*

I left the children in Nain and Anti Alsie's care and went with Glyn to Porthmadog in the car. T. came over from Cricieth where he'd been visiting Lady Megan [Lloyd George], about the Parliament for Wales Campaign, but they also discussed the Broadcasting Council, Independent Television, the Aberdare by-election, and so on. His ankle was still painful, and every step pained him. At Glyn's suggestion [he is a pharmacist] we got hold of some liquid containing lead and opium to wash the ankle, and it did it good.

After enjoying a tasty lunch T. took me to Menai Bridge, calling to see Llanfair-is-Gaer church on the way – we shivered with cold once we'd got there. I worried that he was so lame. T. had Tom Jones's book, *A Diary with Letters*, and we looked through it.

We had a huge tea in the Anglesey Arms, and the Bishop of Bangor [J.C. Jones] called to see us. We went to Llandudno, the men

174

to the *Y Llan* committee meeting and me to meet two of my old teachers at John Bright's school; T.I. Davies and T. Charles Jones. Talking, talking, talking; they hadn't changed a great deal, although I had seen neither of them since 1948, and I was told I looked no older. Very comforting. Being with them gave me a pleasant, happy feeling; friendship, sincerity, fun. They were both extremely kind to me as teachers, and I know this was true for most of my contemporaries, too.

After returning to Menai Bridge we went to Llanfaes Vicarage for a brief chat with Helen and Eric Ramage.

*13 October, Wednesday.*

We spent the morning in Bangor College library, my old haunt. T. worked on J. H. Davies and I worked on Ieuan Glan Geirionydd. I saw some interesting and revealing letters.

Instead of lunch, we ate fruit in the car and started around 2.30 for Denbigh, where T. was to sing in a concert with the Aberystwyth Madrigal Singers. I called at Bethesda churchyard to see my grandmother's grave. She was buried there in June at the age of 92.

A squirrel ran across the road in front of us as we went over Hiraethog. We had tea at Gwyneth and Cyril Richards' house, and Gwyneth came to the concert with us.

*14 October, Thursday*

We went to the Cilgwyn in the morning to have coffee with Kate Roberts. A good conversation and T. enjoyed himself greatly, and the coffee was glorious. We saw over the house, which had been designed by K.R. and Morris Williams; everywhere as neat as a pin.

We went on to Henllan Vicarage to see Cledwyn Owen; he had asked me to write a pageant to be performed in Welsh, but apparently the Welsh was rather a stumbling-block. It wasn't much of a pageant, anyway. We didn't see Myra as she was away. Back we went to Denbigh and called at Gwasg Gee to see Gwilym R.

T. took me to Eglwys Wen so I could read the memorial tablet to Twm o'r Nant, and see the statue outside. I will remember the beauty of the graveyard, with its little trees full of spiky leaves and red berries, and the rain a red tint over it all.

We had lunch at the Castle Hotel, Ruthin, and saw the squire of Garthewin at another table. T. took me to Corwen to catch the train, as he was going to Penycae to see the Rev. Wyre Lewis, and on to Oswestry. It rained all day and I was glad to see William Jones and his car waiting for me in Llandanwg.

*19 October, Tuesday*

We came home yesterday. Poor Pwt wasn't keen to leave Nain's house, but comforted herself by saying, 'but Aberystwyth is nice too.'

*26 October, Tuesday*

Pwt's birthday; she is four years old. Everyone says, 'She'll be starting school now,' but I don't want her to go at all!

She had a happy day and wore the dress Nain had made for her; she had tea and a chocolate cake with white icing, and four candles on it. She blew them out by herself. The Little One took possession of the doll 'Anti' Hefina had sent her (a rag doll).

Once the birthday was over, I turned my mind to the Education Committee's story. Today *Y Cymro* offered a prize of 10 guineas for a short story. I'll have to set to at once to think of a story and write it so that I'll have enough time to revise and edit it, as is my habit. The *Hwyl* stories went to various judges to be evaluated.

Jean Ware came over for a chat. She says it takes her an hour and a half to write an article for the *Daily Post* on Wednesdays, if things go well. She only got 2 guineas for *Campau Dic*.

*5 November, Friday*

Rained heavily all day. Pwt made a cake while I made a pudding; I was forever snatching things out of the Little One's grasp. At one point he spilt a tinful of treacle on the floor.

I lit sparklers for the children in the kitchen tonight. 'Flowers,' said the Little One.

*6 November, Saturday*

In the afternoon we went to the *Cerdd Dant* Festival in the Parish Hall; the children were fairly interested. Eluned Ellis Jones praised one boy's voice, while I thought it was a sort of discordant squeaking!

*8 November, Monday*

I had a letter from Mr Geoffrey Berwick of St. Bees today. He was asking about my article on John Richards and Ieuan Glan Geirionydd, who both attended St. Bees College. He wrote of Robert Roberts, *Y Sgolor Mawr*, who had been there later, and the account in *The Life and Opinions of Robert Roberts, the Wandering Scholar* (1923).

[My article 'St. Bees Theological College; some Welsh connections' was published in the *Cumberland and Westmoreland Antiquarian and Archaeological Society's Transactions*, Vol 2 III 1954.]

### 11 November, Thursday

We had great fun trying to cut the Little One's hair before his bath. I bought Pwt a winter coat, a dark blue one costing £3.9s.6d. She looks a picture in it. I told her it was the same colour as Dada's, which pleased her a great deal.

### 13 November, Saturday

I made brown bread and Sally Lunns for tea. T. and the children went for a walk. Tonight Geraint and Luned Gruffydd came to babysit so that T. and I could go to Professor and Mrs R. O. Davies's house to read a play. It was called *Tarfu'r Colomennod*, and we had great fun and an enjoyable evening.

### 16 November, Tuesday.

It rained, and a whole lineful of clothes got wet; worse still, the line broke and I had to wash the lot all over again. Although it brightened in the afternoon, nothing dried.

Idris Foster called, and cheered me up!

### 18 November, Thursday

T. took me to Lampeter in the car, through the rain and the mist; a dismal enough afternoon, but the hedges were wonderful – rain on the berries and moss on the tree roots, the leaves a delight of different colours, silence, and being with T. was a blessing.

In the old school the Bishop of St. Davids (W.T. Havard) was lecturing on the Church in the eighteenth century. T. felt that he had imported chunks from some history book. I was surprised that he didn't mention Erasmus Saunders. I found it difficult to stay awake, not because the lecture was boring but because the atmosphere in the hall was stuffy, and I'd been up late last night. After tea Ronald Tree [Professor of Philosophy at St David's College, Lampeter at the time] took us around the College. We called on Mrs. Noakes, George's mother, before we went home.

### 24 November, Wednesday

Here I am as busy as ever, full of plans yet somehow I can't for the life of me get to grips with Ieuan Glan Geirionydd's story; all sorts of ideas offer themselves, but none *sticks*.

Tonight I washed the fruit for T.'s birthday cake. I bought a little bottle of rum and poured two tablespoonsful of it on top of the fruit to soak overnight. I didn't see this in a book – it was Dilys Ellis who told me of it.

*Storïau Awr Hamdden* has appeared. [Seven stories . . . edited by Sali H. Davies on behalf of Cardiganshire Education Committee, 1954]. It looks very smart. The list of competition winners is interesting; I'd love to see the adjudication.

### 26 November, Friday

I tried to write an article for the *Western Mail* tonight; I must get T.'s opinion on it. The story is still a nebulous dream.

The birthday cake has been baked and has risen well. I must think about the Christmas pudding now. But I'll put it off until I've got the measure of the story.

### 30 November, Tuesday

Alun R. Edwards' adjudication on the story arrived.

### 4 December, Saturday

I made steak and kidney pie and mince pies. T. took Pwt to see Dr. Gwenan in the afternoon, and left the Little One with me in the garden, and I planted two blackcurrant bushes and three gooseberry bushes.

### 7 December, Monday

Six copies of *Crwydro Meirionnydd* arrived from Llandybïe.

### 14 December, Tuesday

Pwt started at the Ysgol Gymraeg today. I took her there after lunch. She's in 'Miss Lowis's' class. I talked to Hywel D. Roberts [the Headmaster]. Ba-lei and the Little One came with me to fetch her at 3.30. She was tired. [Bai-lei was Pwt's pronounciation of 'Mrs Pyle' when she first began to talk. Mrs Pyle helped me in the house for ten years.]

*15 December, Wednesday*

The Ysgol Gymraeg Carol Service in Siloh Chapel; I took Pwt there.

*16 December, Thursday*

A letter from T. in Oswestry saying that he had seen John Roberts Williams, who told him that my story about Ieuan Glan Geirionydd was among the seven best, out of 126!

*19 December, Sunday*

T.'s birthday. I iced his cake. He went to church at 8 am and 6 pm, and Pwt and I went at 10 am.

*22 December, Wednesday*

Went to Plas Hendre by 7.30 to a Carol evening and it was delightful.

*28 December, Tuesday*

Mrs Rhiannon Mansel Davies called to ask me to autograph *Storïau Awr Hamdden!* [She too has a story in the book.]

I began writing the 'thank you' letters tonight. The *Western Mail* article came before Christmas. I've already thought of another subject to write on, but haven't had time to work on it.

Oh, if only I had two pairs of hands and two heads! – one pair writing and the other knitting; one head thinking about letters and the other spinning stories and articles! But what can I do – with a head like a turnip and one feeble pair of hands?

The story got quite a favourable review in *Y Cymro*.

*Crwydro Meironnydd* looks beautiful and is selling well, as far as I can tell. T. had some very appreciative letters from Wyre Lewis and Tecwyn Evans. Modest and unassuming as he is, he can't understand why people say nice things about him.

*30 December, Thursday*

Nain arrived on the midday train and T. and Pwt went to meet her. Mrs Irene Edwards came to lunch and had fun and games with Pwt.

*31 December, Friday.*

A cold, wet, dismal year as far as the weather goes; the year my grandmother died; but it saw the publication of *Crwydro Meirionnydd* and *Storïau Awr Hamdden*.

The year Pwt started school and the Little One began to walk.

Room to give thanks; *much* room for improvement.

# Violent Husbands

~

*Marian Tawe Davies*

**Marian Thomas** (née Davies) was born in Ystalyfera, at the top of the Swansea valley, in 1930. Her memories of her childhood are of being part of a limitless extended family, as most of the residents of Cyfyng Road seemed to be related to her. As a young girl, under her competition name Marian Tawe Davies, she competed in local and national eisteddfodau and won many cups and medals for recitation. In 1953, she married Gerald Thomas, whose autobiography *Growing up in the Varteg – A Trip Down Memory Lane* was a sell out success in Wales and abroad. Sadly, Gerald died in 2002 after forty-nine happy years together and Marian now lives in a converted police station in Ystalyfera, visited regularly by her four children, eight grandchildren and two (soon to be three) great grandchildren.

A few months after leaving Ystalyfera Grammar School I was admitted to Hammersmith Hospital in London for a thyroid operation and, following a short recuperation period, I decided to help my mother in the small shop which she had taken over on my grandmother's retirement. There was a small room at the side of the shop where many confidences were shared. One Sunday morning, a customer asked if she could stay for a while, as her husband had threatened to kill her and her son. After a cup of coffee and a chat, I suggested that she would be better off if she left him and started a new life. Eventually the situation got so bad that she did so and is now happily remarried.

On another occasion, a customer told me that her husband came one night and told her he was leaving her for another woman. She was so upset that she drank a whole bottle of rum, tore all his clothes to shreds and told him, 'If you leave me, you will have to go naked.' He never did leave her and they remained together until his death. She never forgot, but I suppose she learned to forgive.

At times I would be told of an unwanted pregnancy, but I never betrayed a confidence and if, at a later date, another customer would tell me about it, I would simply say, 'Oh! You do surprise me. Are you sure that it's true?'

I recall another incident involving a family that lived not far from the shop, and the husband continually ill-treated his wife. In those days, there was a tendency to be 'hush hush' about such matters. However, two of my mother's elderly aunts decided to do something about it. So, early one morning, armed with two mops, they went into the home and found him in his underpants and began to beat him with the mops. He ran out of the house but they followed him right through the village and back home again and gave him the 'hiding of his life'.

I am not sure whether the incident stopped the abuse, but at least they gave him something to think about for a long time to come.

## The Divorce

~

*Eva Goldsworthy*

**Eva Goldsworthy** was born in Ogmore Vale, south Wales, on 21 August 1921. She has three daughters. She achieved a BSc in mathematics. The events in her piece occurred when she was a teacher in Holland Park School, Kensington. She now lives in Knighton in Powys. She has published *Practical Maths for the Office* (Edward Arnold 1977) and *A Cautionary Tale (house buying in Greece)* (Carad 2002).

I turned into an alleyway off London's Fleet Street and found myself in a small courtyard. It was flanked by weathered stone buildings and a fountain played in the centre. The bustle of Fleet Street was muted and the trickling water could be heard above the traffic noise. This was a far cry from that functional solicitor's practice off the North Circular Road that I had been used to. I was now in the big time. Owing to my husband Deryk's stubbornness, the case would be held in the High Court over the road and I had come to this place to arrange for a special divorce lawyer and a barrister.

The inside of the imposing stone building was dark and uninviting and as I waited in the lawyer's office, I studied the flock wallpaper, very expensive in its time but now showing signs of age. What would he be like, this man who was going to be so important to me during the next few months? His diplomas hung on the walls, along with the school photograph of a cricket eleven. A small trophy gleamed on a shelf in front of the law books and on his desk was a silver-framed photograph of a woman in riding gear. A far cry from Neasden – not a flying plaster duck in sight!

I was beginning to form a picture of the room's owner – bald, middle-aged, quietly upper class – when in bounced Hooray Henry. This was the term we used in the sixties to describe brash young men. One of their characteristics was a way of speaking that tended to reduce all vowels to a common 'a'. This specimen was no more than twenty-five years old, fair-haired with a forgettable face. I learned later that Hooray's main preoccupation in life was organising the annual Conservative ball at the Dorchester Hotel.

'Well, nah,' he said pompously, 'we must, ah, establish graands.'

'Excuse me?'

'Graands,' he repeated. 'Basics for contention.'

'Oh, grounds!'

Was this the person with whom I had to discuss the intimate details of my life – this comic adolescent?

He cleared his throat and began. 'Would you say that you and your husband were, ah, incompatible?'

'We never got on, if that's what you mean.'

'And what about, ah, in bed?'

'It never really came to much, but I don't know whose fault that was.' (Was that a fair reply? Poor Deryk, maybe I should have tried a little harder.)

Henry made some notes and I counted the bobbles on the wall-paper. Then he looked up. 'Adultery?'

I came out of my reverie. 'What?'

'Adultery?' he said, his pen poised.

'Sometimes.'

'You or him?'

'Not me.' (I didn't think the brief fling with Bob merited a mention and anyway it was after I had run away.)

There was a pause. Henry was obviously expecting more. 'Well?' he said, tapping with his pen.

'I didn't really mind.' I continued, 'It sort of took the pressure off, if you know what I mean. I don't think we ought to add adultery.'

He put down his pen and leaned towards me. 'Madam, do you want a divorce?'

'Of course.'

'Then you have to be prepared to pursue it, ah, vigorously. Plunkett and Green are very strong litigants.'

'Plunkett and Green?'

'His lawyers.'

'Oh.'

'So –' The pen was poised again – 'do you know how many women he, ah, consorted with?'

'Not really.'

Henry frowned.

'Well, perhaps three,' I said hurriedly.

He made another note. He wasn't bad, in fact. For all his brash-ness he had a terrier-like quality. Of course, he must have been a little weightier than he looked to have passed all those exams. He looked down at his list.

'Violence?'

'Not much.'

He sighed and said with exaggerated patience, 'Did he hit you?'

'Yes, sometimes.'

'Any evidence?'

'I ran out one night to Bob's house and he called a policeman for me.'

'That's better. Anything else?'

'He locked me in.'

He made another note. 'Rape?'

'Yes.'

'Fellatio?'

'What?'

'Fellatio,' (irritably) 'It's here in your original testimony. Oral sex.'

'Oh, yes.'

'Sodomy?'

'I don't know.' (What on earth was it?)

'We might as well put it down,' he said.

He compiled a formidable list of crimes and as I left his office I felt that the battle lines were now drawn. It is in the interests of the legal profession to play each side off against the other and, indeed, as the months went by the files thickened. Letters, scraps of paper and diaries were investigated and cross-checked, as if our sad little dilemma was of national importance.

This was a lonely time. Weekly, sometimes twice weekly, there were meetings with Henry and then evenings alone at home listening to the radio. It is ironic that at a time when a woman most needs support she is treated like a pariah. Men avoided me because they didn't want to be implicated and even married friends were wary, but there were just a few faithfuls and one of them was Norman. I had known him since the war years and he had come to our wedding. We didn't see him often because, he told me later, he had spotted the latent violence in Deryk and didn't want to be about if it ever erupted. He was a round Pickwickian sort of man and one of the few people in the country who was both an Oxford physicist and a medical doctor, but although he was clever, he was hopeless as a communicator. Conversation with him was punctuated by a series of grunts, all ending on an upward inflection and begging an answer. How do you reply to a grunt? Norman helped to sort out my finances, was always ready to come round if I had a problem, and thanks to him, I didn't feel too isolated. But there were still bad days and once, when I was feeling particularly low, Norman suggested a day by the sea.

We went to the east coast on a bitterly cold morning and stayed in his holiday cottage. Neither of us had contemplated making love but as we tried unsuccessfully to get the fire to light, it seemed sensible to conserve heat and go to bed. There were only summer bedclothes so we were still pretty cold, which may have explained the debacle, or perhaps good friends don't make good lovers. He couldn't get an erection and I couldn't even begin to get aroused.

'It's supposed to be one of the best erogenous zones,' said Norman, clinically playing with the frills of my vagina, while I visualised the checklist that was running through his head.

We gave up in the end and went out and bought fresh dabs for tea.

One of Norman's virtues was persistence. More for my sake, I think, than his, we tried again in a hotel outside Oxford. The room was warm and comfortable and there were even real flowers on the bedside table.

'Let's have dinner early and then go upstairs,' said Norman.

The meal was very good. We drank a bottle of excellent red wine and went up to bed. We could faintly hear the music from the restaurant and within minutes we were both asleep! I woke and saw the sun streaming through the windows and wondered where I was.

'Good Lord, it's morning!' said Norman.

We drove back to London pure as the driven snow.

The divorce was hotting up. More and more, I went under the arch and past the fountain to have bizarre sessions with Henry. I began to think that he watched too much television. There was the quite unnecessary episode of the private detective. This man was supposed to verify that Deryk was still carrying on with a woman called Jackie. I provided the information, the address of the house and a description of the two of them, and our Sherlock Holmes set off for a twenty-four-hour surveillance. In his report, he stated that it all went to plan up to when he saw them go inside.

'Then,' he states, 'I nipped off for a bite of supper.'

Of course when he returned to confront them 'in flagrante delicto' they had left.

'A pity,' said Henry.

What an inadequate comment! I felt like exploding – after all it was my money they were spending! But, as with doctors, lawyers have to he handled carefully, so I said nothing.

Soon there were encouraging signs that the divorce hearing was getting nearer. I was dreading it, but I also wanted to get my future settled. What would happen if I lost the case? They couldn't force me to go back to Deryk, but without the sanction of the law he would always be like a menacing shadow. And what about the children? For the first time in my life I was acutely interested in the dates of the law terms.

Henry: 'Maybe we will get a hearing before the summer recess.'
We didn't.
Henry: 'It's bound to be before Christmas.'
It wasn't.

The next milestone was for me to be introduced to my barrister. The system seems to be that a solicitor does all the donkeywork but the final performance is given to a prima donna in a wig. Mine was a delicious flamboyant. He leaned back in his green leather chair in an office much grander than Henry's. 'Begin at the beginning,' he said.

I'd got used to discussing the intimate details of my life with Henry but it was difficult to start all over again with a stranger, however gorgeous. Couldn't he refer to the files? There were enough of them!

'Just tell it like a story,' he said, stubbing out his cigar. 'There iss no need to be embarrassed. I haf heard it all before, you know.'

I caught my breath! Those intonations, the hint of a bird in the throat!

'Da iawn (Very well),' I said.

I was back in Paran Baptist Chapel in the Garw Valley listening to the preacher at my grandfather's funeral. Suddenly, that imposing office, the tooled leather desktop, the heavy legal volumes were less intimidating than before. I relaxed and gave a more or less coherent account of my marriage. Every now and then he interrupted me with a sharp question, and at the end of two hours we had finished and I was exhausted. He closed the green leather folder with a smile of satisfaction. It seems that I had passed the test and could be trusted as a witness.

'That iss fine,' said Peter. 'Now let's go out to tea.'

He put on a coat with velvet lapels and I noticed that the design of his tie was just a little over the top even for the late sixties. He was in the wrong century – he would have made a wonderful dandy in Beau Brummell's time. He moved very lightly for a large man. Perhaps he had been an athlete in his younger days. Mind you, he wasn't old even now, my age I should think. We walked under the arch and out into Fleet Street, then turned left towards Twynings teashop. The noise of the rush hour traffic bruised our ears.

'It iss a long way from Wales,' he said and his voice betrayed the *hiraeth* (longing).

For a moment, I fancied that the traffic halted.

'I'm glad you are going to be my counsel,' I said, and if his beautiful gloved hand had been nearer I would have squeezed it.

He ordered tea and toast and we talked about the pebbly beaches where the Severn opens up to the Bristol Channel – Saint Donats, Llantwit Major, Southerndown. He reminisced about galloping his pony on Llanwonno common, high above the valley of Rhondda Fach.

'I had an uncle with a farm on that common,' I said. 'Penyrheol, it was called. My stepfather is buried in the church there but I think the farm has gone.'

Twynings teashop is long and narrow and the tables are very small. We sat opposite each other, knee to knee. I poured out the tea and then, unbelievably, over the Lapsang Souchong, he started to chat me up! His beautifully manicured hand brushed mine as I put down the pot.

'So I thought we might go out to dinner one evening. How about tomorrow?'

It was really very awkward. Here was this man who knew everything, but everything about my life, making sheep's eyes at me. How can one effect hauteur and indifference with someone who knows that you have been fellatioed, cunnilingussed, two-timed and buggered. (I'd looked up sodomy in the dictionary.) Was it plain old-fashioned opportunism or was it a moral boost for a nervous client? Whatever the reason, for the ensuing months and right through the two weeks of the trial, I had an admirer. He brought me flowers and chocolates and we flirted outrageously in pubs and restaurants at a safe distance from Fleet Street. Once or twice he came back to my flat and although we fondled, the sinning stopped far short of adultery. He behaved more like a suitor than a seducer. He even gave my teenage daughter a box of chocolates.

Why did he do it? Did he enjoy the element of risk? Did it give the affair an extra frisson? The risk was certainly there. Plunkett and Green would have had a field day if they had known. I was flattered, I was intrigued, I was overwhelmed by the bizarre situation, but I wasn't attracted. It was the cigar smoke that did it. Each time we embraced I felt that I was being enveloped in a chimney.

I did, however, achieve one ambition – we went to tea at the Ritz. It cost one pound, a vast sum at that time, and the sandwiches and cakes were doll-sized, but the atmosphere was worth it. Soft footed, deferential waiters, ladies in hats, a sprinkling of colonel Blimps, and beautiful young men who seemed much younger than their female companions. To cap it all there was sweet music from a trio of violins playing discreetly behind the potted palms. All this, while outside through the ornate windows strutted sixties Piccadilly!

Their Lordships deigned to be graciously available after Christmas, so my divorce case started in the second week of January 1969, nineteen months after I had run away. I sat in the court amidst the busy to-ing and fro-ing of men and women in billowing black gowns and thought how ridiculous it was that our domestic squabbles had come to this. The defence lawyer was a spry young man. One day, I thought, he's going to run rings round my ageing Romeo. Let's hope it's after this present case is over.

I was rigid with stage fright. The witness box seemed very far away and I needed all my willpower to walk to it and then climb the steps to the dais; I suppose I took the oath but I don't remember anything about it. When the cross-examination began, I answered in a very low voice. Describing sexual experiences had been bad enough in Hooray Henry's office, but explaining them in public was adding another dimension to the nightmare.

'Were you in the habit of indulging in oral sex?' asked Green and Plunkett's whizz kid.

'No.'

'Speak up, please,' said the judge.

'NO.'

'But it did happen on at least one occasion?'

'Yes.'

'Can you describe the incident?' said Kid-O.

'I – I –'

'Speak a little louder, please, so that the court can hear.'

I tried again and saw with horror that Bob was sitting in the back row. Dear Bob. We made love just once. It was soon after I had left Deryk and I called at his house to collect some Labour Party pamphlets. No one else was in and we sat in the kitchen, drinking tea.

'Long time no see,' said Bob.

'A lot's been happening.'

'I know, I heard about it. How are you?'

It was the friendliness that did it.

'I'm, I'm all ri –' But I couldn't get the words out.

He put his arms round me and I sobbed against his blue train driver's uniform, then it seemed quite natural to go upstairs. Suddenly, in that little terrace house, sex became fun. I kept on my suspender belt and stockings and became as titillating as I knew how. Bob was enchanted and later, as we sat drinking more tea, he laughed.

'What is it?' I asked.

He laughed again, a big man's laugh. 'Do you know what Deryk said to me last night at the Council meeting?'

'No?'

'The trouble with my wife, Bob, is that she doesn't like sex. She doesn't even want to kiss when we make love!'

Back in the court Kid-O was getting restive.

'I repeat, can you describe the incident?'

I swallowed hard and began to describe the awful night that I had done my best to forget.

'– and he said –'

'Yes?'

'– and he said that –'

'Yes? Please tell the court.' Kid-O was getting impatient.

'He said that once a woman had tasted it she can't do without it.'

Kid-O was relentless. 'Were you a willing participant?'

'Objection!' said my counsel.

The judge nodded to Kid-O to continue.

'Were you?' he said.

'No, I wasn't willing.'

'Surely it would have been difficult for your husband to, er, effect an entrance if you had struggled?'

I didn't know what to say. I wished the ground would open up.

'Did you struggle?' he persisted. 'I find it hard to believe.'

My suitor was on his feet again but he was over-ruled. This was getting awful.

'Think carefully,' said Kid-O. 'Did you struggle?'

'He tied me up!' I blurted.

'Tied you up! What with?'

'I – I don't know.'

'You don't know?' Kid-O looked round at the courtroom to convey his disbelief.

'A – a rope, I suppose.'

'And where did it come from?' He had a snakelike smoothness now.

'I don't know. Under the bed maybe.'

Kid-O looked round the courtroom with a smile and then back at me. 'Was there usually a supply of rope under the bed?'

'No – yes – I don't know.'

Kid-O leaned forward for the kill. I'd really gone off him by now.

'I put it to you that there was no rope.'

Then I did something I'd vowed not to do. I burst into tears. The incident had so horrified me at the time that I had blocked it out as if it had never happened. Now, in public, in daylight, with more than thirty people watching, I had been forced to admit my humiliation.

The judge was a woman, elderly, with a pale luminous face. She looked like a William Blake God. 'I think we can pass on to the next point,' she said.

I caught reproachful glances from Henry and my swain. No doubt they were wondering what else I had been too chicken to tell them.

'Your witness.'

Throughout the trial I had tried to avoid looking at Deryk. I knew that he was sitting with a Plunkett or a Green and sometimes I saw Kid-O lean towards him, but I studiously made my eyes stop short before they reached him. In our years of marriage, when he had dominated me, I had rarely seen him with groups of people; we had acted out our little comedy alone. But now, as I saw this thin, rather drab man climb up into the witness box, I was amazed. Was this the person I had allowed to cause me such agony? I saw the way his right shoulder twitched, a sure sign that he was nervous. I of all the people in the courtroom would know the questions which he would find hurtful to answer.

My own counsel unfolded his elegant body from the seat and surveyed the courtroom. For a moment, I fancied that he looked like Aneurin Bevan, and thought, Let's hope he had something approaching that man's eloquence. He took a deep breath as he turned towards Deryk and I shut my eyes in dread. This was going to be make or break, and I prayed that he would not let me down. I should not have doubted. He used the whole gamut of surprise, scorn, anger, disbelief, bringing to that English court the *hwyl* (fervour) of the preachers of the Welsh valleys. It was not a contest. It was a massacre, and Deryk's elaborate defences were demolished.

Next day the judge began her summing up, looking even more like a William Blake painting. Through the trial she had said very little and always in a precise, quiet voice, but now her tone was devastatingly censorious. Her criticism of my husband had an Old Testament harshness. One could almost smell the sulphur of the flaming swords as we were expelled from Eden. She went through the evidence item by item and trashed all Deryk's attempts at justification. Before announcing the verdict she congratulated the defence lawyer on his handling of a very difficult brief. (As I had divined, Kid-O was going to go far.) She then in solemn tones gave me my divorce on the grounds of cruelty and I was awarded full costs. There were of course congratulations all round, even Henry looked pleased, but I sensed that the liaison with Peter was over. Maybe he had already lined up another conquest. Good luck to him, no hard feelings.

So that January afternoon I walked away from the law courts free. Free from the shackles of marriage, free from musty offices and the musty smell of law books. I stepped into the world like that advertisement for Startrite Shoes – a toddler walking up a path towards the sun. That was me at forty-five years, setting out to be my own person.

# CHAPTER 6

# UNMARRIED MOTHERS

# The Right to Choose

~

*Dot Clancy*

**Dorothy (Dot) Clancy** was born in 1932 in Newcastle-on-Tyne. She became a trainee nurse, because it was the only place she could go with board and lodgings. She trained in a children's hospital in Hackney, where the events in her account took place. She stayed in the care business for the rest of her life, in between six pregnancies. She started to write and perform poetry in 1976 and has been published in many radical magazines, *One Potato, Two Potato*, a workshop book for schools (Macmillan) and *Rooster Crows at Light from the Bombing – Echoes of the Gulf War* (Inroads Press Minneapolis 1992). She has performed at Glastonbury for the last five years and is currently part of Lampeter Poets and Peasants. She moved to Wales in 1986 and has obtained a BA from Lampeter in Anthropology/Women Studies.

In the fifties, most women were totally ignorant about their bodies and the barrier between married and unmarried mothers was huge. There were other relationships of course, as there always have been, but they were hidden and outside the experience or knowledge of most of us. Most of our knowledge came from the playground or dirty stories. There was no information and no Pill. Only the use of Durex was, in any way, common knowledge and very few young women knew anything about that. The onus was on the man and few young men cared. Agony aunts dealt in platitudes, the general message being 'don't'. If anyone went 'all the way', the general term used then, fear was immense and you lived alone with that fear; having uncrossed your legs, you crossed your fingers. If pregnancy resulted, going to a doctor meant only confirmation. No other help was possible.

Today, of course, many things are different, but two things remain the same – fear and time. That fear still stimulates a false security and the female persona induces its own defence, so that many women cease logical reasoning and do not go instantly to the medical profession for help. When time is of the essence, they are already on the road to defeat and probably already in an emotional trap. Even with an understanding doctor, the stages to be gone through to an abortion take time. To chip away at that time is always going to affect those most at risk, those at the bottom of the heap economically and socially. In fact, the very same women who have been punished throughout the centuries.

Whether we like it or not, many women are not feminists and do not even think about issues like these until it affects them. By then it is too late. Moral Welfare still lives on, regulating the lives of those who struggle at the bottom of the heap. Some women are again and again denied the right to decide for themselves whether they can sustain a child either economically or emotionally. They are forced to reproduce and then conversely condemned for doing so. As far as I am concerned, men and women will never be equal until every child is a wanted child. I have yet to meet a woman who enjoyed an abortion. Abortion is the last resort.

Not so long ago, in 1951 to be exact, I lay down with one of the gods and found myself inside the prisons of Moral Welfare. I was a young student nurse in my final year of training. I knew all about the naughty bits, but I did not connect it with myself. There I was, far from my home in Newcastle, inside the nunnery of the nurses' home in a London hospital. It was Christmas time and the rules were letting their hair down. I caught the eye of the dashing young consultant, just like in the steaming pages of a Mills and Boon, and gave my all in the back of his car under the stars of chronic delusion.

Looking back, it wasn't much of an event, but the monthly bleed failed to appear, which I ignored for three months, telling nobody, wishing the truth away. However, when I passed out on the floor of the operating theatre, under the anxious eyes of the hospital porter, he guessed the truth before I uttered the words 'fallen woman'. Sharp telephone exchanges took place to Mr Almighty, who pleaded career, family, and was I sure it was his? I was then rushed to the family lawyer for legal dismissal and demolition. The grapevine reached Matron who raised her eyes to heaven and sent underlings to clear my room of my disgusting immoral presence. My mother was sent for and informed of my condition, and we left in the cold dawn, unable to look at one another. No word was said of Mr God. Boys will be boys, and hierarchies must be upheld.

My parents were distressed, puzzled, ashamed, and basically wanted the problem, me, somewhere else. As far as they were concerned, and for that matter, most people at that time, there were good girls, bad girls, stupid girls, but not their girl. So I left with a small suitcase, a small amount of money, and what now appeared to be a small growth.

There was not enough money. To get money you had to work, so I arrived at the Labour Exchange with a wedding ring; but all that glitters is not gold. This was firmly pointed out to me by the loud ringing tones of a million clerks shouting 'Miss' and a million turning heads. For a few days they sent me after jobs, jobs they knew I wouldn't get. We played the game. In between, in the room I had managed to rent, I took vast quantities of gin and quinine sulphate, and I lay in hot baths. I was very sick and very drunk and nothing shifted. Everyone had a remedy, or knew somebody, but really nobody knew anything, least of all me. I had seen the results of interference on the wards, where septic abortions were commonplace. I had helped put up the drips, washed the kidney dishes, flushed the foetuses down the drains in the sluice, condemned the back street abortionists. I also knew that with the right amount of money and the right connections it wasn't a problem for those who made the rules. This is not radical or me going on. This is fact.

Eventually the Labour Exchange, in their graciousness, sent me to the National Assistance Office and inside one of their grey confessional booths, I coughed up my sin. They coughed up some small change, and despatched me to the Moral Welfare. The Moral Welfare was staffed by superior women who enjoyed other women's discomfiture. They wanted details. Did I stand up for it, was it regular, and worst of all, apparently, did I enjoy it? Sorry, sisters, this is how I explain why I find it difficult to stand in a circle and hug all women; but I'm getting over it. One final question was apparently of major importance: what was my religion? It hardly seemed relevant at the time, but now going down the road from which there seemed to be no turning, I replied Roman Catholic. We were apparently in luck there. My lapsed religion was the frontrunner in fallen women. The big G was now in charge.

The main reassurance seemed to be that only good girls got pregnant. I didn't quite follow that at the time, but apparently bad girls didn't get pregnant because, 'they knew'. I was twenty, nearly twenty-one, young for my age by today's standards and I didn't know boo from a goose, but I did know I didn't want to be pregnant. I had no idea about having a baby, or about the responsibilities of caring totally for another human being and having to make decisions about their future. No one mentioned that.

Mother and Baby Homes were supposed to be secret, though how you can keep a row of dodgy large prams and lines of off-white nappies in suburban back gardens a secret is beyond me, and of course we weren't hidden: what we were was in custody.

The home was full. It was always full. It seemed there were a lot of good girls around. We came in all ages and one shape – bump. In return for our keep – there was little maternity benefit in those days – we cleaned and washed, cooked and gave everything a double coating of Ronuk. Nuns are into prayers and Ronuk: if we were going anywhere, we were going shining. I won't go overboard and say we were ill-treated. We were fodder for conversion, and our bumps were Catholics.

I don't know what *he* was doing at this time. Getting on with his career, kissing his wife in the morning, and being Jack the Lad in the operating theatre, I daresay.

I grew. I became aware that around me, others got thin and had babies on their breasts; and that after six weeks, they cried more – crying was endemic – and they started looking out of windows. That strange meetings took place. That those babies were dressed up in their best. That cars came and left with babies. That the Irish girls had to deliver their babies to a convent for adoption, back in the village we call Ireland. That they were scared of excommunication, hell and damnation. That young girls left with red lips and grey faces, looking old and ill. That now and again a woman, any one of us, went raving bonkers and we all held her down and wept with her.

However, it wasn't all misery. We stole food from the larder when the nuns were at their offices. We giggled, sang popular songs, played silly games and we dreamed of getting out. We hardly mentioned men.

It was a hot summer. I started to hate nuns. I understood why missionaries got killed. I started to think about this bump that was ruining my life, marking my skin and kicking and wriggling in my belly. For the first time I knitted. I knitted booties, mittens, jackets and bonnets. I became Madam Guillotine, knitting him into every stitch of vengeance. This baby used up an entire sheep.

I was two weeks late when the pains started and, like everyone else, I was hustled out to the local hospital for delivery and recovery. He was big, nearly ten pounds, healthy and hungry for life. In the ward, I shrank down in the white bed, amongst all the legal women surrounded and drowned in their gift-wrapped flowers. No one came. No one rang. Visiting time was a different time of hell, a time to dive under the bed clothes and pretend you didn't care. No one was unkind, just the system, and the pity and the knowing looks. I made a meal of the 'baby blues' and they shuttled us off into a side ward. Mustn't upset the 'happy mums'. I was glad to get back to the nuns, the praying and the Ronuk.

I fed him. I washed him. I loved him. Six weeks flew by. It had already been arranged with the family lawyer and the nuns where he should go; it was nothing to do with me. They were elite folks, with a luxury nursery all prepared for him. He would have every-thing money could buy and his name had already been put down for Eton. The couple who were adopting him had it all – except fertility and I had provided that for them. Everything was arranged for them to collect the baby. The baby was primed and ready in all his knitted gear and I was in another room with my case all packed and ready for my release. The trouble was they were late – a luncheon party had overrun and held them up. But now, suddenly I wasn't so sure about giving my baby up for adoption. In an instant, I swept him up and tucked him under my arm and amidst the wails of the nuns and the cheers of the girls, I left.

The rest was long and hard, not the fifties you see with your rosy nostalgia, before women grew up. At five he died of leukaemia in the year of Windscale. I grew up with the bomb: we saw its mushroom cloud and we felt its heat on our skins. I felt it killed him, and no one could give me an answer as to why. It sent me to Aldermaston, to Greenham, to Holloway. Subversives aren't born. They grow out of history, which takes a long time to write and when it is written is always about those in control. This bit of history was not so long ago, though I thought it was behind us. I had foolishly reckoned without the Moral Welfare Brigade. I don't know about the rights of babies in kidney dishes, but I do know about the can of worms I stumbled on in the back seat of a car. Nobody gave me a choice, and when they had chosen for me and talked about God and the sanctity of life, they didn't try to help. All they did was punish.

This is dedicated to all those women out there who know how it was, and know also that the only reason for it, was to control us. At the time I was angry and often thought about writing it out, but things changed and it seemed those times were over. It seemed silly to write about what was commonplace and had been going on for centuries and ignored. Now I am angry again, as it seems we have forgotten and the Moral Brigade are back where they always are, judging and controlling.

On behalf of all those women and their suffering, I say, how dare you put back time just to polish up your rules?

# An Unmarried Mother in the Nineteen Sixties

~

*Eirlys Ogwen Ellis*

**Eirlys Ogwen Ellis** was born at Cochwillan Farm, near Bangor, in February 1937 and lived there for the first nineteen years of her life. She trained as a dietitian in England and worked at the London Hospital, Whitechapel in London during the 1960s. She now lives with her husband John in Pill, a small village near Bristol. She has published various articles and poems and in 1994 her autobiography *The Voyage Home.*

For the first nineteen years of my life I lived at Cochwillan Farm, Half Way Bridge, near Bangor in north Wales. Two generations of my family had been born in this farmhouse which was rented from the Penrhyn estate. My maiden name is Eirlys Ogwen Ellis and all my adult life I have done some written work in that name. I had a secure and close family upbringing with my parents, my elder sister, Enid, and my brother, Noel. Although we had lived through the Second World War we were very happy. We were often visited by our various uncles, aunts and cousins. I attended the primary school at Llandegai, passed the eleven plus exams and spent seven years at the Bangor grammar school for girls. I consider that I had quite a good education. Then I became a student at the Gloucester training college of domestic science. This was quite a formidable establishment and there I undertook a two-year course in institutional management.

All very nice and straightforward one might think, but it seemed that from a very early age I had a mind of my own and I could be quite determined. Perhaps that is the reason I have had an unusual life with many twists and turns.

I became a post-graduate student at Leeds General Infirmary in 1960 undertaking a course in dietetics in order to become a State Registered Dietitian: I was quite a pioneer as there was not a course available in Wales at this time. I was only the 162nd dietitian to qualify in the whole of the British Isles. The course was very interesting with lectures in diet therapy, nutrition, anatomy and physiology, chemistry and microbiology. We had lectures from the professor of medicine at the infirmary, a very interesting man who understood the work and training of dietitians. In order to study for this course I was awarded the Rose Simmonds Memorial Prize, given by the British Dietetic Association – £250 to cover my books and living accommodation for eighteen months. When I undertook my six months' practical training at the Royal London Hospital in 1961, I lived on one pound a week as everything was all found. I considered myself very fortunate as I had a wonderful career as a dietitian throughout the 1960s.

To go back to Leeds, I lived in a house belonging to the hospital with a number of young women who were either students or on the staff of the catering department. We all got on well with each other and we used to go to the university 'hops' for entertainment.

One evening I met Hassan, who was to make me pregnant before I could even think about such things. I don't remember how we really met, we started talking and there was instant rapport. He told me about his family in Sudan and his twenty brothers and sisters – his father had had four wives! Hassan's mother died when he was young: she was a beautiful woman and he had loved her very much. He was a British Council student studying for his M.A. at the University; he had already gained his B.A. from Cairo University. He was a very handsome man with shining, dark hair, beautiful teeth and tribal scars along his cheeks. He came from a tribe in southern Sudan but his family lived in Khartoum; they were all very clever and well educated.

In August 1961, I gave birth to a beautiful baby boy named David. Hassan had returned to Sudan before the birth and I was left to cope with it all and I have not heard anything of poor old Hassan in forty years. Me, an unmarried mother at the age of twenty-four with no idea of how my life, or David's, was going to unfold. Finding myself pregnant at this time was so traumatic and I was so scared of how I was going to break the news to my family.

My mother was not well and I was five months pregnant when I told my father, one evening when I was home for my Easter holidays. The poor man was so upset. I will never forget the look on his face. He must have thought, Not just in the club but a black man as well. There were only a few black students at Bangor University at the time; not many coloured people had discovered north Wales. My poor father was horrified and went straight to bed, one of the worst experiences of my life.

My family were not as strict as people made out but the way things were dealt with were quite different from the twenty-first century, where teenage pregnancies and single parents seem to abound. My mother took the matter very well. I did not speak to her about the problem until she and my father came to see me in a home for unmarried mothers in London. I begged my father not to meet Hassan. That ordeal I just could not cope with at all, I was so scared! Hassan went home to Sudan without his son (imagine that to a man of the Islamic faith), without me and without his degree. We had both cried together over what happened, as we were not having an affair.

Illegitimacy takes place the world over; children can be conceived in all manner of ways both within and out of wedlock – just watch the 'soaps' on television. I feel very strongly that children born outside of marriage should not be termed 'illegitimate'. I used to hate the word. My little David was, and still is, the most beautiful little soul. I am glad that the law has changed so much in their favour though it still has some way to go.

I have jumped ahead in time – my college lecturers were very good to me; I was not thrown out of college, as had happened to many girls. I was well, ate a very good diet and I was put in touch with a doctor in Leeds who arranged for me to go to a mother and baby home in London at the end of my course. This was run by the Church of England Adoption Society. How things have changed. Young girls of today have no idea of all the secrecy involved. I could have had David adopted into a children's home, but *not* into a family, because children of mixed race were not considered suitable for adoption by white parents in those days. My family and I had different ideas anyway; I was taking my baby home to Wales. My mother was marvellous: she could be very strong when the need arose and I could be also.

The young women with me in the home all came from good homes but some of them had their babies adopted at six weeks old. There was a lot of heartache and I have seen girls cry at the thought of letting their children go. All those married women in the Mothers' Union, who thought us a lot of sinners from the word go, knew nothing of the reality of what we went through.

There were twelve young women in the home; we spent six weeks there before the birth of our babies and six weeks afterwards. There was a matron, who was a nurse and a midwife; a cook, who was drunk most of the time; a cleaning lady and handyman. There was also a chapel where the local vicar had words with each one of us, trying to show us the errors of our ways. I did not like his tone of voice as we were all, according to him, tarred with the same brush and terrible sinners. The cook had connections with Sudan – her husband had been in the army there. She taught me to hold a baby's head properly and told me that I should tell David about his father later on. I shared a room with a vicar's daughter and, believe you me, getting pregnant as a single woman could happen to anyone. We girls are not always to blame, whatever people think.

The home was run to quite a strict regime but we were given a great deal of assistance with coping with the birth and the care of a young baby. I met some very interesting young women who each had a tale to tell. We were young, healthy and quite resilient. We were all in the same boat and it was hard times on one and all. Sometimes we cried or even laughed as we sat in the rear garden surrounded by large, black prams.

David was born at 3 am at the Lambeth Hospital in London and I had a remarkably pain-free delivery. A lovely pupil midwife assisted in the delivery and she thought that I was very brave going through it all. Her best friend had killed herself when she became pregnant and her family threw her out. I was lucky as my family helped me bring David home to Wales.

My parents came to see David and me in the mother and baby home, and although they must have been terribly upset, they never said a word to me about the mess I was in. My mother told me to bring David home to Wales and give him to my sister and brother-in-law, as they had no children of their own. I feel that my mother was right as I would have had a difficult time on my own. I had no money and the welfare rights were not as they are today. Unmarried mothers had a very difficult time bringing up their babies at that time; they often wore wedding rings and called themselves 'Mrs'. I was saved a lot of heartache. It was a tradition for the girl's mother often to bring up a baby as her own and the baby would grow up believing that his mother was his sister. It still happens today in some families. David was a beautiful contented baby and we all loved him for his smile and sweet personality.

Because of this turn of events, I was able to finish my training and embark on quite a successful career as a dietitian. There were a few problems – the main one being 'don't mention that son of yours'. It was difficult but it was all right. I used to go home to Bangor once a month and see my little treasure. I loved him very much and I found it very difficult to let him go.

I worked at the Royal London Hospital in the East End of London for nine years. It was the most interesting and rewarding period of my life. I ended up as the deputy chief dietitian and somebody told me that I was the strictest member of the staff. Poor things, I always thought that my boss deserved that title. She knew about

David but I was not allowed to talk about him. I am sure that quite a few people knew of his existence but nobody said a word. No wonder I was to develop quite a peculiar private life really.

In 1967 I was awarded a Winston Churchill Memorial Prize to study aspects of diet therapy in the United States and Canada. I had a wonderful experience as I spent six months travelling all over America and Canada. Wonderful countries and people but I was glad to get home, as I did not particularly like the lifestyles. During this time I sent David postcards from so many places that he pinned on a large map on the kitchen wall in Cochwillan. He told me later that he learnt to read English from them. Imagine such a career had I been a single mother, it would never have happened. David had a secure upbringing and it has been a privilege to have him for a son. My sister told him that I was his mother when he was eight years old and I am greatly indebted to my family for helping me along the way.

My story does not end there, as in 1971 I was appointed chief dietitian to the University Hospital of Wales in Cardiff and I was dietetic adviser to all the hospitals in that city. Again I was told not to mention David, as I would never have got the job. I do hope things have changed. Many women manage to bring up their children now, but I do think that it must be very difficult for them. They have my greatest respect, as I do not think that I could achieve that in life. My time in Cardiff was really my 'road to Damascus', as I became very ill. I had a dreadful mental experience that still haunts me. I worked very hard and was mentally and physically exhausted. I made the terrible mistake of becoming pregnant again. What a disaster! Are dietitians and unmarried mothers not allowed a private life? I had a legal abortion in Bristol in February, 1973 – a week after my thirty-sixth birthday. My boyfriend and I were devastated and the depression set in. Later I was diagnosed as being a manic-depressive and have never recovered properly from the trauma of it all.

I lost my wonderful career, my second child and my mother in a matter of eighteen months. I did, however, get married in August 1973 and despite dire warnings have lived to tell the tale.

# Lessons in Life

~

*Margaret Smith*

**Margaret Smith** was born in Hospital Road, Bury St Edmunds, in 1938, daughter of a Welsh father and English mother. She lived in Newport for many years and now, in retirement, lives in Lincolnshire. She has three cats and fifteen rabbits, the latter descended from wild rabbits the cats brought home. She has had poetry published in *Beyond the Boundaries* and *Target*, short stories in *Cambrensis* and an article in *The Lady*. Most recently she won second prize in a competition run by Age Concern.

There is no right time to tell your father that you are unmarried and pregnant. It was three years before the swinging sixties would attempt to open up the world to so-called equality for women. Meanwhile, there I was, nineteen years old, an adult in today's world, but a mere irresponsible child in 1957.

My father had left South Wales in the late 1920s to seek his fortune in England. He was tired of seeing the poverty and unemployment in the valleys and managed to transfer from his job as a linesman for GPO telephones to Brighton on the sunny south coast of England, a far cry from the gloom and smoke of the steel works in Ebbw Vale, where he had last been in digs. He found himself transferred to rural East Anglia, where he met and married my mother. May was the daughter of a farm worker, poorly educated and no intellectual match for Arthur. Perhaps this suited him, for he firmly believed that a woman's place was as close to the kitchen sink as possible.

'How can you know anything?' he would chide my mother. 'You've never been any further than the farm drive.'

He ridiculed Len and Herbert, my mother's slow brothers, who were content to shovel horse manure for the rest of their lives. I believe he secretly envied the family; they were a close community who had the freedom of the countryside, clean air and regular home-cooked food on the table. Arthur's arrogance would not allow him to admit to this.

It would not be easy to reveal the news that I was with child to my father. Neither could I tell my mother, who had singularly failed to tell me about periods. I had never revealed to her that I had started them! My elder sister, Joan, could not be trusted to be a confidante. Had it not been for a friend at work and the support of her mother, I believe I would have ended my life. Mrs Gillie and June became my lifeline; the family had been evacuated from war-torn London and had suffered great hardship. It was at Mrs Gillie's suggestion that Ian, the father of my unborn child, should be per-suaded to be involved in telling my parents. To this end, she bravely approached his adoptive mother, who was something in the medical field and quite severe in her manner. She showed little sympathy and wrongly believed I was the scarlet woman who had been keeping him out till four in the morning.

I wished I could have rubbed vanishing cream on the developing lump. Facts had to be faced. Ian had reluctantly agreed to help reveal the unwelcome news to my parents. 'Well, there then, I thought as much,' said my mother in her best country manner.

My father, the arrogant Welshman, was surprisingly quiet. He thought he was about to get rid of his troublesome teenage daughter. 'I suppose I'll have to give permission for you to get married then.'

'But I don't love her enough to marry her,' Ian blurted without a sideways glance. Father had managed to put the newspaper down and, not wanting to comment on Ian's remark, walked away, closing the door behind him. It was obvious that any affection the father of my child had for me was pure lust and the desire to get into my knickers as often as possible. How could I have been so gullible? Ian's words that day still echo through my head forty years on. This was the man I loved and trusted. I had surrendered my virginity to him and conceived his child.

My home background was far from supportive. From the age of nine I was given the responsibility of caring for my epileptic sister after she had contracted meningitis at twelve. I was always called on to supervise a *'grand-mal'* attack, which could be a terrifying expe-rience, as Joan flailed about, smashing ornaments and rolling her eyes. My brief at night was to report back on any fits she might have. Sleeping in a double bed made it easy to watch her twitch and convulse in the most appalling manner. I was too terrified to move, or to tell anyone in the morning of these nocturnal events. It would have been easy to have placed a pillow over her face and put us both out of our misery.

Joan was unaware of her fits and outwardly behaved perfectly normally. She had inherited our father's arrogance and bullied me unmercifully.

'She's been ill,' my mother warned.

Joan was not allowed out on her own so I became her nursemaid. I was much prettier than my sister, a fact much resented by her. Boys became my favourite subject and I did not want to be seen with an older sister with spots who could not dance and thought boys and rock and roll were both equally disgusting. She would report back to my father that I was kissing a boy in a doorway and Dad would storm out after him brandishing his walking stick. All I wanted was to get out of this oppressive atmosphere of the terraced house where my father's Edwardian upbringing caused him to treat my mother like a second class citizen. He had married late in life when he became tired of living in digs and needed regular meals, someone to wash his clothes and warm his bed. Women were not allowed to have opinions.

When I was thirteen and just developing breasts my father arrogantly poked me in my left bosom with a sharp pointed finger. 'And you, young lady, are not allowed to have an opinion until you are as old as I am.' His face flushed and he left me feeling sore and embarrassed. He died of a heart attack at the age of sixty-two. My mother had been told that since she had been given the vote she must place her cross next to the Labour candidate's name. 'You never saw the bread queues in Wales during the twenties,' he shouted. 'Then you'd understand, and that bloody Churchill . . .' Arthur had served in Palestine during the Great War. He had been the first and youngest volunteer from Newport.

My father and I had many arguments. My mother and sister took his side and I ended up with a good hiding for speaking out of turn. This included the day of my first period, when I was severely beaten across the buttocks for daring to disagree with my parent. My most traumatic experience was having to return to school after the summer break clutching a report book in which my father had written his comments on what had been a good report from my teachers: *'Nothing is good where better is possible!'* I later discovered this was the motto of his school in Maindee. Not once did he come to the school to discuss my progress. My sister had left school at fifteen because of her illness. It was not considered appropriate that I should have additional privileges.

I wanted to be a writer, but was told to find a job or my father would steer me to the family tradition of GPO telephones. At sixteen, my headmaster, Mr Fawkes, helped me find a job in a veterinary hospital as a laboratory assistant. Although I loved animals I had little scientific knowledge and mathematics was my weakest subject. I loved the work and gained more information on laboratory technique by attending college one afternoon per week. I was more interested in the veterinary side of the work and, just before falling pregnant, I transferred to the hospital as a nurse. My father had developed late onset diabetes and had to inject himself with insulin twice daily. My parents both believed that, since I was to become a veterinary surgeon, I could perform this task.

My next comment was considered totally out of order: 'Why don't you do it, Mum? He is your husband. What about Joan? She's had hundreds of injections.'

'You cheeky little . . .'

I didn't wait to hear the rest.

Late one evening an argument developed with my father and I ran out of the house. I was wearing my pencil line skirt, swagger jacket and my first pair of high heels. I could not go back home – my pride was hurt. I did not notice the footsteps behind me at first. It was not unusual for girls to be approached by soldiers from the barracks. It was not until he pushed me down a side street and grabbed my bag that I realized all was not well.

I knew nothing about sex, had never heard the word 'rape' and had no knowledge of the male anatomy. My education was about to be completed. I was dragged by my pony tail on to a coal heap, where he removed my shoes and undid his trousers. He dragged the metal heel of my shoe across my cheek. I realized I had to be my own salvation. He was having some difficulty with his implement and made trips to the wall to urinate. I seized my opportunity to run but without shoes it was difficult. I engaged him in conversation and persuaded him to take me somewhere more comfortable. I retrieved my shoes. He retained my bag and twisted my arm behind me. I had told him I was sixteen. Why hadn't someone told me it was the legal age for sexual intercourse? As we headed into the town centre my prayers were answered, in the form of a policeman walking towards me.

My assailant did not protest as he was marched off to the police station. I was interviewed in a cell by a policewoman. My parents were not present. My attacker protested that he thought I was a prostitute. I was reprimanded for wearing unsuitable clothes and told to dress more appropriately in future. I was taken home and the matter was never discussed.

I became more determined to leave home. My mother continued to look at me with contempt. Just an arm around my shoulders and the ability to share my experience with somebody would have helped. My sister, now fully recovered from the effects of meningitis, became the figurehead of purity; I was soiled goods to be taken out of the window and hidden. Joan was told to keep an eye on her younger sister. My role as nursemaid and carer was over. Joan asserted herself with the vigilance of a Victorian parent. I had to leave this oppressive atmosphere. Perhaps I could join the WRNS but that, like university, was still two years away. Most of all, I needed love and affection and the support of my parents.

Having left school, I grasped the opportunity to meet new friends of both sexes. While Pat Boone sang 'Thee I Love', Ian, my knight in shining armour, appeared. I had met Ken at a dance and he asked me to find a friend to make up a foursome. My friend Muriel was to be Ian's blind date. There was an instant magic between Ian and I and we managed to sneak our first kiss, despite being with different partners. I soon decided that this handsome trainee accountant was the love of my life and with a little 'Friendly Persuasion' we became lovers. We talked of becoming engaged at Christmas on my nineteenth birthday. But by that time I was pregnant and I discovered that Ian was not the love of my life but a Jekyll and Hyde who had been seeing other girls.

Once my family had been told and Ian had denied paternity, the situation was taken out of my hands. Aged nineteen and five months pregnant, I found myself facing solicitors, who arranged to proceed with an Affiliation Order against the father of my child, the man I loved and believed I was to marry. The vengeance of my family now took precedence. Miss Todd, a shrivelled-up spinster, was appointed my social worker. No one asked how I felt or what I wanted to do for the sake of my unborn child.

Arrangements were made for me to go to a mother and baby home in Cambridge, where I would give birth and the baby would be adopted. Two girls from the department store where my sister worked had been recent inmates at 48 Bateman Street. I was to pay for my sins and left for Cambridge on a March morning in Miss Todd's car. My mother accompanied us and made small talk with Miss Todd while I sat terrified in the backseat. The door of No. 48 opened to reveal a figure reminiscent of a character from the Addams Family. Sister Sylvia welcomed us with a sickly grin and we were introduced to Matron Stubbs, who retreated behind a desk and shook my mother's hand. Her grey habit signified that she belonged to an order of Protestant sisters. She was much nearer to God than the rest of us and knew all there was to know about the sexual sins of wicked teenagers. The middle-aged matron passed me back to sickly Sylvia and I was ushered to a dormitory containing more than a dozen metal bedsteads and allocated one just behind the door, before being given the grand tour.

'Leave your suitcase. Someone will show you where to put it. Make sure nothing is left on the floor,' a reedy voice monotoned.

The house appeared deserted as we traipsed up and down flights of stairs. There was a communal bathroom containing several Victorian-style baths on legs. I had no intention of exposing my eight month bump to anyone, so bathing was not on my agenda. Sister Pauline was in the nursery, where several small cots were arranged around the large airy room. Pauline really cared about us and our babies. She was in her mid twenties and had a round face with curly auburn hair. We passed the chapel where we were to pray for our sins to be forgiven; on down more flights of stairs to the basement kitchen.

'This is the entrance you will use in future.'

I belonged below stairs. I thought of the girls who must have scrubbed, cooked and cleaned here over the centuries, little realizing that I would soon be on my knees with scrubbing brush and bucket. The girls' sitting room revealed the whereabouts of the other residents.

'This is Margaret. She has just arrived. I'll leave you to get to know the others.'

I was to become a member of the Bateman Street gang. The sentence was twelve weeks, six before the confinement and six after. Being unmarried and pregnant was a great social leveller. It was a strict regime. We were allocated the menial tasks of cooking and cleaning which were done on a rota basis. I had no experience of either and no desire to learn. Soon I was outside in the cold riddling the ashes from the numerous fire grates into a dustbin by the cellar steps as though I had done it all my life. We all helped and supported each other. There was a resident cook called Peggy of masculine appearance with enormous hands and a tufty beard. She was a woman of few words but considerably more culinary skills than the young mums. Cooking for large numbers is a definite skill; trying to make custard without lumps in a witches' cauldron I found impossible. I was happier on my hands and knees with a bucket, scrubbing brush and bar of Sunlight soap. The joys of the laundry room were to come when my baby was born. Unending piles of nappies, all to be hand-washed in enormous sinks and forced through mangles before being hung out to dry.

After a few sleepless nights, I began to settle into what was rather like a boarding school. We giggled under the blankets and had midnight feasts after lights out. In ages, we ranged from fifteen to twenty-seven; from nurses and secretaries to farm hands and factory workers. There was a distinct gulf between those who were already mothers and the ladies in waiting. Those still pregnant envied the new mums their waistlines. Most girls had been persuaded to have their babies adopted. The home ran in conjunction with a Church of England children's home. I felt it was a baby factory; adoption was the end result. After six weeks the adoptive parents called to collect the baby. Today was Janet's turn. Pain and tears welled up together from her heart. 'I can't watch her go.'

Later Janet was to discover that she was unable to have any more children.

The door closed and the voices died away. The cord was to be severed; the unkindest cut of all. The baby she had borne, and loved for the past six weeks, had to be given away to strangers, glimpsed only through the chink in the curtains. On the morning of that last day, Janet had dressed Jenny in her best clothes and given her a farewell cuddle before Sister Pauline whisked her away.

Dot became my closest friend; we had arrived in the same week and our babies were due within days of each other. She was in her twenties and worked as a telephonist. The father of her child was married. Her mother was a frequent visitor and I obtained permission to go into the town with them. It was good to see how other families accepted the situation.

Although most of us knew how babies were conceived, avoiding pregnancy had not been uppermost in any of our minds. Some girls had fallen victim to the American occupation of East Anglia and the promise of prosperity in a distant land. Mary married her Yank, even though the baby was adopted. I believe he actually visited her at No. 48.

Marion was fifteen. We doubted if she was literate. It was rumoured that she had been the victim of the farm workers in the village. Marion had never seen a bath and we watched in the communal bathroom while Sister Pauline showed her the complexities of hygiene.

Maggie was engaged to a young man who seemed unaware that she was pregnant. She was lucky and put on little weight and continued working as a lifeguard. The baby was the result of a brief liaison with a Canadian Mountie who was appearing at a local festival. He returned to Canada unaware that he had left part of himself behind in England. Maggie continued with her life.

Jackie worked in a meat factory as a sausage twister. During one of our midnight parties, she explained, 'The sausage meat goes in this machine and a tube thing fits on the other. Every so often you grab it and twist it into a sausage.' We all dissolved into hysterics followed by loud hushing, as we feared an invasion by Matron might ensue.

Meals were served in the sitting room around two rectangular tables. We sat knitting baby clothes and listened to Perry Como crooning 'Magic Moments' while Pat Boone warned us about 'April

Love'. Each Sunday we were paraded before the local community at church. We sat in the back pews and giggled our way through the service as the priest waved the incense burners about and we pretended to choke. Locals stared at us as though we were lepers.

Tuesday was clinic day, when we waddled to Mill Road Maternity Hospital. We blended in with the other mothers as we waited to be examined by gorgeous Doctor O'Shaunessy. After one such visit I was admitted, as I was past my due date. The next morning my membranes were ruptured and by lunchtime I was in labour. Just before 7.00 pm on 11 April 1958, my son, David Antony, was born. His father Ian was attending college a few hundred yards away. My mother and sister visited a few days later and the word adoption was mentioned. I realised that this was the reason I had been sent away. My mother was aware of the overwhelming maternal instinct that prevailed on the birth of a child. She had the same feelings for her first grandchild. My sister, Joan, felt the shame I had brought upon the family and would *never* forgive me.

Duties changed on return to No. 48; Dot and I shared a room with our new-borns and were responsible for waking the household and serving early morning tea to the staff at 7.30 am. One day we overslept. The stare from Gorgon Stubbs turned us to stone. 'We lost ourselves in the piles of wet nappies.' Dot seemed resigned to losing little John. I watched through the curtains as more tearful partings took place. Patty had signed her baby's adoption papers and prepared to go back to modelling underwear. News arrived that her baby had failed the medical and was to be sent to a children's home. Patty was heartbroken but had no family to help.

A stubborn determination welled up within me and when I was summoned to Matron's office I prepared to stand my ground and refuse to sign adoption papers.

'Sit down, my dear, your mother's on the 'phone. She has some bad news for you.'

'Margaret, is that you? Your dad's in hospital. He's had a heart attack.'

It was not unexpected as he had suffered from angina for some time, but I realised that it would be considered my fault. Since retiring from the GPO, my father had taken on a small pub called 'The Nutshell'. It was an ale-house without accommodation and required much physical effort. Gladys, my father's sister, told him it would kill him. My mother now had to take responsibility for running the bar while my father was hospitalised, until the brewery could find another tenant. I took the opportunity to offer to come home to help, bringing baby David with me, of course. I left my new-found friends at Bateman Street and prepared for the struggle to keep my love child. I visited Dot at her home in Cambridge and kept in touch with many of the girls for some time. I do not regret my stay at No. 48. The memories will stay with me for the rest of my life.

My father recovered from his heart attack, and became very attached to his grandson and would take him for walks. 'He never did that with you,' my mother commented. My mother doted on him and even my sister seemed to warm to his presence. My father had only a half pension from the Post Office. I would have to find a job. My circumstances would make it difficult but my father could pull a few strings and a few weeks later I was sent to Canterbury to train as a GPO telephonist. My life had come full circle and I had become a prisoner of circumstance. I never consciously noticed my father smirk. I never saw David's father again; he did not appear at the affiliation hearing where he was ordered to pay two pounds a month.

David was an intelligent boy who went on to obtain a Ph.D. in Biochemistry. He was ashamed of being illegitimate and blamed me. I have not seen or corresponded with him, or my two other sons from a disastrous first marriage, since 1992. My sister could not let the past lie and ensured that full details were made known to my daughters-in-law and my present husband. I realize now that adoption would have been the best choice.

# CHAPTER 7

# WORK

# Teaching in a South Wales Valley Comprehensive in the 1960s

~

*Eiluned Davies*

**Eiluned Davies** was born in Llanharan in 1943. She graduated with honours in Welsh from Swansea University in 1966 and completed a teaching diploma in 1967. She married in the same year and started her first job in Aberavon. She lived and worked in Cardiff, Bridgend and Porthcawl before 'emigrating' to Surrey for six years. She completed a second degree in Sociology, which she has since taught at A level in two Cardiff schools. Now a widow with two adult children, she retired to Cyncoed, Cardiff. She has sent several articles to newspapers and magazines, and has had each one published so far. Now she intends to dig out the stories she has been writing over the years and never had the confidence to send off.

In September 1967, I began my adult learning career – not as a pupil, but as a teacher in a God-forgotten comprehensive in a deprived, valley town near Port Talbot. The well publicized research by a local doctor on the dire state of the health and well-being of the impoverished inhabitants of the area should have given me an idea of what I was to expect – but nothing describes better than the experience.

I was fresh from university with a certificate to say I could teach. But this was for real. We wore gowns in the classroom – a symbolic request for respect – and I inherited a chair-leg from the previous teacher in room four to enforce respect, and used it on the very first day to try to achieve silence from one class for long enough for me to at least introduce myself, but badly scarred the front desk-top in the process.

The kids were bussed to school from the remote colliery villages which were clamped to the steep valley sides. That bus ride was the furthest most of them ever travelled. Few had ever been out of the valley. Absenteeism was rife. Only a third of children came in on a Friday.

'Market in Maesteg, see, Miss. Martin's on Dad's china an' I'm on the paper stuff,' explained his twin to the new girl in the chalky gown. 'I'll get you six bog rolls for a shilling, Miss.' I duly paid, in advance, for fear of reprisal.

When my first term's supply of exercise books had diminished to zero, after three weeks of continually replacing 'lost' volumes, I discovered that mams were in the habit of tearing out the 'used' pages to ignite the morning fires. Kids appeared day after day with cleaned out, ever thinning books. There was then no evidence of any classwork activity to prove to my 'probation' lecturer when she came that anyone ever appeared in my lessons. I spent a large proportion of my first term's salary on buying sets of replacement books from Woollies in Port Talbot before I learned the trick of collecting them after each lesson.

I taught Welsh. The top streams were bright – within weeks they were saying '*Dw i'n hoffi frothi coffi*' with a passion – even if they hated it. But with the lower ability bunch we had picture stimulants. This entailed pinning up some ancient pictures on the wooden easel for them to copy and label. For weeks they drew wonderful copies and labelled all the features in each room of the blue and white, smart, detached house in the series. We came to the bathroom picture; they copied it. I asked them to write five sentences about theirs. They chewed their pencils. I hassled them to finish and one girl cried. I went to her desk. 'Please, Miss, we 'aven't got a bathroom,' she sobbed. The lesson stopped. It cost me a huge bag of sherbet bombers to make up to them in the next session and to thank them for my own learning experience.

John sat in the front in that class, when he was in school. He was twelve, thin, pale, strained and towered over me. Robert, with a severe curvature of the spine, shared the old, two-seater desk. They slid and bumped each other, joked and giggled when Robert's hard, hunched back hit John's bony jaw. I reprimanded them in Welsh.

'That's "shut your gob", John,' translated Robert, correctly.

Monday, first lesson, one week, saw the book distribution ceremony.

'Martin?'

'Not here, Miss.'

'Robert?'

'By here, Miss.'

'John?'

'Dead, Miss.'

'Don't be naughty, Robert,' I rebuked, but his best mate had indeed suffered a fatal heart attack at the weekend, 'down his gran's house'. Death was part of their lives in that valley. I'll remember that lesson for *another* thirty years and the stone tone of Robert's two word response.

Mrs Price was the 'Remmy' teacher, when *she* was in school. Her charges were remedial in all aspects of sixties life. Friday was to be a lesson for the girls in how to bathe. The school had installed a bath in her department. She gave instruction lessons on how, when, how often and why one should bathe. She sent home a list of requirements for the lesson. They were to bring soap, a towel and talcum powder as an optional extra. On Friday it was Mrs Price who learned that most had never stripped naked before and that she should have explained the procedure *before* they got into the water, having taken off only their shoes and socks. It was 'dirty Diane' who taught Mrs Price to be more explicit in explaining the use of talcum powder on a *dry* body and that it was dispensed through the *small* apertures in the lid, not the large one. Mrs Price was not seen then for two months. She took full advantage of her sick leave allocation every term. She never did complete the hair care and manicure lessons and they missed out on the Food and Diet course. So their children's children will still have chip buttie breakfasts and smoke suppers, and still be coughing.

The doctor author died of overwork and in the middle of a third book on his research in the community. I wonder if anyone acted on it? I wonder too if all the children in the school today have seen the sea?

# Teaching in a Welsh Medium School

~

*Heulwen Williams*

**Heulwen Williams** was born in Rhymney in 1922. She trained as a teacher at Swansea Training College during the war before teaching in various primary schools in Shropshire. She became involved in the movement to establish a Welsh medium school in Rhymney in the early 1950s, later taught at the school, and was Head teacher from 1972 to 1984. She still lives in Rhymney with her husband and continues to be active in the local community. She has previously contributed to *Struggle or Starve* (Honno).

During the course of my teaching career I taught in many schools – in Wellington, Shropshire (1942-4), Cwmsyfiog in the Rhymney Valley (1944-7) and in Willesden, London (1947-9). In 1949, I married and returned to my hometown of Rhymney and once again worked for Monmouthshire Education Authority, teaching in a number of the valley's schools – Cwm, Phillipstown and Elliot Town in New Tredegar. Of course, all these schools in which I taught were English medium schools. But once I returned home, I became involved in the Welsh medium education movement. I taught large numbers of children through the medium of Welsh on a Saturday morning at the Upper Rhymney Infants School between 1950 and 1955. I did this as a volunteer teacher, along with other like-minded people who all gave their time without payment.

The Welsh language means a great deal to me. I was brought up in a Welsh speaking home and I attended a Welsh chapel; even when I was working in London, I attended the Welsh chapel in Radnor Walk, and met up with other young Welsh speakers. Once I was back in Rhymney, it was the minister of our chapel, the Reverend Rhys Bowen, who was himself a dedicated advocate of Welsh medium education, who got me involved in the movement and who was responsible for my becoming a volunteer Saturday teacher.

During the week, I taught my children in the English medium

schools Welsh songs and dances and switched on the BBC's plays and lessons for them. An inspector who came to one of the schools was so enthusiastic about my work that he returned and brought me Welsh children's books. They were few and far between at that time. The Saturday morning school was also inspected regularly. The inspector, Mr Archie Lush, reported back to the Monmouthshire Education Authority and this must have contributed to the authority's momentous decision to establish the first Welsh medium school in this border county. It was a small class, because many of the children who had been in the voluntary school had now gone to local English medium schools, due to their age, but it was a significant step forward and a very exciting development for those of us who had worked hard to campaign for it. It started in the Middle Rhymney Infants School in the autumn of 1955 – just in time for my daughter, who was born in December of that year.

My life changed somewhat when I became a mother. I was very fortunate; I had my own mother and father at hand, my sister with her family nearby, my mother-in-law and many friends. It was a very happy family life together for us all. We had outings in our first family Austin 7 on Saturdays, and Moreia chapel on Sundays, of course, with gymanfas and eisteddfodau. I also belonged to a local drama group and attended evening art classes.

At the time, many women gave up their careers completely upon marriage and married women were not allowed to teach until the war. Very few women with children were fulltime teachers. However, after some years, the local head teachers were short staffed in schools and I decided to do some occasional teaching, while my parents and my mother-in-law would take over the care of my daughter – and, of course, I had the support of my husband.

In the meantime, we moved house, and when my son was born in 1961 and my daughter had started at the Welsh school (Ysgol Gymraeg Rhymni) I was a very busy parent of the school and became secretary of the Parents' Association. We held our meetings in Dallanegras, the local Italian café, in a little back room. We organised events for raising money so that we had funds. We knew we had to support the school financially and pay for the Welsh Nursery School and its teacher, Mrs Jones. Mrs Jones and her husband used to light the fire in the chapel vestry where the Nursery

School was held, as well as cleaning it. Again, I worked locally thanks to my wonderful parents and mother-in-law and, of course, my husband, who supported all I wanted to do. Some of my occasional work was in Ysgol Gymraeg Rhymni, and when a post became vacant in 1965, I was made permanent and my son was able to come with me.

The school was growing thanks to English speaking parents who wanted their children to have a bilingual education. I had a very large class with all the infants in a large hall, with the Head's little office in one corner, and all and sundry passed through while my children were busy painting and playing – sand, building blocks, educational toys, in the book corner, and so on. But I was very happy as I had worked in a big hall before in my old school in Gibbon's Road in London – a hall which we shared with the senior school because of the bombing. I played the piano for the whole school for morning service, singing and music and movement. We were delighted that our children were being educated bilingually. New Welsh books arrived in the school. Visitors came to see us – after all, we were the only Welsh school in the county of Monmouthshire. Students came to us to do their training from other parts of Wales.

We met up with the other Welsh schools in the valley, Senghen-nydd, and later, Bargoed, established by the Glamorganshire Education Authority, at the local Urdd Eisteddfod. We also travelled to other parts of Wales to the National Eisteddfodau. We worked hard to raise funds to pay for the buses and we were one big family setting off: parents with their babies, grandparents and supporters. It was very much like our Sunday school trips to the seaside. One time, we were going up to Rhyl and when we got to the hotel we found that we had been booked in for the wrong week. The school children were all right. But what could we do? Anyway, the hotel said they would push us in but that we would have to share rooms. Well, what a to do! The mothers had brought their finery to dress up, but what a hope. At bedtime, a group of mothers in their curlers came dashing down to tell me that their room had a hole in the ceiling and they could see the sky. There wasn't much sleep that night. The talking and laughing went on for hours. The Eisteddfod and all its attractions and excitement made up for the fuss. Also, the children had good adjudications. Of course, they didn't reach the stage.

Every Eisteddfod trip had its own adventure. In Aberystwyth in 1969, the rain was pouring into the marquee. The children solved it by paddling in their socks while the adults had plastic bags over their shoes, the town having sold out of wellingtons. Some people even had their umbrellas up inside the marquee. On another occasion we were all in the coach ready to go home when one of our girls had to be called for over the tannoy. She, if you please, was washing her socks in the toilet because they were dirty and she would have a row from her mammy. She had spent all her money on decorations for her hair. On arriving back in Rhymney we had to knock her mother up, as she had gone to bed – she had a lodger there, working on the open cast.

Then, when we went to Llanelwedd, we were competing in the folk dance competition. It was very important that we had the whole party of children who had been taught by Mrs Jessie Williams, a well-known folk dancing teacher. But when the bus called for one of the boys, he was still in bed. I had to help him get dressed and we gave him his breakfast on the coach. We could not compete without him and would not be able to fail Jessie. It was with Jessie and the folk dancing team that we *did* get to the stage and won second prize. Jessie said that if the children hadn't gone to compete in the netball competition we would have come first! She didn't like coming second.

Our gymanfas, held for all the local Welsh schools, were the highlight of the year. A committee selected the folk songs and hymns for us to learn and we all joined together in one of our many large chapels. When the gymanfa came to Rhymney, I had to prepare the children for readings and recitations from the Bible for the beginning of the gymanfa. We had the famous conductor of the Treorchy Male Voice Choir, Glynne Jones, for ours. The children loved to sing, and it was a joyous experience. We also had twmpath dances for the parents, when we had a 'caller' to give us instructions and a lively band. This was a good family affair with plenty of food made by the parents.

Every summer we were visited by the Bristol School of English. The head, John Neuman, was a friend of my brother. He brought us students from different parts of the world. They were delightful. They loved to hear the children perform in the Welsh language. In their turn, they sang in their own languages too. The parents provided the food; they gave them a real Welsh welcome. The farewells were indeed very fond and tearful ones. It all started with John bringing two Russian students to my parents' house on a Sunday in the 1950s. Mam was flabbergasted, but luckily had a dish of beetroot cut up for tea, and plenty of bread and cheese, of course. We had to go to the evening service in the chapel, but obliged them before we went by singing, *Hen Wlad fy Nhadau*, the Welsh national anthem. As the years went by, the number of students grew until they came every year to our home in a large coach. The neighbours in the street helped and we had everybody sitting on the floor or on the stairs while myself and my daughter entertained them with Welsh songs. Eventually, it was transferred to the vestry of our chapel and the schoolchildren and their parents took over. The children loved it.

The first Welsh medium secondary school in South Wales, Ysgol Gyfun Rhydfelen, opened in 1962. Until then, our children had no choice but to go from us to local English medium secondary schools. Once Rhydfelen opened, we had to find a way of paying the transport of the children from Rhymney to Pontypridd. We applied to Monmouthshire, but while we were waiting, after an appeal in the Welsh newspapers, we received some cheques towards the cost of paying for a car – mostly from the Glyndwr Fund which was in existence at that time, and whose meetings for Welsh parents I attended in Pontypridd. Although the parents paid towards the cost at the outset, we knew that we had to press for the cost of transport as there would be more pupils travelling the following year. After much lobbying and having managed to gain the support of the councillors, we were eventually granted the transport by the Monmouthshire Authority.

The Rhydfelen link became very important to us. When I became Head of the Welsh school in 1972, I attended meetings and courses with other head teachers, and there was a strong Parent and Staff Association too. We performed oratorios in the chapels under the direction of Mrs Lily Richards. Music was also very much part of our home life. We loved all the early Welsh pop records as well as the classical ones. Our family life was a very happy one.

I had a very satisfying teaching career; the classroom with the children seemed to be my second home. But of course, my involve-ment with the Welsh medium education movement in Rhymney was very close to my heart. I became passionate towards this cause, because of my own family upbringing and because we had succeeded in bringing up our children bilingually. I wanted other children to have the same opportunity. My deep appreciation is due to my predecessor and successor and to all teachers, parents and sup-porters, including my family, who made such a venture possible and who had such faith in its success.

## Nurses Move Fast but do not Run

~

*Brenda Curtis*

**Brenda Curtis** was born in 1934 in Watford, Hertfordshire and trained as a nurse and midwife in London. She has since gained an Open University degree in Social Science and is presently studying English at Aberystwyth University. She married in 1959, had three children and is still arguing with the same husband. She enjoys writing short stories and poems and this is her first published piece.

I had studied the prospectus for a whole impatient year and now, at last, here I was walking through the Henry VIII gatehouse into the quadrangle. A fountain splashed gently and spring sunlight filtered through six giant plane trees. Elegant Georgian buildings flanked the square and a clock on the George V block chimed the hour. From my reading I knew this to be an Augustinian foundation established in 1123 by a monk called Rahere, with paintings by Hogarth and Sir Joshua Reynolds hanging in the great hall. St. Bartholemew's Hospital, London, one of the oldest hospitals in the world, was reformed in 1546 by Henry VIII who granted a Royal Charter that charged nursing sisters to avoid 'scolding and drunk-enness' and to keep the poor 'sweet and clean'.

In 1953, at the age of eighteen, I was embarking on a four-year nurse training course and had just completed ten weeks in a preliminary training school at a country house in Hertfordshire. With forty-four other young women, I had been introduced to the theory and practice of nursing and such mysteries as hygiene, bandaging, Sick Room Cookery, Household Duties and Ethics with Nursing Etiquette, as well as human biology and chemistry.

The first lesson was how to wear the uniform: a mid-calf length, blue and white striped dress made of heavy cotton, a separate starched white collar, a full length white starched wrap-around apron with bib, a stiff blue and white striped buckram belt, thick black stockings (tights were not yet available) and regulation black leather lace-up Oxford shoes. The cap, that icon of nursing history, was required to cover as much hair as possible. The distinctive Barts bonnet, a miracle of origami, took several weeks of practice to perfect and was pleated so that two 'duck tails' turned up at the back and shame on anyone whose tails drooped. The final glory was an enveloping navy blue, scarlet lined woollen cape, with straps that crossed over the chest.

And so commenced the attempt to transform forty-five individuals into a collective, highly skilled professional body of women through a regime of strict discipline and obedience. Every day we went to the classroom in full uniform to receive instruction from sister tutors, also in uniform, who wore long sleeved, royal blue dresses and white starched organza caps that floated out behind like wind socks.

The second instruction was that we must always wear a deodorant. We were told that we would be doing hard physical work and patients would not appreciate smelly nurses. Make-up and jewellery must not be worn and we were commanded never to run. Nurses move fast but do not run. Every day we were given daily household duties. One day I was singing as I cleaned a bath and a Sister put her head round the door, telling me not to sing while I worked as it might disturb the patients. We were taught how to prepare a meal for an invalid, how to coddle eggs, make junket, cut crusts off thinly sliced bread and lay a tempting tray. Carrying the tray, we had to practise opening a door and closing it behind us without spilling anything.

We delved into the complexities of making a bed with somebody in it, our colleagues acting as surrogate patients. Many hours were spent bandaging each other, learning the intricacies of such specialties as 'hip spikers' and other specific patterns that I have long forgotten, cotton bandages having been long supplanted by modern materials and techniques. The medical use of leeches remained on the syllabus and two fat specimens lived in a jar in the practice room. We were scrupulously addressed as 'Nurse' followed by surname and tended to follow this tradition until personal friendships blossomed. My working class background and local day girls' grammar school in Watford seemed a world away from the people I was now getting to know and my life opened up to a kaleidoscope of unimagined influences.

Nurse training in the 1950s was based on military and medical models and not only were we discouraged from questioning authority, we were trained positively not to. In class, tutors would frequently interrupt a lesson to pose the rhetorical question, 'And who is the most important person in the hospital?' We were supposed to chorus, 'The patient,' but we knew the real answer was, 'The consultant.' It would be at least another decade before nurses started to devise and conduct their own quantitative and qualitative research methods and evolve independent professional models of nursing care.

Now I had come to London to start work on the wards with real live patients. A porter directed me to the Nurses' Home in a corner of the quadrangle and I found my room on the third floor. It was furnished with a small rug on dark brown linoleum, a bed, a locker, a built-in dark wood wardrobe, a desk with one hard chair, a bookshelf and a washbasin with mirror above. A narrow window opened onto a side street, with a view through bombed buildings across flattened acres of the blitzed City of London. In my suitcase I had a battery radio, a gift from my parents, and from an aunt a heavy biography of Florence Nightingale. I put the radio on the locker and the book on the shelf above the desk. What more could I want? I was in heaven. My private place, a retreat in which to think, read, study, sleep and often, it transpired, cry myself to sleep. The radio was a great solace but I don't think I ever read to the end of the biography. On the ground floor there was a large comfortable sitting room and a smaller, more private one with a grand piano that I would enjoy playing. Television was not yet in universal domestic use in Britain although sets were placed in every ward for the coronation of Queen Elizabeth II in June 1953.

Meals were taken in the large dining room and food was good and plentiful. Britain was still struggling with post-war shortages and during our first year we were allocated individual weekly rations of butter and sugar which we carried around in jars in our baskets.

As a first year student I worked a forty-nine hour week and received a 'training allowance' of £200 per year less national insurance and superannuation. Residence was compulsory, with a further £100 deducted for board and lodging. Duty started at 7.30 am and finished at 8 pm divided into split shifts, with three or four hours off duty during the day and one evening off before a rest day. Twice a month, as a treat on a day off, it was possible to request breakfast in bed, which a maid would bring to our room, but it was more fun to go to the dining room, even if late, where friends might be met or made and outings arranged. We were free to go out in the evenings after duty, but we had to sign back in at the Porter's Lodge by 10.30 pm. Late passes were allowed twice a week when we had to return by the Cinderella hour of midnight.

My first ward was male surgical and my first challenge was to give a blanket bath. I remember worrying about which flannel I had used for the patient's face and which for his 'privates', as his genital region was euphemistically called. There was a complicated procedure with sheets, worthy of a magician's sleight of hand, whereby I had to wash every part of his body without ever leaving him exposed. Meal times in the ward were another ritual. Sister would dish up the appropriate selection and quantity of whatever the kitchens had sent and we would watch as she deliberated on which ailing old man would get a bottle of milk stout on his tray. The National Health Service had only been in operation since 1948 and old, more generous ways persisted.

It wasn't long before it was my turn to escort patients to and from the operating theatre. It took a while to get used to the terrifying hiatus before an unconscious patient coughed and successfully spat out the airway. On operating days it was difficult to obey the 'no run' rule as I took my turn escorting patients to and from theatre at the same time as giving premedications *and* keeping an eye on intravenous drips. And *then* I might be admonished for having too much hair showing!

We were reprimanded if we succumbed to exchanging personal chatter with a colleague over a patient, for example, while making their bed. This was a hard lesson to learn because we were young and eager for life, yet we shared many moments of laughter with our patients. One of the last duties of the day was for the lowest ranking student nurse to accompany Sister to the 'museum'. This was a glass cupboard ventilated through an outside wall where urine specimens and samples of faeces were stored for daily inspection. It was the student's job then to dispose of them.

Days when consultants did their 'rounds' entailed a frantic race to finish dressings and make beds before the great man made an entry, followed by his retinue. Just before 10 am, Sister would cast an eagle eye down the rows of beds in the long Nightingale ward to check that each counterpane was correctly mitred and that all the bed wheels were turned parallel to the bed end and facing inwards. We would often go off duty exhausted but exhilarated and occasionally saddened. Some Sisters bullied us, others treated us with kindness, humour and example but they were all fiercely dedicated women, devoted to their job and to Barts.

We worked hard but also played hard and often went out after finishing duty in the evening. I loved dancing and my favourite was the quickstep, but I found the custom of having to wait for a man to ask me to dance very frustrating. However, around 1954, Bill Haley and his Comets burst on the scene and everybody began to dance, all over the place, partner or no partner. You may be wondering, what about sex? Well, I wondered, too. The contraceptive pill was over a decade away and Family Planning Clinics were just that, for women with families. Sex was dangerous and no way was I going to jeopardize my career. Some girls took risks, but it would not have occurred to me at that time to carry a 'french letter', even if they had been widely available.

I qualified as a State Registered Nurse in 1956 and after a further year, collected the coveted Barts certificate and silver badge with its black and white enamelled crest. After finishing my final shift of duty, I went straight out to a jeweller and had my ears pierced.

# Early Work

~

*Jude Brigley*

**Jude Brigley** (née Roach) was born, brought up and educated in Maesteg. She is Head of English and Media Studies at Cardiff High School and is Chief Examiner for A level Media Studies. She has written on education and edited two poetry books. Teaching remains her vocation and her passion, although she hopes to write more in the next track of her life.

When I was growing up in Maesteg, I liked making family trees and one of the things I liked to list was occupations. It interested me to know that my great, great grandfather had been a gamekeeper on the Picton estate in Pembrokeshire and that some of my ancestors had come over from Ireland to work on the roads. Most interesting of all were the stories about the women of the family who had worked in Laviers' Stores, a 'posh' shop for that era, which in the twenties charged families for training girls like my Auntie Nan in book-keeping.

Throughout the fifties, my mother worked in Leslies' Stores, the old Laviers, which had been taken over and developed as a general store selling everything from toys to furniture. It had a glamour for me because of its history and my mother was full of stories about its day-to-day life. She provided a sort of docu-soap on shop life. Like the woman who came in and asked for pantses and knickerses without catching the irony of my mother's, 'What size pantses and knickerses would you like?' Or my mother telling young girls in the store that if you had had sex then tiny hairs grew on your palms and then sitting back and watching them peep. Or closing the shop one Christmas because everyone else had drunk too much and had one by one retreated to the back room. My mother made the world of work exciting, like a video replayed each night. Her counter was her domain and everything was ship-shape and the stock listed in charts.

On Saturday evenings, I would wait on the corner of Talbot Street, happy to see her returning from work, flushed, it seemed to me, with the excitement of the commercial world. I waited, especially close to Christmas, passing the time by looking in the chemist's window at pretty bottles and wrappings and wishing I could buy them for her. I did odd jobs for people in the neighbourhood, running errands to the shops. Running to the Home and Colonial for half a pound of butter for Mrs Price or as far as the Star or Maypole for Mrs Davies' special tea brand. And each time I did, there was a shiny silver coin to show for it and soon there was enough money for a Christmas present from the chemist's, such as apple blossom perfume or talcum powder or soap.

Then my mother switched jobs, working only at weekends on the indoor market stall but leaving me full of wonder and with a life-time obsession with department stores.

From the age of fourteen, I worked in Maesteg Market helping my mother on the dairy produce stall. It made me feel important but I hated handling the meat. Early Friday morning, my brother and I would help my mother to unpack the van from Carmarthen. Carmarthen – the very name conjured up rolling green fields and dairy cattle eating lush grass under blue skies. There were two products which I particularly disliked: one was brawn and the other the trays of faggots. The peas had been soaked over night and gave off an unmistakeable smell like a pea gas.

I was extremely proud of my mother as she stood behind her immaculately organised counter. Everyone seemed to know her and her pleasant talk and jokes brought many people to the stall. I could not match her banter. On summer days, the inside market seemed like a prison and I longed to be reading or just walking with my friends. My mother did not understand me. Sweet to her was the banter and chatter of the stall and when we finally got home, she would entertain the family with the stories she had picked up that day, while I sat in sulky silence. Worst of all was the repacking of greasy, empty trays when my brother would reappear to get rid of the rubbish. However, at the end of the day, was a pound from Sid Thomas, which seemed like a lot of money and had at least been earned. I did not like the world of work.

Later, as a lay preacher I was given the same amount for preaching a sermon. A teenage speaker of what now seem platitudes, this work was more congenial. Indeed, it did not seem like work, for it was pleasant to me to stand amongst the highly polished wood of the chapels giving my thoughts, which were usually extempore. It was not hard to speak aloud and soon I was double-booked morning and evening. I did not do it for the money, but it was a job of sorts for, as the old deacon told me, 'a workman is worthy of his hire.' I believed that to be true and wished for a way to use those skills for a living. I toyed with the church idea but could not hold on to the faith. People who I admired did jobs which were a vocation, not just payment. Gareth Daniel was our preacher and his sermons often packed the chapel. I still remember him talking of the writing on the wall: I almost saw it. Word people attracted me, which was why I liked the chapel, the school, the youth club; places where work meant using your words carefully, skilfully. It was then that I wished I was a writer and I created a street newspaper. I did not do it for money but it was a kind of job and one which was a labour of love as I banged it out on my old typewriter and posted it through doors.

Later, it was back to the market as my mother, with her influence, got me a job working for Peacocks. In my sixties student way, I used to come home and claim it was soul destroying and that I spat on money. It is true I was bored of being told that there was only one way to fold pants, but I found that there were ways to make it more congenial, by using the imagination. I used to play games, such as pretending that I was laying out goods for refugees or that these were stores at the time of war. Such games pass the time. When the manager went to lunch, I made tea for all of the staff on the grounds we were entitled to a tea break. They thought me pushy, especially when I suggested having a union. They did not have the confidence. However, I fitted in well with them all, made them laugh and they thought me a daredevil. They were long summers, which taught me the importance of a wage packet.

If I thought that shop work was tedious, I had not lived until I got the call from the dole office to go to Revlon of New York, Paris and Maesteg. The worst aspect for me sounds ridiculous now – it was wearing a cap. As a cool, hippy chick, the cap was an embarrassing curse. Clocking in was another odd idea, which made me feel like a trapped thing. The factory was extremely clean and sterile. To me, who had been a fumbler from birth, it was a terrifying experience at first. It was as if my brain had stopped functioning and everything

I was good at was stripped away and I became a careless, useless person incapable of the simplest task.

This was brought home to me when a woman demonstrated to us, in a careless, easy gesture, how to make a box. To me it was like magic and I struggled to follow. 'Stealing is wrong,' she told us new girls. 'Thieves will be caught. You would never catch me stealing – well maybe the odd lipstick.' We watched her with open admiration as even her cap looked good on her and Revlon's finest technology was applied to her facial features. I did not last long in her section. I was moved to another line where I was told, 'The eye shadow box will come down the line. You drop in the refills and a piece of foam, close the box.' My worried face must have told a story. 'You can always take a few boxes off,' she added.

An hour later the sweat dripped off my back and boxes were piled around me. I could not do the simple job to save my life. The line had to be stopped. I felt like a child who cannot learn tables or whose spelling is deviant. I have never felt such a disaster. I was moved after that to the stores. Some people said it was because my auntie was manager of the shop. I don't know. I was much happier there, making up orders for shops like David Evans and John Lewis. That captured my imagination as I thought of the box reaching the store and being opened and the contents displayed. And who would buy the fine shiny wares? In the stores there was joviality. There were men who teased students about sexual shenanigans at college and we spun them plenty of stories. In the stores, there was no moving belt, just filling up orders in the leisurely fashion our leader showed us. Soon I was clocking in, taking long toilet breaks and, when the whistle blew, throwing everything down wherever it lay and getting the hell out of there. No working when time was the master.

Work taught me what I couldn't and what I had no intention of doing. The money earned in such jobs was valued much more than my salary these days. Mostly, I liked the people I met and I understood their frustrations. Little things seemed big and boredom made me feel mischievous. I was a prankster in all my jobs because humour was one of the few ways available for coping. Summers were always long then and I often think of those who are probably doing that same grind to this day.

# CHAPTER 8

# THE
# SWINGING SIXTIES

# Sleeping with the Enemy

~

*Molly Parkin*

**Molly Parkin** (née Thomas) was born in 1932 in Pontycymer, Garw Valley, south Wales. After Art College, she worked as a teacher, artist, author, journalist (Fashion Editor of *Nova*, *Harpers & Queen* and *The Sunday Times*; agony aunt for *TV Quick*), broadcaster and TV personality. She has had a raffish romantic career with two ex-husbands, nine ex-fiancés and a galaxy of glorious lovers, plus two daughters, three stepsons and four grandchildren. This has been rewarding research for her ten novels, one volume of verse, one cookery book, one compilation of journalism and one autobiography (so far!). She has recently returned to her first obsession – painting. Molly's sister, Sally Gough, writes about her life on page 162.

My life exploded in the sixties. It was as if I had been on strangulated hold until then, trying to subdue my soaring spirit to the hushed confines of the Welsh chapel, gratifying a devout grandmother to whom I was devoted. Embracing strict conventions espoused by my highly-strung mother and the academic impositions of two orthodox aunties, the headmistress and the schoolteacher, I was in thrall to their collective female power; always the people pleaser and failing miserably.

My older, only sister fitted their bill perfectly throughout our childhood. The stark contrast in our school reports summed it all up. She was the well-behaved little lady, the pleasant and friendly pupil. Mine carried the terse comment, 'a disruptive influence'. Much of my scholastic career was spent in the school corridor, banned from class for general bad behaviour. It was to prove, however, a fertile preparation for the painter and writer to be, left alone for long hours with that most inspirational companion, my own imagination. I came effortlessly top in English Composition and Art.

We laugh now about how different we were as children, Sally and I, but we always shared the same sense of humour. Though resentment of this universal approval for my perfect sister simmered in me for years and gave me the role model to kick against, she says she envied my naughtiness, my nerve in questioning everything and answering back, and generally being an uninhibited, exuberant pain-up-the-arse.

But the sixties gave me the opportunity to mix with kindred spirits, all those other pain-up-arses who had never quite fitted into their families. Round pegs being forced to fit into square holes, now leaping from conformity with blood-curdling relish. At last we could be ourselves and let our creativity rip, full strength.

I'd just come out of the English upper-class marriage, which had always been my mother's ambition for me. My father's too, but he died before enjoying the exalted circles which they'd both aspired to and which my smart marriage would provide. They willed with all their might that I should 'better myself'. A heavy burden. But their marital plans for my future bore confusing messages for a child reared between the coal-mining Garw Valley of industrial south Wales and the seedier suburbs of London.

In both places the upper classes, so-called moneyed swankers and wankers, lived on another planet far beyond us lesser mortals. Though my parents voted Liberal because of Lloyd George being Welsh, we were Socialists, who saw to each other. All toffs were Tories, who looked out for themselves. We were Labour, who believed in progress and opportunities for all. They were Conservatives, opposed to change, dedicated to preserving the status quo. They were Ancient. We were Modern. They were the enemy.

And in south Wales, in Pontycymer, which was always my most favourite place in the world (and remains so) the rich and privileged meant the English and they really were the enemy, not just the class enemy, but the actual enemy, a tribal thing to do with race. It boiled down to a question of national identity. We had fought them in battle and lost, for God's sake! They had stolen our land and destroyed our language. They had driven us to the hills and underground to hack out a living in the coalfields. They had forced us to crouch like animals for our daily bread. And the bitterness and the bile at the very thought of the English was something apart. This was what united all Celts. We were told that when we emerged from the womb in Wales, back in the 1930s, where racism ran rife and the English were reviled as no other race, save for the Germans during the war.

So why would my parents want to elevate me to their midst for the sake of their own social pretensions, sacrifice me to the enemy? And not just my parents, my granny too. When I answered, using my mother-tongue, in this Welsh-speaking household, she was the one who reprimanded me, 'Speak in English, *bach*. You are the one going to England for us, to find the fame and the fortune, isn't it.'

Why couldn't I be allowed to stay in Pontycymer with my granny in chapel and my *Tadcu* (Welsh for grandfather) Noyle, tending his roses? And my *Tadcu* Thomas, Sam the Post, tramping the mountains and sucking on toffees and seeing to the world. And sitting by the fire toasting bread on a wire fork with my other aunties, not the headmistress or the schoolteacher, but my favourite ones, Auntie Eunice and Emily, school cleaners, who kept chickens for boiled eggs to go with the toast. And their sister two doors away, Auntie Maggie, who knitted and had three different kinds of Co-op cake on the table for breakfast – jam sponge, ginger and iced fairy with silver balls. I loved it up in the valley. I never wanted to leave.

My background has been described as Welsh working class, and we did all have outside lavvies at the top of the garden, if that proves anything. I'm proud to claim it all as my own, but the facts are more complicated than that. Like most valley families, mine is all of a mixture. We boast teachers, preachers and miners. I can add commerce because of Auntie Bess, Wool shop, and Auntie Lizzie, Cats, who sold kittens. My cousin Miriam, who died in childbirth barely an adult, had gone to England as a downstairs scullery maid, which was thought a step up. My paternal grandfather described himself as a civil servant: he was Sam the Post. When asked in interviews if I descend from a literary line, I answer truthfully that my grandfather was a man of letters.

But my own father, son of Sam, was a frustrated writer and painter, and that is the truth. I have actually led the life that he had envisaged for himself. It didn't make things easy between us and there had always been tension: ours was a deeply unhealthy relationship. Beatings to break my spirit. Fondlings to tie me to him. Secrets which had to be kept from my mother . . .

But he couldn't break my spirit, nor obliterate my creativity. He watched me write and paint effortlessly, win a five-year scholarship to Art School and whilst there the coveted travelling scholarships which would take me on a tour of Italy: the Sistine Chapel, the canals of Venice, Michelangelo's statue of David, the frescoed murals of Giotto. He listened morosely and took refuge in the pub. Most parents are proud of their children's achievements, but not always. Not if they've ached for the same themselves and been denied the chances. He claimed that writers and painters, like musicians and poets, can cross any class barrier, that social opportunities would never be denied them, that they transcend forbidden circles and choose their own company. Creativity brings its own rewards.

Now, in the wisdom of age, my heart goes out to my dead father.

Each fresh sketch of mine as a child, each scribbled line as a teenager, later (mercifully, death spared him this) my published novels, poetry and journalism and public exhibition of paintings, would have been as salt to the wound. I wonder how many such blocked artists must endure this pain from their children, trapped as they are in their own adult years of abject conformity, denied the glorious release of self-expression and never succeeding in being true to themselves. I would have been like that if I hadn't broken free. If the sixties hadn't happened for me.

I recently watched a television documentary on the late Anthony Eden, former Conservative Prime Minister, and I finally had a true glimpse of what my mother wanted for me. Urbane, sophisticated, suave, as handsome as a god, beautifully shod (shoes were always important to my mother), fanatically well-groomed, with exquisite nails. He was the kind of man she felt she should have married. He must have been what she glimpsed as a young girl, sent away to boarding school from Pontycymer (unusual then) by my grandmother. For my grandmother had begun life in a real Welsh Castle, Craig-y-nos Castle in Abercrave, and had been part of the good life and inherited wealth. Her family had owned the surrounding hills as far as the eye could see, only for my male forebear to lose it all through alcohol and gambling. She remembered waking up on the next dawn in the humblest dwelling on the edge of the estate no longer theirs. The shame and humiliation never left her.

Her mother married three times and ended up in the Garw Valley, with my grandmother and her four sisters. They all married, my granny to my grandfather, who was known as John the Bump because his mordant sense of humour raised a laugh when he lowered the cage of miners down into the pit, bumping them on the final stage. He earned a top wage for that position of responsibility, but had worked from the age of ten in the mines for it.

My granny, with the zeal of lost-land-owning in her blood, scrimped and saved to buy up most of her street of miners' cottages. When pit catastrophes came or strikes with no pay, she was able to tell the tenants not to worry about the rent. She put her religious faith into acts of kindness. She is an example of generosity to me still, long after her life is over, and she was a shining beacon in the valley.

My mother was the only one to survive of her twelve children. In one month alone she lost three babies under the age of six. So she saved enough money to send my mother away to school, away from the rain-soaked valley where TB was rife, to the Vale of Glamorgan, where the climate is less harsh. There my mother mixed with the cream of society, gazed at the fathers and grandfathers who arrived at the end of term to whisk their daughters away to luxuriant mansions, whilst she went back home for the holidays in Pontycymer. Some contrast. The charming gentlemen must have fanned a fascination for the likes of Anthony Eden, a predilection which ruled the rest of her life. And mine.

Meanwhile, my father was storing up similar malcontent for himself. Having successfully lied his way into obtaining a commission in the Royal Flying Corps, the equivalent of the Airforce then, he adapted easily to the life of a young officer. The very best years of his life, he always claimed. He'd sworn he was of age, though he was only fourteen, and that he was as a skilled horseman as if a country boy. The only ponies he'd ridden had been the wild ones at the top of the mountain, hanging on for grim life, bareback. But his charm would always get him through and the twinkle in his eye. And the way he looked just like Cary Grant with a dimple in his chin – and this was when Cary Grant was still Archie Leach in mid-England, before Hollywood got to him. My father invented the mould.

So, after school at Miss Culverwell's Academy for Young Ladies in Cowbridge, my mother went back home to become the chapel organist in Tabernacle, Meadow Street, Pontycymer, with nothing to look forward to. And after the good life of a young officer, with the fine taste of fiery liquor still on his tongue, and smooth leather brogues caressing his toes, my father returned to Park Street, over-looking the tennis courts in Pontycymer. His cousin invested his service annuity funds training to become a doctor in Cardiff. My father spent his cash on solitary boozing up the mountain, unsuc-cessfully trying to write poetry. Then descending to boast of the good times. There was nothing else to look forward to. My parents were perfect for each other. Their circumstances had designed it to be so. They fell in love and were wed from an aunt's house up in Watford. From there they fled to London, where they really believed that the streets were paved with gold. They were a mirror image of each other's dreams and fears and frustrations. They planted their mutual ambition in me.

My own marriage was a whirlwind affair, following closely upon the death of my father. I was unhinged by this loss and wasn't thinking straight when I met my future husband. My mother was desperate for a male in the family to replace her husband, even if it meant the man would be mine and not hers. She beseeched me to follow the rules laid out for me in earlier years. That he should be a public schoolboy. That his university should be only the very best, either Oxford or Cambridge. That he would have been a com-missioned officer whilst doing his National Service (an obligatory two year stint in the Armed Forces for all eighteen year olds then).

My first husband supplied all the requirements. But I must add that we did fall passionately in love. Now, almost fifty years later, the bitterness of divorce long forgotten, I have to admit that I see why I fell for him. We are friendly. We meet at grandchildren's events and sometimes in the Chelsea Arts Club, to which we both belong. We have a genuine fondness for each other and a mutual respect, and we still laugh at the same things. He has been a warm and loving father; his daughters adore him.

He is English, very, and when I met him he voted Conservative. We quarrelled about this, but I married him anyway. He was exactly what my mother had ordered. My father would have genuflected at his largesse and the note of natural command, and writhed with pleasure at his cultured voice. I know he would. I did myself. He was blond, with blue eyes and a chiselled, cherubic mouth. He loved classical music and good literature, and fine wines and expensive tweed and polished shoes, and money and breeding and friends with vast estates and titles, and castles in Scotland. And this is how and where we spent our time together. We went to the continent before the masses did. And stayed in Manhattan, the first of our lot to do so. We honeymooned in Paris and cruised the South of France. Breakfast in Nice, supper in Cannes, and a trip over to St Tropez for a glimpse of Brigitte Bardot, big at that time, the sex-goddess of the world.

We lived in the very centre of Chelsea, off the King's Road, with our two delicious daughters, half English of course, who attended private schools (the greatest anathema to me, a grammar schoolgirl). I was now a highly successful landscape painter, in the Abstract Expressionist style. Our home was a Mecca for all that was upper class and fashionable, until the permissive sixties poisoned my very own domestic idyll. I kicked my husband out for flagrant infidelity and sued for divorce, viewing his behaviour as a betrayal of our wedding vows before God. Beneath it all, I had remained a child of the chapel. My granny would have been proud of me.

So there I was, mother of two and still in my twenties, at the start of the sixties, single again and about to explode. Ready to blossom into being myself – immaculate timing. The first thing to go was my affected accent, the strangulated vowels of Margaret Thatcher, which I'd adopted and strived to maintain for the seven years of my marriage. I'd had to speak very slowly when I gulped too much champagne, for fear of losing my 'h's, as in "appy', and my endings, in case 'Dancing" became 'Dancin'', for instance. When you've affected a posher accent than the one you used in childhood, there are many ghastly pitfalls. A pal of mine in similar circumstances said she always got unstuck at 'sprouts'. And another said that it took her ages to cancel out the 'ov' in 'getting a book off ov the shelf' (which probably should be 'from the shelf' anyway!). Added to which I was not only aiming for an upper-class accent, but an upper-class English one – come to think of it, is there any other?!

So I could relax, not fearing any more that I would be letting my husband down by revealing my origins. Instead, it was time to flaunt them. The lower orders were rising, they were finding their true voice, like me. After all, we had Harold Wilson at the helm, the Socialist Government was in power again. With the impact of the Beatles, screen stars like Albert Finney and Rita Tushingham, and sirens like Shirley Bassey from Cardiff, it was considered fashionable to sport a provincial accent: the voice of the people. Even young Etonians affected a twang and took to dropping their 'h's just to be part of things.

Cockney models like Twiggy were photographed by East End fashion photographers: the famous trio, Bailey, Duffy and Donovan. Cockney hairdressers like Vidal Sassoon gave hairdressers a social kudos, dictating the shapes of heads for each season. His simple cuts for straight, shining hair swept the world, and did away with the discomfort of sleeping in curlers and following in your mother's permed footsteps. Carnaby Street revolutionised clothes for young men, with the camp and casual designs of a young man from Glasgow, John Stephens. I dressed my own moppets in scarlet leather mini-dresses and knee-high boots from Kids in Gear, Carnaby Street. Mary Quant ruled the King's Road before moving to Knightsbridge. I'd been at Art School with Mary Quant, the first to dress in her youthful designs. And now I embarked on my lifelong, still enduring friendship with Barbara Hulanicki, who, with Fitz, her husband and partner, launched the wildly successful, groundbreaking fashion emporium, BIBA. This was where the daughters of duchesses really did do battle with the daughters of road-sweepers, stars such as Bardot, and teenyboppers from the typing pool, all equal, tearing the latest batch of backless mini and maxi-dresses from the rails, trying them on in the frenzy of the communal fitting rooms. Democracy, indeed.

It was in the world of fashion then that I made my name in the wider sense, though I was already known in the art world. A vast canvas of mine, an abstract oil painting in cadmium yellows and lemons, called 'Spring in New York', had been purchased by the Contemporary Arts Society and was then housed in the bowels of the Tate Gallery in London.

But when I kicked my husband out, my painting Muse left with him and I was traumatized by the double loss. I didn't paint again for another twenty-five years, not until the late 1980s, when the Muse returned in my new-found sobriety. I'd given up drink, drugs, nicotine and rampant promiscuity. Those destructive habits, which had afforded me such delights in the sixties, had become such dangerous addictions by the end.

So, having earned so much from my painting, I now had no income as a newly divorced single parent. I light-heartedly turned to what I could do with ease and very little involvement of the heart and soul. I needed money for me and my children. I did the first thing that came along. I supplied BIBA with hats and bags before opening my own boutique off the King's Road in Chelsea, one of the very first boutiques to open in London. It was an instant success and within a few months I sold out for a sizeable sum. News of my boutique had travelled. I mixed in exciting circles of people doing their own thing.

At one of the celebrity-strewn parties that I was constantly invited to now, this one was at Len Deighton's – author of *The Ipcress File*, a novel to be made into a film starring the young cockney actor, Michael Caine – I met a publisher from IPC. He was seated beside his pal David Frost and listened intently to my piss-take of the fashion trade, on how to start and sell a boutique and make a bomb in a matter of months, no sweat, as I'd just done. He subsequently confided that he'd been impressed by my attitude, my get-up-and-go, my lack of neurosis, so rare around fashion circles. And the undoubted fact that I looked so, so good in what I was wearing, which, in fact, was simply my usual kind of outfit: everything hurled on bar the kitchen stove, with strategic items removed just before leaving the house to enable normal mobility. Lashings of Elizabeth Taylor black eyeliner, of course, and a fringe or a hat drowning any suggestion of eyebrow. It's the look I have affected all my adult life and it has never let me down. Enough said.

The following day, he rang up and invited me to lunch, then on to meet the editor of the revolutionary new glossy magazine for women, *Nova*. They offered me the position of Fashion Editor on the spot. There was no way that I could have turned down the salary. Several years later, I moved to be Fashion Editor at *Harpers & Queen*, then became Fashion Editor of *The Sunday Times* in 1969. It was a meteoric rise in the effete world of fashion journalism, especially for a fashion maverick like me. My training as a dedicated painter had nothing to do with Parisian haute couture. The frivolous aspect of vast amounts spent on a single glove-and-handbag set stuck in my gullet.

My only previous job, until marriage when I was enabled to paint fulltime, had been serious and profoundly satisfying to the soul: teaching Art to deprived children at a secondary modern school at the Elephant and Castle. At Art School we students of fine art, such as sculpture or painting, were taught to despise 'the commercial crew', those students of fashion and design and illustration: we found them superficial and therefore contaminating. We worshipped at the ethic of 'Art for Art's sake'. Hard cash and making a living didn't come into it. Our talent was God-given and as such had to be nurtured in its purity. I swooned at the high concept. It could have been my granny talking.

Yet here I was in this despised world of fashion, garnering just about every covetable award for my work, culminating in Fashion Editor of the Year for my pages on *The Sunday Times*, when I left in the early 1970s to become a novelist. I was a legendary figure in fashion journalism, irreverent in the extreme, because at rock bottom I just didn't care. In truth, I was faintly ashamed. I knew that my granny would have said that I was squandering my talents. So would those tutors from college. The conscience is an uncomfortable companion. It wasn't a proper occupation. It wasn't a calling, a career. It wasn't a compulsion, not like painting was to me. I couldn't treat it seriously. But the sixties provided the backdrop for that attitude – take the money and run – and I was surrounded by people who felt the same. We were all only there for a laugh, and the drink helped that. I wasn't ruled by the normal anxieties and fear of management or the editor. I could take risks and work on instinct, always ahead of the latest trend. In fact my pages caused trends to happen, though I was blithely unaware, or too busy having fun to care.

And this was where the sixties were important to me. They were irreverent times, like the twenties. There was a lot of laughter in the air, drug or drink induced, no matter. Everybody was in employment, there was no housing crisis, we were not at war, though concerned with America and the Korean conflicts. But that war wasn't ours.

We demonstrated but we didn't fight. We cried bitterly over the assassination of Kennedy, but it didn't happen here. Our own ship was in order. We were safe and everybody was swinging.

I had no abiding interest in the world of fashion, never had and still don't. My own bizarre style of dress is still actually merely that of a post-menopausal art student, nothing more or less. Apart from Barbara Hulanicki, I have no friend from that world. My chosen companions are from the literary and visual world, other artists or poets and writers. The world of fashion has always felt too superficial for me and yet it was that that made it the perfect vehicle on which to ride with the wind in the sixties. It supplied me with the where-withal, the power, the prestige, the opportunities and the contacts, to surf the excitement, to satisfy my hedonistic appetites, to fly my kite until my feet left the ground. I was the sparkling hostess of a party which lasted the entire decade. It almost killed me.

Many of my friends and lovers never survived the sixties. They perished in a sea of alcohol. They overdosed on drugs. They died of disappointment by their own hand, preferring suicide to financial failure. There were many victims of that time.

Looking back I wonder sometimes if the sixties weren't a total waste of time for me, in terms of my development as a serious artist. The spurious fame that it and subsequent years in the limelight brought me, feels meaningless now, an empty aftertaste. I know for certain that I would have painted more paintings, probably better ones, if I had continued throughout the sixties, up until now, unin-terrupted. I'm doing them today instead. Even so there's a gap which can never be filled.

Maybe my real error was marrying out of my race and back-ground under pressure from my mother, believing her when she said it would bring me happiness and a better life. People pleasing.

But that charming, courteous, cultured Englishman gave me the devoted daughters of our mixed marriage. And for the profound blessing of them alone, and the infinite joy of all our sweet grand-children, it was well worth this wise Welsh woman sleeping with the enemy. I can forgive myself now.

# Redefining the Sixties Myth:
## Letters Home to Swansea

~

*Jen Wilson*

**Jen Wilson** was born in Swansea in 1944 and left to live in Streatham, London, in 1968, and then Newcastle in 1971, before returning home in 1974. She had her first gig as a solo pianist at fourteen and played in various jazz, blues, R & B and rock bands, such as The Tempos, Jenny and the Giants, Last of the Brownies, ROOTS Trio and Wilson & Morgan's Café Society Ensemble. She is Director of Women in Jazz, based in Swansea. Her current research is on the history and influence of African American music and culture in Wales from 1850. Publications include pieces in *On My Life* (Honno 1989), 'Birth of an Archive' (*Minerva* 1995), *Swansea Anthology* (UWP 1996), 'The Skiffle Craze' (*Planet* 1998), 'Devil's Music, Swansea Clerics and the WI: Jazz in Wales 1930s-1940s' (*Planet* 1998). She is currently working on *Devil's Music in Wales 1840-1940* under consideration by the University of Wales Press.

The decade witnessed the transition from the last gasp of post Second World War austerity to self-indulgent psychedelia. For others on the roller-coaster ride from Ministry of Social Security to Family Service Units, from Department of Education to Psychiatric Social Worker at the Department of Social Services, life carried on as normal. 'You've never had it so good,' said the Conservative Prime Minister Harold Macmillan as he led us from 1957 into the sixties. Excuse me? Harold Wilson, the Labour PM who led us out from 1964 to 1970, himself briefly flirted with the swingers until his Prices and Incomes Policy and 'the pound in your pocket' finished him off, to be replaced by another Conservative PM, Edward Heath, 1970-1974. At least Ted played the piano.

The Second World War had only been over fifteen years. I had no idea at the time. I was aged sixteen in 1960 and my father had protected us well from his personal horrors with the Royal Engineers:

D Day, the Liberation of Paris and his confronting the concentration camps alongside 'the Yanks'. Pa's mantra whenever it occurred to us to ask war questions was, 'Let it be,' – to be echoed by Paul McCartney in 1969. Ma kept house, which included Gran, in one of the terraces above Swansea Bay and scrubbed the front steps before eight each morning. Ma dressed herself and me fashionably from Butterick patterns costing 1s 6d and remnants from Lewis, Lewis. Most girls I knew looked like their grans.

My brother John, six years older than me, was completing National Service in the Royal Army Medical Corps in Nairobi and Mombasa. A drummer of the modern jazz school, he went by the name of Mbongo, having managed to ship his drum kit overseas. We got our musical bent from Ma, who played chapel chords on the piano (she came from Pontycymer) and Pa, a Swansea boy, who played ukulele in Oxford bags. They both did a mean Charleston. Pa drove the South Wales Transport bus route 33 from St. Thomas (working class) to Tycoch (middle class). Their handles were short forms of Mama and Papa given by John, cynical of middle-class pretensions belonging to some of his old grammar school contemporaries.

As a family, we wrote profusely. We had no phone nor did anyone else we knew. Letters whizzed in and out, with Ma replacing them in their envelopes, as she saved everything. John's eight-piece band, the Jazz Senators, which had practised Saturday afternoons in our front parlour, staggered from one drummer to another in his absence and eventually disbanded. Letters to John from members of the Senators announce themselves as 'Hey Daddyo!', 'Hey Man!' and are full of gig rates (10 shillings, a pound or 25 shillings), the latest threads ('cool' shirts in stripes with button-down collars) and which cat was cutting up who on the bandstand. They sign off with Dad, or the tag from their latest infatuation on Blue Note. Steve the guitarist who'd gone off to seek his fortune in London writes of, 'hocking the horn at Uncle Joe's', and promises to pay John the money he owes.

I busily kept John informed of the state of play with my own piano gigs at the Glanmor Jazz Club. Although licensed premises, I had been playing 'intervals' there since the age of fourteen. As far as we all were concerned, we'd been swinging since bebop got invented in 1948. Remnants of the Jazz Senators escorted me to the club, thereby relieving my parents of any doubts as to my wellbeing, and relayed my progress to Africa. Still at school, I remained quiet and mostly sullen, ever since the day they locked the piano when the Deputy Head found a crowd of girls jiving to my lunchtime boogie session. I wore thick black stockings and black ankle boots at Swansea Secondary Technical School for Girls, copied from the London girls I'd seen on my trips to Ronnie Scott's in Soho. The Head thundered in Assembly, *'You girl, are lowering the tone and decorum of the whole school.'* I entered a short story about jazz for a school Eisteddfod and never heard what happened to it. I failed O levels except English Language.

However, I did spectacularly well on the secretarial course with 97 per cent in shorthand and started work in the shipping and export department of the British Anthracite Company on Swansea docks at £3 10s per week. On my first day I wore my red and black striped dress, black stockings, black Cuban heels and my new, draped-shoulder, silver mohair coat from C & A. Working there previously on Saturdays at fifteen shillings had kept me in clothes and enabled me to give Ma five shillings. I ran the shipping and export department when my two bosses were frequently out of town; securing eta's (estimated time of arrival) on telex, booking berths, typing bills of landing, and nipping over in taxis to get documents signed by ships' captains. I did not realize at the time, but this was Swansea's dying coal and shipping industry. I was frantically busy, but sneered at by ancient men in Accounts who remembered the days when hundreds of ships were berthed in the docks.

I also had a little thing going with Tony from Port Talbot, Jenny and the Giants – a five piece; we did the Friday trad night at the Glanmor with Tony performing Armstrongs on trumpet. We got a regular booking at The Pines until they refused to up the rate so we took the proffered twelve shillings and sixpence and quit, taking the club members with us. I also did several solo numbers at the Wednesday Modern Music Society, membership five bob. Ma wrote to Mombasa, 'Jen accompanied Russ John with a blues "Going Down the Road Now Feeling Bad". She did "Highway 49" last week. Russ is still singing down the cellar, Ma.' Art, saxophonist, also wrote to Mombasa, 'The hepcats have been crowding in.

Having had your golden-haired sister to take the stand has certainly given her a big incentive to play good jazz. She's gone down well and with Russ singing those funky blues everybody's lapping 'em up. Well here's 4/4 in your eye.' Russ, who wouldn't be seen dead without his black polo neck, black pants, black leather jacket and crew cut, accompanied himself on guitar and sang in the short-lived Colony in Mansel Street, a sophisticated night spot before its time, with chequered cloths and candles in bottles and the rougher Cellar Bar in St. Helen's Road. Russ had three paintings exhibited at the Glynn Vivian during his *'blue period'*. Trad jazz was the pop of its day, but the good authentic sounds of Chris Barber and Ottilie Patterson were diluted by the bowler hat and waistcoat brigade.

I knew something was wrong but couldn't quite put my finger on it. I was introduced at the club as, 'the only girl in Wales to play like a man,' and asked to, 'play ballads, much more ladylike.' I ignored the advice. No girl or woman spoke to me in the jazz club. At the day job, handing in impeccably typed letters, a boss said, 'good girl', but the office boy was called Mr. Phillips. The commissionaire, keeping an eye out for the director's Bentley so he could do his Tank Corps salute, passed sneering comment on my beehive hairdo and shades. I got my hair dyed to trouble him further, beige blonde with pink highlights in Bryn-y-Mor Road by that one that looked like Phil from the Everley Brothers. We all booked him.

Ma posted *Melody Makers* to Africa while Gran, a regular at Band of Hope, went on Billy Graham Crusades with coach loads from Mount Pleasant Chapel. When Sister Phoebe called to save me, Ma kept her talking in front of the big family bible in the parlour, supplying tea and homemade cherry cake. LPs cost £1 16s 8d and I had to save up for weeks if I wanted Mose Allison, Nat King Cole or Thelonious Monk, which I recycled on piano at the club. Ma wrote, 'Hurry home, boy, you're having your nose put out of joint . . . but between you, me and Pa, Jen has a lot to learn, mum's the word.'

I had boyfriends my own age lasting no longer than a week. If they didn't know what instrument Mose Allison played I was not interested. I didn't get up to much mischief as Pa on his regular routes around the town always knew where I was and what I was doing and was also kept informed by his colleagues. No escape.

Relationships with girls were far more fraught, especially those girls belonging to the guys in my new band, The Tempos, the only R & B outfit in town with a two-sax line-up when everybody else was doing the Shads. The guys were kept on a tight leash and I was ignored, for they all knew I had to sit on somebody's lap in the one car that got us to gigs.

There was one chap, Mike, from the old Senators clique, who kept hanging around. He'd gone to sea when I was twelve and had resurfaced when I was seventeen. He occasionally roadied The Tempos' gear into gigs, wore the latest from New York (he'd been on the New York/Sydney route) and sported a blond Gerry Mulligan cut with regulation shades. The band girls, in sugar-glazed petticoats, summer frocks and perms, glanced sideways and breathed easier. The big news was the purchase of our guitarist's Wah-Wah pedal, a pioneering effort at great expense. The two front saxes sported suits and magnificent quiffs, held in place with copious amounts of axle grease. A wow with the fans. I wore a snazzy little silver lamé outfit run up by Ma, with a box jacket and tight skirt with a slit sporting four inches of midriff. We hid the band outfit from Pa.

John returned from his exploits with African drummers, to find his sister eighteen, a dispersed Jazz Senators and a need to earn fast money. He auditioned for The Fireflies rock band and defended his actions to an appalled Steve who had decamped to Canada: 'Yup, I'm in a Shads group. Before you rip this letter up in disgust hear this. Playing this stuff is far more exacting and demands far more concentration than just jamming or sessioning at the jazz club, some of these rock drum breaks are tricky things man, 3 bars some-times and tempo changes. A big drag for playing a melodic instru-ment, but for drums, man, this is the best sharpening up practice there is.' The Fireflies were snapped up as support band for the Rock Tours with Joe Brown and Marty Wilde et al that came to town, with John the only rock drummer capable of performing 20-minute drum solos. Terry Williams, late of Dire Straits, is testament to this, having sat at his feet as a spotty youth in the Tivoli, Mumbles, to watch The King.

The Tempos also flourished, supported by the landlady of The Oystermouth Hotel, near the jail, who gave us her upstairs room for weekly rehearsals. We played youth clubs, community halls and occasional 8-1 am dances at the Langland Court Hotel. We included lengthy rock and blues *'interludes'* for these. As we didn't know any waltzes we played 'Silent Night' and 'God Save the Queen'; with two saxes wailing, nobody recognised the tunes. With by now a fair grounding in jazz, I coached the saxes in improvisation and how it worked over the chord structures.

Things still weren't quite right. Pa abruptly switched off the TV when *The World at War* came on and left the room. I had watched news footage of CND marches and was transfixed by the marching bands at the head. I would have gone, but pianos weren't portable and I didn't want to march by myself. I was inarticulate discussing politics with Pa. What had he done? He wouldn't say. Ma kept the peace.

Dave, our tenor sax, was going to university, another was rushed up the aisle, and The Tempos gradually drifted apart. There were no jazz courses or summer schools for me and they wouldn't have accepted me anyway without a music O level. The Tempos' occasional roadie and ex able seaman and I decided to get hitched and buy a boat. Tax rebates of £160 were the incentive and there was a rush on for marriages. We booked the Registry Office, but backtracked rapidly at the furore. Ma, who looked stunning on her wedding day in her dress she made herself and satin shoes, resigned herself to a daughter who had no interest in posh frocks. Six days before the wedding, Ma fell off the stepladder distempering the scullery ceiling and broke her arm. She refused to go to the doctor, remembering how she discreetly placed scarce money on the hallstand when the doctor had to be summoned. Pa went nuts as he was on overtime and was going to do the ceiling. She was hauled off to the doctor's. John, who had just taken delivery of his new white Ford Corsair, which was intended to drive me to church, crashed it on black ice and attended the wedding with his face bruised and battered. During the March storm, I was snug in a beige suit with a mink collar and Eva Bartok hat, with Mike resplendent in a dark blue Italian three-button mohair suit, with red waistcoat and black knitted tie. Ma commented, with her arm at an angle and her sleeve split, 'He might have put something tidy on.' Pa secretly hired an Austin Princess to whisk us from the Mermaid Hotel, Mumbles (Dylan's old hangout, roast chicken at fifteen shillings per head) to the station. The car was crammed with relatives, all yelling along with the Beatles' 'She's Got a Ticket To Ride' blasting from the car radio, their new single being promoted and due out in April 1965. Ma waved gamely from the platform at my collarless black leather coat, no hat and no gloves. We did *April in Paris* for real.

We moved to London. Our top floor flat in a large detached house in Streatham was just around the corner from Cynthia Payne's brothel, at which she serviced the clientele armed with their Luncheon Vouchers. Carol and Silloo from Mike's department were in the big ground floor flat with Australians in the middle flat. Mike, newly qualified with A levels (correspondence course) and the Home Office Letter of Recognition in Child Care, the 'cutting edge' of professional social work qualifications, was instantly employed at Lambeth Social Services and assigned a piece of Brixton by his senior, Don, an Asian thrown out of Idi Amin's Uganda. I landed a job at twenty pounds a week, twice my Swansea salary, at a publishing house off Fleet Street. I was a 'Girl Friday', PA, to the managing director. Unfortunately, after two high-powered interviews, the job entailed sitting at a leather desk with onyx lamp keeping the 'riff-raff' from the printing section out of his office, delivering his coffee in the silver service at 11 am and preparing the cocktails at 5 pm. Within three months I was out of there, and I successfully landed a job with less money at Family Service Unit.

Pacifist Service Units were set up during the Second World War to enable conscientious objectors to undertake non-military work for the benefit of the community. After the War, they dropped the pacifist connections. We were housed in a semi in a street trying to keep up appearances, and took referrals from local authorities, NSPCC, Home Office etc, families needing extensive casework. I was administrative secretary running the house, comprising co-ordinator, five caseworkers, students on placements and volunteers. On the ground floor were kids' playrooms and groupwork rooms, upstairs were interview rooms and office. 'Swinging London' were the new buzzwords but they hadn't filtered down to any of our families.

Freda ran a tight ship and enthusiastically gathered a new intake of freshly trained, keen social workers around her. I found the two-line switchboard under a huge pile of donated clothes: nobody had known how to operate it. Well qualified administratively and with an abundance of good sense instilled by my parents, I coped with the day-to-day traumas arriving on the doorstep, keeping clients' files and interviews updated, compiling rotas on who was cooking unit lunch (a big feature of FSU democracy), organizing kids' holidays at Toc H Camps, running fund-raising events and paying household bills and salaries.

My casework colleagues were young, dedicated, and committed to making inadequate political policies stretch to embrace their families. Pat arrived from Manchester with John and got themselves installed in a little flat over a shop in Brixton. John worked as a designer at the Hampstead Theatre, where Willie Rushton and Anna Massey were starring. John promptly asked Rushton home to tea but he never showed. Greg arrived spectacularly each morning draped in Marius Goring's green velvet cloak from a Shakespearian production, purple velvet pants, tie-dyed tees and flowing locks. Fred, gentle and crumpled in cords, and Tina, his Scandinavian wife, lived in the small flat in the attic with their twin babies and kept watch on the house after office hours. Ingrid, who had wandered the African bazaars, arrived on her bike in cheesecloth and long plaits. Hilary, also from Wales, was the eldest, nearly thirty years old, and the most experienced of the caseworkers. Carol and Silloo, the local authority contingent in the ground floor Streatham flat, came from Ipswich and Bombay respectively. Our various flats welcomed new friends and colleagues; Anglo-Caribbeans, Europeans, Asians, Africans and African Americans. Hilary, a Welsh speaker, and I flew the flag for Wales by hosting Welsh days at the Unit with *cawl*, Welshcakes and daffodils.

Their work was intense and committed, often traumatic and they were sometimes threatened. Unit lunch was the time to hang loose and chill out. Wednesday mornings were set aside for the Unit meeting, when household, admin or personal chips on shoulders were discussed and resolved. I took the minutes and soothed dramas with balm of tea and chocolate biscuits. Greg, always up with the latest, invited Ed Berman of Interaction to 'get rid of our inhibitions' and one afternoon we all lay on the floor with the curtains drawn, holding hands and screaming as directed by the large American in violet octagon specs.

The families visiting the Unit were classed on official documents as Problem Families, ESN (Educationally Subnormal) or Inadequate. Freda hated those terms and referred to our families as simply families with problems. I wrote home twice a week:

Dear Ma and Pa, Mrs A burst into my office yesterday and asked me if I had a gun as she wanted to shoot her old man. I said 'sorry' so she demanded a bread knife. Freda came in to rescue me and I made tea. She happily accepted and settled for a nice chat instead. Mrs B who is fifty-one, told her caseworker she was pregnant, her ninth. One of her daughters, aged sixteen, is also pregnant – both babies due within two weeks of each other. Mrs C's husband has just had a stroke and is trying to get out of hospital, as he is worried about his thirty pigeons he keeps on his council flat balcony. Last Tuesday, responding to a thundering on the door, I was confronted by Y, a beautiful but faded lady with long black hair. She looked about fifty but I learned later she was thirty-six. She dangled her fag, grinned warmly and asked, 'Do you want to see my scars, love?' and slowly inched her thin skirt up her thigh to reveal her and her lover's initials carved where her knicker elastic should have been, if she'd been wearing any. 'My, that's impressive,' I said. 'Fancy a cuppa?' and got her in off the doorstep. I kept her mollified while she awaited her caseworker's return to sort out her financial and emotional affairs. She thought my Welsh accent 'funny' and remarked, 'You're not like them posh ones we get sometimes, I like you.' One of Pat's huge families, who don't have hot water, have a weekly bath here. Persuading the Gas and Electricity Boards to reinstate heating and water is one of the main functions of the caseworkers. We've got a new volunteer, Martin, spending a year with us before going to Brunel University. He drives a little sports car and gives kids treats in it, he looks like Buddy Holly and says, 'This'll knock the edges off me.' Mike had to go to one of his client's funerals in Brixton. I got a bit worried as he didn't come home for two days. He looked terrible and said the funeral was still going on. They told him, 'This is how we bury people in the Caribbean, we celebrate their time with us.' All for now, love Jen.

Mike and I were asked to volunteer one night a week at the newly set up Brixton Advice Centre on Railton Road, a community hall staffed by multi-ethnic volunteers from the Housing, Health, Social Services agencies, and legal practices. I took clients' details and ferried them into the right interview room. Gradually, the white volunteers were replaced by black ones coming off the new social work courses.

Part of my job was to keep the clothing store in order and one day a suitcase of Biba and Mary Quant originals were donated at the door by a young lady who said she had put on weight. Pat and I sighed over the purple shifts with hoods, the little sleeveless striped numbers, the satins with leg-o-mutton sleeves and, watched carefully by Freda, we stacked them in the section marked Special Treats/Girls. 'Handy for our mums to give their daughters at Christmas,' she said, grinning. Ma and Pa were up on a visit, I took Ma to Biba's and we spent a giggly day in Kensington Church Street, trying on maxis, feather boas and stetsons in their darkened interior. Ma didn't like the communal changing room. I didn't much either, not since somebody tried on the dress I was wearing when I came in and hissed that she'd seen it first.

Silloo married Ernst, a German journalist in Brixton Registry Office. The reception was held in Carol and Silloo's flat, with the doors thrown open on to the huge back garden. Ernst kept bowls of his sauerkraut in our bath overnight. Will, Carol's boyfriend from Ghana who was doing something with computers, supplied the soundtrack from his collection of Stax and Atlantic labels and the throng grooved the night away. We looked splendid: Mike in his pearl grey mohair suit, ruffled shirt and lace cuffs, me in my little oyster satin Biba number and orange feather boa. Silloo was stunning in a scarlet and gold sari. Crocheted dresses – more hole than crochet – were very much in evidence. Things heated up when the African contingent strutted their stuff. The scent of hash drifted over the garden.

29.5.1969: Dear Ma and Pa, Charlie Watts nearly ran me over on Streatham High Road last week, he came hurtling around the corner in a shiny black Mercedes. We went to the Tate, dead crap, pile of carpet in a corner. Mike said, 'It's underlay.' He should know having been a carpet fitter. All for now, love Jen.

5.9.1969: Dear Ma and Pa, Saw the Pop Art Exhibition at the Hayward Gallery, some a load of old cobblers, but we liked the soft typewriter, the Warhol soup cans and coke bottles, and the Portable War Memorial sprayed silver which played 'God Bless America' and dispensed ice-cold cokes. Bernard Levin was looking at it. After that we went to see Tubby Hayes at the Bull's Head, Barnes, best 5s 6d worth of jazz for ages. All for now, love Jen.

I missed my piano dreadfully.

The swinging London of the Chelsea Drug Store, Desmond's Hip City (where the Black Panthers hung out), Electric Avenue, Carnaby Street (we never bought our clothes there) was a world away from the families we knew, liked and respected and who had just 'slipped through the net'. As far as our families were concerned, some of whom had never been on the tube, who purchased their eggs singly in paper bags, and sent their kids up the chippy to buy a penn'orth of batter, swinging London didn't exist.

And that niggling worry that things weren't quite right? Women gave it an official title in the 1970s: feminism.

# Ah, the Swinging Sixties . . .

~

*Jenny Sullivan*

**Jenny Sullivan** was born in Cardiff too many years ago, but now lives in Raglan. Having left school at fifteen, she returned to education in 1993 and has since completed a PhD in Creative Writing at University of Wales, Cardiff. She has written several novels for children: the *The Magic Apostrophe* trilogy, *The Back End of Nowhere*, *Following Blue Water*, *Gwydion and the Flying Wand*, *Magic Maldwyn*, and *Who, Me?* and *Me and My Big Mouth* the first two parts of the second Magic Apostrophe trilogy. In addition, the picture books *Siôn and the Bargain Bee*, *Two Left Feet* and *The Caterpillar that Couldn't*. Jenny also writes short stories, plays and poetry for adults and children – and for fun.

When at the ripe old age of fifty, I finally, belatedly, fulfilled a life-long ambition and made it to university, my mid-twenties fellow students couldn't believe I'd never swung. 'Listen,' I said, 'if there was any love, I paid for it one way or another, if there were any drugs, they came in prescription bottles from Boots, and apart from the mini-skirt, trust me, the sixties totally passed me by.'

There were boyfriends, of course, one in particular, who turned out to be a faithless heel, but my memories even of him are faint. There were arguments with Victorian-vintage parents – 'You are *not* leaving this house with a skirt up around your backside!' 'What time do you call this to come home?' And, most numbing of all – 'Don't you bring trouble to my door, my girl!' I wasn't quite sure what the trouble referred to actually was, until much later.

There were some memorable moments of conflict – and I was sixteen when the sixties began, a year out of school. There was never a possibility of taking O levels and certainly not A levels or university education. University wasn't for the likes of us, although education was the thing my father valued above all else. For males, that is. He had this theory that, because girls' bodies were smaller, their brains were proportionately smaller, and too much education would addle their grey matter permanently. The sad thing was that my next sister up, Ruth, did her O levels as a young mother, then her A levels, then the Open University, then a teaching certificate at Cardiff. Then, at fifty-one she was diagnosed as having early onset Alzheimer's. Ironic or what? Anyway, it proved his point. When I got my MA in 1994, both she and my father were dead, having died during the academic year.

The first memorable sixties occasion was when my mother quoted me at me, and, after a second's puzzlement, I realised that she had been reading my secret diary. It was her duty as a mother, she said, even if I did hide it in the drawer under my knickers. I'm not sure why it was a duty, since if I'd written it down, it was too late anyway, but hey. Anyway, I've never kept a diary since. Maybe that's a boon for posterity. Maybe not.

The second was when she found a box of Tampax in my aforesaid knicker drawer. The reaction was, in retrospect, hilarious, given that I'd bought them furtively in a chemist far away from home – and almost crippled myself trying to insert them in totally the wrong place, so innocent was I, but it didn't seem hilarious, then. Her reaction was terrifying.

'Dear God!' she said, in tones of utter horror and disgust. 'Are you using those things? Don't you realise that no man will ever look at you now. You'll never get a husband. You aren't a virgin any more!'

It took me a while to work out what she meant, and for a good few weeks I felt despoiled and worthless and considered suicide. Then a kindly typing-pool workmate reassured me. 'Listen, my love,' she said, patting my hand, 'you're a virgin until you've had a man up you, not a Tampax. And trust me, men are much more fun.' Philip Larkin had a phrase for it, concerning parents . . .

The third moment came at the ripe old age of twenty-four. Living at home with the parents in Cardiff began to be unbearable. I'd split up with the afore-mentioned heel, and was back to dating. My best friend was away nursing, another friend had married her soldier boyfriend. ('Had to!' said my mother meaningfully. 'Oh, her poor mother . . .')

Me, I was still living at home, totally fed up with being quizzed about my movements whenever I left the house; and waited up for by Mum in a flannelette nightie and no teeth, her asthma inhaler at her side and a bottle of aspirin in her hand; and made to be home by half-past ten. Then my cousin, six months younger, asked if I'd like to share a flat with her. Would I? Do monkeys climb trees? We spent a whole evening making wondrous plans. She was (and still is) a thoroughly respectable, ladylike girl, shy, quiet, and wouldn't say boo to a goose. Even my mother wouldn't object to me moving in with her own sister's child! And then I told her . . .

First there was a ten-day silence. Mother wept ostentatiously in corners, father looked grim-faced because mother was weeping. Then, when I could stand it no more and was reaching the point of silent screams, from behind her handkerchief, she sobbed, 'What do you want to do in a flat that you can't do at home? The neighbours will think you're a prostitute. I won't be able to look anybody in church in the face any more. I'm so ashamed. None of your sisters behaved like this. They all got married before they left home. They were good girls. Where have we gone wrong with you?'

Not surprisingly, given my upbringing, I abandoned the idea of leaving home and suffered in silence until I married – a year later. I could have made a disastrous mistake just for the heaven of getting away from the parental control, but thank God I didn't, and thirty-three years on I love him more than I did on our wedding day.

My own three daughters, aged twenty-nine, twenty-eight and twenty-two, are all happily unmarried, two of them living in London with lovely, sensible partners. The eldest, the stroppiest, the most explosive and the most vulnerable of all my darling girls, was a primary school teacher, and a good one, but stressed out by the strain of working in 'Ackney, she quit and is now ecstatically working as a museum education officer. The middle one, the one whose life seems to be lived on an even-tempered plateau, who is funny, feisty and not quite as tough as she thinks, is happily co-habiting with a very large, very talented, amazingly sensible professional musician she's known since she was eleven. And my timid, retiring, baby? Well, she's just graduated from university and will be (is!) a drama queen. Her teacher partner has rapidly sussed out the dynamics of our family – that is, we're all completely mad.

They all phone me at least once a week and we chat for hours about all sorts of things. I utter words of caution if I think they are about to leap into something that might prove dangerous, give advice when I'm asked (and yes, I admit it, sometimes when I'm not) love them to bits – and let them lead their own adult lives, pausing only to bail them out when the going gets tough.

If they ever ask me, 'What did you do in the Swinging Sixties, Mum?' I'll tell them. They probably won't believe me any more than my student friend did.

Swinging Sixties? Don't make me laugh.

# Missing Out

~

*Margaret Lloyd*

**Margaret Lloyd** was born in 1930. She spent most of her life in Merthyr Tydfil and took up writing after retiring as a health visitor. She has had several poems and articles published in anthologies, including *Parachutes and Petticoats* and *Struggle or Starve* (Honno) and *Women to Woman* . Her hobbies include travelling, writing and enacting historical cameos with friends.

The 'swinging sixties' is a phrase often accompanied by nudges, winks and dreamy-look memories of pop concerts, hippies, free love and Mary Quant. How could I have missed out on it? Did it have anything to do with being a young mother of three in Merthyr in the 'frustrating fifties', still controlled by the ethics laid down by my forceful extended family? Any sign of abandonment on my part was crushed with a simple, 'What would the neighbours say?' How I envied the rest of the female population in their mini skirts and tights, looking like Hollywood versions of winsome medieval pageboys. Anything over two inches above the knee was regarded as 'showing off' by my mother and quite unsuitable for a mother of, now, four, although I was still only in my early thirties.

The height of degradation of not belonging to the swinging sixties scene came on the night my husband informed me that we were to meet a friend of his and his current girlfriend, prior to going to the annual works' dance. Panic set in! What to wear? I had nothing that would compare with the local crop of Mary Quants. I rummaged for an old dress bequeathed to me by an aunt, considered to be a smart dresser in the family, and started to darn the slit in the material. My tears were not only for my poverty but for my lost youth. My grief was reinforced on meeting the said friend and his companion, a vision in blue patterned satin. The figure-hugging creation she was moulded into ended above the knee, decorated with a bow. Eat your heart out, Marilyn Monroe! I cringed in my darned drab brown frock as the men ogled, smirked and dreamed, and the lady swallowed her Bloody Marys with aplomb. Inevitably, nature called and the vision asked me to go with her to the Ladies. Was she being friendly or did she feel sorry for me? I asked myself.

I was rather taken aback when once in the cloakroom she asked me to unzip her dress, explaining that it was so tight she was unable to pull it up. I watched goggle-eyed as she stepped out of this amazing garment to reveal the thickest woollen vest I had ever seen outside my Granny's chest of drawers! We returned to the table. 'What's wrong with you? You look like a cat with cream,' said my husband. 'Nothing,' I said, thinking about the black satin basque with its saucy suspenders I was wearing under my plain exterior. I spent the rest of the evening in a state of euphoria as I watched the dolly birds iced in luminous greens, pinks and yellows, twist and twirl around the dance floor. What hidden passion-killers lurked beneath their fine feathers? I asked myself. Ah, well, nothing is as it seems in this world.

Some days later my husband informed me that his friend and the lady had parted company, she alleging that he had tried to rape her after the said dance. 'No way,' I cried. 'Not unless he was carrying a pair of scissors.' My husband put my remarks down to female envy. Well, I couldn't tell him, could I? We girls must stick together.

By the mid-sixties, we were able to afford a family holiday in the north Wales resort of Rhyl. We set off with visions of beautiful mountains and historical castles only to find Rhyl a place of sand, sea and bingo. Still no sign of the swinging sixties, apart from my older sons having Beatle haircuts and me abandoning my curlers for a blow-dry hair-do.

Bank Holiday hit us with Flower Power. We had decided to go to one of the sea-front shows. We walked along the promenade admiring the well laid-out flower beds of blues, reds and yellows, comparing it to our own drab valley (landscaping hadn't yet arrived). The setting sun washed the world in a soft sense of wellbeing: life was good. The evening was complete as we chuckled at the innocent humour of Richard Hearne and his 'Mr Pastry' antics and left the theatre anticipating a quiet stroll back to the boarding house. But alas, in our absence aliens had invaded our simple world. Our beautiful flowers had disappeared; only the footprints of a thousand sandals graced the beds. FLOWER POWER had arrived. The whole place was swarming with strange beings in flowing robes, unwashed hair and beads. Clan recognition seemed to be by the flowers sprouting out of everyone's ears. The spectacle of colour was broken only by the beetle-black of the local constabulary trying to force their way through the mêlée. Their Alsations looked equally bemused.

My four-year-old son looked at these apparitions in disgust and said in a very loud voice, 'You are not supposed to pick the flowers – that's naughty,' but like all four year olds, having given his opinion, he announced he would walk home upon the seating attached to the sea wall. The rest of us gathered close around, rather overwhelmed and not a little frightened of this weird crowd who pushed and shoved on all sides, despite their repeated chants of,

'Peace Man.' Our little lad strode purposefully on along the wall, a picture of correctness in his multicoloured school cap and matching blazer (an outfit of which he was particularly fond and refused to relinquish even on holiday). Then came the impasse. A group of lounging hippies blocked his path. We held our breath. Who could challenge such power?

'Well,' said our intrepid manikin, 'You are in my way.'

They stared at him.

He held their gaze. 'Are you going to move?' It was a command rather than a question.

No reply – just blank stares.

Then this sixties version of David sighed and with authority oozing out of every inch of his two foot nothing frame, said in a very loud voice, 'I wish to walk along here now.'

Stunned amazement replaced contempt as in complete silence, Goliath, arose, stepped aside and allowed the diminutive person-ification of the establishment to proceed along his chosen path. Thus ended my brush with the 'swinging sixties'. To me, they were more like the screaming sixties, as I yelled at the family to cut down the volume on the transistor, screeched in despair as the Rolling Stones were played for the umpteenth time on the record-player and squawked my head off at teenagers about getting their hair cut.

There is just one thing I am eternally grateful for to the swinging sixties – the invention of tights, which meant, of course, not having to wear suspenders any more.

# CHAPTER 9

# POLITICS

# Danger – Revolution in Progress

~

*Siân Edwards*

**Siân Edwards** was born in Barry, Glamorgan, in 1948. She graduated in Welsh in 1970 and Philosophy in 1971 from UCW Aberystwyth. She was the Literature Officer for the Welsh Arts Council, 1971-74, and writer in residence with TIE companies Coracle, Milford Haven and Frân Wen, Harlech. She is a founder member of the editorial board of the political magazine *Radical Wales* and active in the women's peace movement. She was Plaid Cymru parliamentary candidate in Cardiff South in 1983 and 1987 and chair of Plaid Cymru from 1992 to 1993. She is now a freelance translator, film researcher and editor, and production editor for the *Journal of Law and Society*, Cardiff Law School.

In the spring of 1963, we were visited by my hero, Gwynfor Evans, who called by to welcome us to Carmarthen after our move from Barry Island. In Barry, I had read every Plaid Cymru publication I could lay my hands on, particularly *Wales Matters to You*, a three-penny compendium of statistics outlining how Wales was economically disadvantaged without a government or economic policy of her own. I used to rage at the unfairness of it all, and couldn't understand that everybody in Wales wasn't as outraged as I was. I desperately wanted to take part in the struggle for self-government. The first step would be to join Plaid Cymru, but I thought only adults were allowed to. (Well, you couldn't vote till you were 21, so what was the point of being in a political party?) When introduced to the great man, I shyly asked how old you had to be to join the party. He appraised me nervously and ventured, 'Thirteen?' Safely fourteen and a quarter, I beamed and was signed up on the spot.

Our first campaign as the Carmarthen Plaid Cymru Youth Branch was against a piece of blatant discrimination. In those pre-Sex Discrimination Act days, Carmarthen hostelries (of which there were plenty – a different one for each week of the year, in fact) were plagued by that misogynist concept, the men-only bar. Our campaign consisted of four boys from our youth branch going into one of these dens, and ordering six pints of beer. Then we, the two girls in the branch, would race in, leap on to bar stools and try to get as much of our pints down us as possible before being thrown out. ('Typically Carmarthen' was the fact that a group of rather young-looking fifteen and sixteen-year-olds downing beer was never an issue – our crime was much worse than under-age drinking: violating hallowed male space and breaking the last great unwritten rule of Carmarthen social etiquette – 'ladies don't drink pints'.)

The branch developed by leaps and bounds – leafleting, pavement politics and toilet politics (letters about the disgusting state of public loos), Plaid *twmpathau dawns* (barn dances) organised for local youth on Saturday nights, which brought in a heap of money, selling our *Ddraig Goch* and *Welsh Nation* newspapers at the market every month – more money for our branch. In fact, our bank balance was positively embarrassing compared to that of the impoverished grown-ups' branch, so we decided to make a (substantial) contri-bution, to help them out. Our cheque was handed over to some amazement. When asked, 'Where on earth did you get this?' our inscrutable Youth Branch treasurer replied, 'Green Door,' (who, carrying all our branch funds, had come in at seven to one).

We were engulfed in electoral politics in 1966. On the eve of the General Election, we set out for Lady Megan's hustings meeting in a packed Market Hall, ready to engage in debate. We soon realized that there was to be no debate, just speeches, so we started heckling. We raised a Red Dragon and began angrily questioning her, as a representative of the Labour Government, about the Vietnam War. The response was furious. We were surrounded by middle-aged men, with dull-red mottled faces and spittle-flecked lips under flat caps, two to each of us, picked up by the arms like toddlers and dumped unceremoniously outside. All attempts at engaging our people-carriers were met with angry mutters of 'Little nippers . . . shouldn't be allowed . . .' Dai Goddard's mother attacked some of them with her handbag, trying to make them put us down, but we were corralled into a corner to be lectured on our bad behaviour by Labour's enforcer in Carmarthen, the late Lotty Rees Hughes, while Lady Megan spoke on, unimpeded.

No wonder they thought it shouldn't be allowed. We were so passionate in our cause that we raced home from school to go out on the knocker straight away, without bothering to change from school gymslips and blazers. It annoyed a lot of the Labour party – whose idea of a young member was anybody under fifty – but it seemed to impress a lot of the people we canvassed, who thought it was a novel, and rather good thing, that school kids should be so passionate about politics, and know something of what they were talking about. (*Wales Matters to You* was by now committed to memory, statistics ready to be rattled out on every doorstep.)

Carried away with our own enthusiasm and imbued with a youthful sense of fair play – i.e., if you put in as much work as we had for months, we deserved to win – and obviously having the best candidate in Gwynfor Evans, we were absolutely shattered when we failed to win the seat. That Gwynfor had increased the vote was barely a comfort. But then, with Lady Megan's untimely death, another chance presented itself a few months later with a by-election in Carmarthen.

If we'd worked hard before, this time it was frantic day-and-night stuff. My Lower Sixth English teacher told me off one morning for having put a ladder up the side of her house in the early hours (I was just picking up her nephew, secretary of the youth branch, who lived with her, to go out for a spot of late-night flyposting), but with more amusement than anger. The campaign galloped on. Home from school, out for an evening's canvassing, home again, go to bed, pretend to sleep, then sneak out to stick up posters, paint walls, fences, road bridges, make it seem that there were even more of us than the hundreds who had poured into the constituency.

More than once, short of transport for our night's work, my parents' car had to be commandeered, snuck out of the garage underneath the house, freewheeled, lights unlit, down the hill, engine not started till we got to the bottom of Springfield Road. We did a beauty on Bancyfelin Bridge – undercoated, gone over, and glossed – magnificent. I had been keeping look-out while the artists were at it, and it was only when I was called over to admire it that I saw the mistake – *CYMRU RHYDD,* instead of the correctly mutated *CYMRU RYDD.* Why the hell hadn't we stuck to 'Free Wales'? (At least, we hadn't ended up with 'Palid Cymru', a favourite typo in our hand-duplicated leaflets and flyers.) But it couldn't be left like that. After another frantic bout of undercoating, filling in and glossing, and with dawn greying the sky, we ended up with the very unusual *'I GYMRU – RHYDDID!'* (For Wales – Freedom!) which graced the bridge for many years.

Then an amazing thing happened. After this summer of extraordinary intense political activity, we *did,* this time, get our reward. On 14 July 1966, Gwynfor Evans won the Parliamentary seat of Carmarthen for Plaid Cymru with 16,179 votes – Plaid's first ever Westminster win, and perhaps still to this day the most astounding victory in the history of political Welsh nationalism. It was a glorious and unforgettable time. I guess it also spoilt us for politics after that. It seemed that the hard work principle – if you put in the effort, you get the result – had been vindicated. It rarely was again in my experience in politics – the price, maybe, of enjoying too much success too young!

I went to college in Aberystwyth the following year, and joined the Plaid branch, but college politics seemed very tame after the real thing. Most of the college battles and campaigns were concentrated on the Welsh language (the campaign for a Welsh-language Hall of Residence, Cymdeithas yr Iaith demos, occupying magistrates' courts, painting road signs). I felt passionately about the language, of course, but couldn't help feeling somewhat frustrated, as a Barry girl, brought up in a very anglicised area which I loved dearly and was the heart of my Wales (and one of the great joys of more recent years has been to see the election of Plaid Cymru councillors in Barry). I spent a lot of time arguing with Cymdeithas yr Iaith types who didn't seem too bothered at being under English rule for the foreseeable future, as long as the government – be it right-wing Tories or Brit. Labourites – supported the Welsh language and backed its future financially and legislatively. I was desperate to see us building up a truly national movement, reflecting both language communities, that could properly express what was distinctive about Wales – our collective, socialist heritage, our concern for the education, health and welfare of all our people, our passionate desire for world peace and international co-operation – and win us self-government, to implement these principles and rebuild our shattered economy.

At the same time, painting road signs was certainly more fun than most of the political activity that seemed to be going on at the time. There was the thrill but ultimate disappointment of the Rhondda West (1967) and Caerffili (1968) by-elections. We hitched down every weekend – the joy of crossing Rhondda mountain with its hand-painted road sign 'Danger – Revolution in Progress' – and threw ourselves into the campaigns. Plaid Cymru did off-the-Richter-scale well in both these Labour strongholds – but didn't win, and some of the momentum was lost.

The sixties ended for me in February 1970, when a group of us from Aberystwyth travelled overnight to London and demonstrated in the High Court against the jailing of Dafydd Iwan. We were charged with contempt and sentenced on the spot to three months imprisonment, spent a week in jail (women in Holloway, men in Pentonville) in a state of shock, and got released on appeal (all but three who refused to be bound over). I finally joined Cymdeithas yr Iaith in the Eisteddfod that year, out of shame. We had all been welcomed back in Aberystwyth as Cymdeithas heroes and honoured with a special chapel service (doubly embarrassing for me, being neither a Cymdeithas yr Iaith member nor having ever darkened the doors of any chapel in Aberystwyth).

It wasn't until 1979 that I got seriously involved with Plaid Cymru again. I returned from Catalunya where I'd been living for a while, managing, in the process, to sit out the political horrors of that year (the dreadful, divisive and dishonest devolution campaign, the lost opportunity of the Referendum vote on March 1 and the election of Margaret Thatcher's Tories in May) to find that there was now a bunch of energetic and committed women such as Carmel Gahan, Eirian Llwyd, and Rosanne Reeves, amongst others, active in the party. They were fighting to modernize and energize Plaid Cymru by rejuvenating the moribund Women's Section and forcing Plaid Cymru to take women's rights and equality issues more seriously. Then political life got interesting again – but that's another story!

# A Political Life

~

*Hilda Price*

**Hilda Price** was born in Cadoxton, Barry, in 1920, the youngest of five children. Her parents were both theatrical performers and, as a child, Hilda was a member of a touring dance troupe. In the 1930s, she worked as a clerk in Sherman's Pools in Cardiff and during the war she became an airframe fitter at RAF, St Athan. She married in 1944 and has one daughter, Mair. Hilda has been an active trade unionist and Communist Party member for most of her life. She has published her wartime memories in *Llafur, 6*, No. 3 (1992) and has appeared in television documentaries for Channel 4 and HTV Wales.

I got married during wartime, in 1944. The war ended in 1945 and everyone looked forward to a lasting and prosperous peace. The Labour government was elected by a landslide in 1945 and many changes were made for the better. There were improvements to housing, education, health and welfare. The National Health Service was set up and the coal mines and railways were nationalized. It was a time of huge optimism in Britain. Internationally, the United Nations was established, as an association of states to promote peace, security and co-operation. It seemed to me that after the appalling poverty and unemployment of the 1930s and after the carnage and horrors of the war, we were at last on our way to building a new world for humankind.

Personally, my life was brightened by the birth of my lovely daughter in 1948. At the time we were living in lodgings. We shared a three-bedroomed terraced house in Pyke Street, Barry, with another couple, who had two children, and with the lady who owned the house. Each of our three households had one living room and one bedroom and we all shared the kitchen and the bathroom: the lavatory was outside at the bottom of the garden. There was no hot water in the house, only cold. So for personal washing and for washing our clothes, all the water had to be heated in a bucket on top of the gas stove. But then, in 1949, after five years of living 'in rooms', we were allocated our own council house.

People today do not realize the sheer joy it was for a family in the post-war years to move into a council house with all its 'mod cons'. We were so excited to get our house on the Colcot estate in Barry. The house was semi-detached with three bedrooms, two good-sized downstairs rooms, a well designed modern kitchen complete with gas cooker, a gas boiler for washing clothes and a pantry with a very cold slab for keeping food fresh. We had an upstairs bathroom and toilet. Outside we had a large garden and the whole estate was clean and tidy with well kept roads and pavements and plenty of open green spaces. Our rents were inclusive of rates and water rates and the local authority, with its own direct labour force, carried out reasonable repairs at no extra charge to the tenant.

But not everything was rosy. Some foodstuffs and coal continued to be rationed for a time after the war. The demise of wartime industries meant a drop in the level of wages and the end of over-time for many workers. Women were often the first to lose their jobs and some people found it impossible to get the money even to buy the rationed foods to which they were entitled. I was concerned about these issues and, together with a group of local women, raised them with our MP, the Conservative Raymond Gower. He wasn't interested.

Our group had other concerns too. Our estate was located on the edge of the town, a long way from the main shopping centre, so transport and access to shops was a prime issue for us. We pressed local councillors to take action on this and by the late 1950s, the council built a small shopping centre at Winston Square on our estate. It was convenient for us all and we could now buy food and clothes and go to the chemist shop within our own locality. I suppose what would surprise people most today is that these shops were built with *public* money.

I have always been interested in politics and this led me to join the Communist Party in 1941. I attended many meetings where we discussed the current political situation and also working class history and its relationship to the problems of our own time. During the war, of course, the Union of Soviet Socialist Republics (USSR) was our ally and there was a great deal of interest locally in the situation there. We held many open public meetings in the Unity Hall on Broad Street, Barry, with speakers such as Will Paynter, the South Wales Miners' leader, and Idris Cox, secretary of the Welsh Communist Party. These meetings were very well attended. We also organized bazaars and fetes to raise money for the newspaper, the *Daily Worker.*

In the 1950s, under the auspices of the Cardiff branch of the British Soviet Friendship Society, artists from the USSR were invited to perform in Wales. We held a huge concert in Barry's vast memorial hall, where we listened to their choir and soloists. The hall was packed and it was a magnificent show. A ballet company from the USSR came to the Cory Hall in Cardiff. It was a beautiful performance, but I remember wondering how on earth the dancers managed to move so beautifully on that knotty, old wooden stage.

In the 1950s, the threat of nuclear war hung over us all. I supported the Campaign for Nuclear Disarmament (CND), which was set up in the late 1950s by philosopher Bertrand Russell and Canon Collins. CND was a non party political organization, which advocated the worldwide abolition of nuclear weapons, and sought unilateral British initiatives to help start the multilateral process to end the arms race. I went to Cardiff and heard Bertrand Russell speak in the Cory Hall to a meeting that was so packed that the crowd overflowed on to the street outside. In 1961 a huge demonstration was held in Cardiff. Many people, including the writer Elaine Morgan, sat down in the road outside Cardiff Castle and blocked the traffic. The rest of us marched down Queen Street with our banners. There was strong support for CND amongst the general public, and from trade unions, political parties, the Quakers and many other religious groups.

By 1963, I had decided to work outside the home again. I took a job as a nursing auxiliary in Lansdowne Hospital, Cardiff, for two years and after that at St. David's Hospital, where I stayed for sixteen years. I enjoyed the work and learnt a lot, though at times it was physically very hard. I made new friends and the work itself was rewarding. I was a member of the Confederation of Health Service Employees (COHSE). I recruited lots of new members to COHSE, including many nurses, and every week I collected in the membership money. Eventually COHSE amalgamated with the National Union of Public Employees (NUPE) and is now part of Unison.

The long war between North and South Vietnam (1954-1975) horrified me. I wanted to do my part and I willingly joined when a medical team was set up in the old Transport Hall in Charles Street, Cardiff, to organize a blood transfusion service to send blood to North Vietnam. I encouraged some of my nursing colleagues to join the team too. Many people gave their blood, including local dignitaries and members of parliament.

I have been politically active all my life and I am still at it, even though I am in my 'twilight years'. I remain a member of the Communist Party of Britain, though it is difficult for me to get to meetings in Cardiff. Nowadays, I concentrate on the problems of pensioners locally, in Barry and the Vale. I am a member of the Vale of Glamorgan Pensioners' Forum and in 2000 I was a delegate at the Pensioners' Parliament held in Blackpool. It is widely known that pensioners are not happy with their lot and would like to see their pensions linked to earnings, without any means testing. Amongst pensioners' other concerns is public transport. The availability of bus and rail services varies enormously across the country and transport is a key issue for older people.

But life is not all serious. Our pensioners' group enjoys the odd social evening too with a chat, food and even a little drink, as we listen to the music of yesteryear.

# The March

~

*Penny Anne Windsor*

**Penny Anne Windsor** is a Cornishwoman who has lived in Wales for many years. She teaches creative writing and literature in a wide variety of adult education groups and is presently studying for an MA in Education (Lifelong Learning) with the Open University. She is widely published as a poet and short story writer, including two collections of poems published by Honno. She has had stories in *The New Penguin Book of Welsh Short Stories*, *Luminous and Forlorn* (Honno), *Mamma's Baby (Papa's Maybe)* (Parthian) and *Cambrensis*, and had stories broadcast on Radio 4. She has recently completed a collection of her poetry for schoolchildren *A Cut Above the Usual*, as a result of receiving the Irma Chilton Award for Children's Writing in 2000.

It was in the late sixties that I became 'politicized', as they say. I remember furious arguments with Heda, my socialist Scandinavian friend, about the way Britain was shipping goods to Rhodesia – as it was then – via South Africa. Having been reared on the *Daily Telegraph*, which I thought balanced because it mentioned Harold Wilson every now and then, and equipped with vague ideas about Justice and Equality, I took for granted the integrity of the government. It was, I think, on the grounds that I believed people told the truth. How naive all this sounds! It went with a whole set of ideas about black and white people being the same under the skin and policemen being there to help you find your way when you are lost.

Perhaps it was the combined influence of Heda and Black Mao – a benign and gigantic Jamaican Trotskyist, who she had met at 'meetings' – which led me to Trafalgar Square that day, to join a demonstration against the Vietnamese War. It was the first demonstration I ever took part in and I was bemused by the big crowd, by the intermittent heckling of the onlookers – 'What about the

Russians?' 'Go and live in Moscow' – by the banners proclaiming that one group was the socialist party from Woking or the miners' union from Wakefield or the young communists from Cardiff, by the slogans which swayed through the marchers in great waves – the terrible simplicity of 'Yankees Out', or the primitive rhythms of 'Ho Ho Ho Chi Min'.

We marched down Oxford Street and into the narrow side streets leading to Grosvenor Square. Packed tight against strangers, I had no will of my own. I could only move forward. Word came back that a delegation of protestors had been turned away from the American Embassy. The marchers became restless. It was suggested that we storm the building and the crowd began to move forward again, people toppling over each other and into policemen. Someone fell. A policeman's helmet was knocked off. There were screams as some of the marchers tried to turn back and found they couldn't. Protestors were running across the space in front of the Embassy, weaving around the police, until, finally caught on the steps, they were brought to the ground and flung into the back of Black Marias. I grabbed the pole of a banner, which seemed the only stable point in a falling world and by one of those unlikely coincidences, found that the man holding the other end was someone I had met briefly in Geneva the previous spring.

We had only exchanged a few words when I was swept away again, like seaweed, through the small hedge and into the park in the centre of the square. Here, trapped on each side by the crowds which blocked all exits, I watched mounted policemen ride their horses at us. People screamed and fell and tried to hide, clinging to benches or trees. As one of the horses came towards me, I was flung again back into the crowd, which had begun to turn, spewing me out eventually into Oxford Street, where I sat down in the road among strangers, nursed my bruises and decided that policemen did many other things besides rescuing lost children and giving directions to tourists.

A few months later I took a clerical job in an office working for Voluntary Service Overseas. The office overlooked Grosvenor Square. I watched the models shivering in skimpy clothes for photo shoots. Office and shop workers ate sandwiches. Leaves fell. It was never quite the same place again.

# Zionist Identity

~

*Stella Schiller Levey*

**Stella Schiller Levey** is Cardiff born and bred and has lived there all her life, save for short spells in London and Israel. She is married with two daughters and five grandchildren. She is currently a mature student of BA (Hons) in English Studies at the University of Glamorgan. She won the Michael Parnell award for Creative Writing in 1999. She was formally a warden at Janner House, Cardiff, adult literacy tutor and marriage guidance counsellor, also a former researcher for a University of Wales social work department handbook on drugs. She was the founder editor of *Bimah* (many times award-winning magazine on Welsh Jewry) and is currently its literary editor. Published in many magazines and journals, including *Cambrensis*, *Cajex* and *Bimah*, she is the Welsh correspondent to the *Jewish Chronicle*.

Looking back, I see that the main memories of my youth centre on the 1950s. I was born in Eton Place Nursing Home, Canton, Cardiff, on 14 August 1937, the younger daughter of first-generation British parents. My father was born in London's East End, the youngest-but-one of nine surviving children of Polish parents, and my mother, born in Warsaw, Poland, was brought to this country around the age of nine months and was the eldest of five. Being products of the early twentieth century, they had rather Victorian attitudes, although at times they were given to the odd modern gesture.

I am Jewish and my mother came from a pious background. My father obliged her by compromising on the main religious issues of home and family so I had a relatively strict upbringing. We were bombed out in 1943 – the last bomb on Cardiff dropping on our house, one of a row of four – and we were lucky to survive. In the years between then and returning to our rebuilt house, we lived in Llandaff and Fairwater, so that regular synagogue attendance was not possible. It was too far for us to walk (travelling on a bus on

*Shabbat*, the Jewish Sabbath, was forbidden) and Hebrew classes on Sundays and weekdays were not possible as we didn't have a car for some time to transport us. So my mother brought up my sister and me to observe Jewish practices and she paid teachers to instruct us in reading and writing Hebrew. Rising each morning and going to bed each night had separate prayers, and there were blessings for food, fruit, vegetables, wine, seeing lightning, new crockery – you name it, there was a blessing for it. After lunch on *Shabbat*, I would have to sit with my mother, having said *Grace After Meals*, and read and translate the *Ethics of the Fathers* to make me a good person as I grew up!

Most of what was going on in the ordinary world passed me by to a certain extent. That is not to say I did not have friends. I belonged to *Habonim*, which was a nation-wide Zionist youth organisation, and we had a ball with weekend and summer camps and singsongs around the fire, indoor or out. I graduated in my early teens to the Junior Cardiff Jewish Youth Society, which met in Windsor Place synagogue in the basement (it's a wine bar now) and got to know the Jewish youth who lived 'on the other side of the river'. (If you came from Riverside or Canton you were a downtown girl.) Often crowds of us met in the Cadena or Kardomah cafés but I couldn't afford to do this often as I had very little pocket money. We had lost most of our possessions in the bombing and it took years for my parents to recoup. Therefore, money wasn't splashed around. Nevertheless, we did have treats and, indeed, by the time the fifties arrived we could actually go abroad to Blankenberge in Belgium for our summer holiday. My father did indulge me in a racing-style bicycle with drop handlebars when I was sixteen and groups of us would go cycling on Sundays, sometimes as far as Lydney in Gloucester. We had simple outings but a lot of fun.

I had a lot of fun, if that's the word, during my six years in Cardiff High School for Girls in The Parade, the top school to be in at that time. I had won the Craddock Wells scholarship with the highest marks in Cardiff, but my father wouldn't accept the financial reward as he would have had to state that he earned less than £20 per week. This he refused to do. Later, my parents were extremely disappointed with me for not going on to university, but I didn't wish to be a teacher and there was no career mistress to discuss any other possibilities. So I went to Cardiff College of Technology and Commerce in Cathays Park for a year and passed out top with a secretarial and language diploma and started my first job, which I hated, in Norwich Union Insurance at the top of Churchill Way for the princely sum of £4 14s 6d per week in 1955. By the time I had given some of my wage to my mother towards the housekeeping and after tax and National Insurance stamps had been deducted, I had hardly a penny to bless myself with. Luckily, at that time my father would occasionally go to London to do some buying for his drapery business and if my mother accompanied him I would profit by a smart dress or two.

When I hear some of my friends reminisce, I realise that a certain amount of the fifties 'club life' in town was absent from my life but what you didn't know about you didn't miss. I rarely frequented such places as the Whisky Agogo in St Mary Street or the Marina ballroom in Penarth (hunting grounds for those wanting to 'pull') but groups of us used to go to the dances at Bindles every Saturday night just as soon as the boys learned to drive and could borrow their fathers' cars. My father always used to wait up for me and look out of the front room window in case I sat in the car with my boy-friend, so there was little opportunity, if any, to sin!

We had our own Cardiff Jewish Youth Society which was 'swinging' for its time and it competed with another Jewish club on the other side of town. Our dances used to be packed on Sunday nights – we used to sit on the windowsills and it was a far cry from present times, with the current dearth of Jewish youth in Cardiff and other small communities. Boys and girls used to come from Merthyr and the valleys and we had intercity trips to Swansea, Bristol, Reading, Birmingham and other towns. Many marriages were forged in the Cardiff Jewish Youth Society. We used to play tennis in Llandaff Fields and repair to the Gourmet Café in St Mary Street for coffee – from a machine! The only time I ate upstairs in the Gourmet was when I got engaged and my fiancé Gerald treated me to a *spaghetti milanaise* – a novelty in those days – all for the sum of £1 15s plus a huge five shillings tip.

I learned to drive when I was seventeen and passed first time. I was only allowed to borrow the car on Sunday mornings to visit my grandmother and various cousins so I was unable to be too adventurous – although I drove a bit recklessly at times. I started going out with Gerald when I was sixteen, on and off, until we got engaged in 1959.

In fact, before then, my parents decided to send me away on a 'working' holiday to Israel in 1956, when I was nearly nineteen, as they thought I was spending too much time with Gerald, seeing him twice a week at the Canton cinema! So I sailed from Marseilles to Haifa with a suitcase of cotton shorts and tops and this time I didn't feel out of things with a range of simple clothes and shoes. Even one of the girls I had always envied, coming as she did from a wealthy family, envied me in turn as she had brought all the wrong attire, with her starched frilled net petticoats and fashionable full-skirted dresses. I had an eye-opener of a holiday, starting with rising at 4 am to go to the kibbutz's banana groves to grovel in the mud and slash dead leaves off the banana plants, so the sun could reach the huge hands of bananas. I travelled around Israel in the eleventh year of her formation as a state, slept on the Lebanese border at Rosh HaNikra, got shot at in a group by Arabs for trying to take photographs at the time of the Suez Crisis and travelled from Tel Aviv to Jerusalem on the floor of a train carriage, accompanied by a soldier with his machine-gun mounted on a stand and pointing out of an open window as we passed inches from the Arab border. That was adventure!

I returned to Cardiff two months later, Gerald and I having decided that absence had indeed made the heart grow fonder. We decided to get engaged towards the end of the fifties, but plans for our marriage in 1960 had to be postponed owing to a change in Gerald's job. We then hoped to get married on 1 January 1961, if only because my beloved grandmother got married on New Year's Day back in Poland in 1901, but the date was unavailable, so I had to opt for the 15th. Our wedding was typical of Jewish weddings of the day, with a ceremony in our impressive synagogue in Cathedral Road whose Victorian grandeur lent itself beautifully to the nuptials.

I was very surprised indeed to find I was expecting a baby at the end of 1961. Just before my elder daughter, Jocelyn, was born, some local new Jewish wives and mothers set up a branch of the world-wide Women's International Zionist Organisation (WIZO for short). We called this social and fund-raising group 'Young Ziona'. Now, after forty-one years and the word 'Young' having been dropped (we refuse these days to be called 'Old Ziona'), I find that membership of 'Ziona' has been an integral part of my married years and social life, whereby, by dint of hard work, we have raised thousands upon thousands of pounds for underprivileged Israeli and Arab women and children. The money helped to found crèches, playgrounds, health centres and after-school clubs for children of working mothers. It also helped to train immigrants into the Israeli way of life and how to speak the language so that they could integrate into society. We have had marvellous times raising money and even travelled in groups to Jerusalem for triennial conferences in latter years. I cannot see my social life without it now, whatever else I do.

# ABOUT HONNO

Honno Welsh Women's Press was set up in 1986 by a group of women who felt strongly that women in Wales needed wider opportunities to see their writing in print and to become involved in the publishing process. Our aim is to publish books by, and for, women of Wales, and our brief encompasses fiction, poetry, children's books, autobiographical writing and reprints of classic titles in English and Welsh.

Honno is registered as a community co-operative and so far we have raised capital by selling shares at £5 a time to over 400 interested women all over the world. Any profit we make goes towards the cost of future publications. We hope that many more women will be able to help us in this way. Shareholders' liability is limited to the amount invested, and each shareholder, regardless of the number of shares held, will have her say in the company and a vote at the AGM. To buy shares, to buy books directly, to be added to our database of authors or to receive further information about forthcoming publications, please e-mail: post@honno.co.uk or write to Honno:

**'Ailsa Craig',**
**Heol y Cawl,**
**Dinas Powys,**
**Bro Morgannwg**
**CF64 4AH.**

# www.honno.co.uk

# Parachutes and Petticoats

## Welsh women writing on the Second World War

edited by Leigh Verrill-Rhys and Deirdre Beddoe

Often poignant and at times wonderfully funny, this anthology is an evocative record of Welsh women's lives during wartime.

There are memories of air raids, Mickey Mouse gas-masks and of mothers feeding families on Spam, snoek and dried egg. Contributors include Welsh Wrens, WAAFs, ATS and Land Army girls, and also conscientious objectors who suffered job losses and imprisonment. There are accounts of nurses who followed hard on the heels of the D-Day landings and who helped the survivors when Belson was liberated; of war workers in munitions factories and in engineering; of evacuees, some basking in the love of a surrogate Welsh Mam; others meeting coldness or sexual abuse; of refugees fleeing Hitler and finding new homes in Wales.

From the horrors of blitzed cities and bombing raids on the small towns and villages to wartime romances, GIs and jitterbugging, *Parachutes and Petticoats* reveals an intriguing kaleidoscope of experience.

ISBN 1 870206 12 6

£9.95

Also from Honno Autobiography

# Struggle or Starve
## Women's lives in the South Wales valleys between the two World Wars

### edited by Carol White and Sian Rhiannon Williams

Drawing on the memories of those who were girls and young women during the inter-war period. *Struggle or Starve* vividly recreates the lives of working class women at a time of hardship and poverty. It mingles fragments of reminiscence by previously unpublished writers with extracts from published autobiographies – some, like Elizabeth Andrews's work, long out of print – to portray women's struggle, not just for survival but for dignity, recognition and wider opportunities. The book cleverly develops a strong sense of narrative whilst its chapters, arranged thematically on topics such as 'Childhood', 'Little Mothers, Little Skivvies', 'Out to Work' and 'Women and Politics', combine to build a picture of a way of life which, though gruelling and often dispiriting, was nevertheless illuminated by the warmth of family ties and friendship.

The critical introduction situates these women's individual experiences within the wider social and political context of a period of mass unemployment and labour unrest, when the only real choice open to the majority of valleys women was struggle – or starve.

*'This is a delightful book. It is moving, poignant, funny and a very good historical record – what we have here is the authentic voice of the women of the valleys themselves. These accounts are characterized by a freshness and a direct appeal to the reader which books about the same
topic written by historians can never attain.'*
Emeritus Professor Deirdre Beddoe, University of Glamorgan

ISBN 1 870206 25 8

£9.95